With Compliments

Manoharan

[signature]

07/12/12

CANADA

CANADA

A NATION IN MOTION

Samy Appadurai

authorHOUSE®

AuthorHouse™
1663 Liberty Drive
Bloomington, IN 47403
www.authorhouse.com
Phone: 1-800-839-8640

Published by AuthorHouse   09/27/2012

ISBN: 978-1-4772-7476-7 (sc)
ISBN: 978-1-4772-7475-0 (hc)
ISBN: 978-1-4772-7474-3 (e)

Library of Congress Control Number: 2012918292

CONTENTS

FOREWORD

by
Dr. Andrew Linder

It is my very great honour to call to your special attention a man I have admired since I met him a decade ago, Mr. Samy Appadurai. He is a scholar, community activist, educator, policy advocate, and the host of a popular television program on Tamil One (Rogers.868). He could match the populist mayor of Toronto for the many calls to which he responds helping those who have difficulty understanding and joining that "Canadian Mosaic" which is accurately described as in motion, its trajectory not fully determined. That is why we need to listen to someone who sees matters equally from the perspective of an unstable world looking at Canada and from the point of view of a proud Canadian enchanted by and grateful to the land which gave his people refuge, as it had successive waves from its Scottish, British and Irish immigrants which followed the French to that astonishing variety of cultures which have arrived and continue to arrive to a land accurately and ironically described in Samy Appadurai's first work by its title, *Canada—The Meat of the World Sandwich* (2009).

Of supreme value in this work is its author's deep attachment and gratitude to a country which gave his people an opportunity to feel at home that other nations deny, even when they grudgingly allow refugees fleeing dreadful conditions to enter. "Mr. Samy", as he is widely known in his community, takes to Canada like a duck to water. It is touching and all too rare to find at the beginning of a serious work on public policy, the author repeating the oath he took when he became a Canadian citizen. Clearly, Mr. Samy believes that his citizenship confers not only the benefits that make our country so attractive, but beyond that, obligations which we may pledge unthinkingly. Not so Samy Appadurai.

He is a man after my own heart, an "educator" in the best sense of the word, *a pundit*, "a teacher", as it meant in my youth, remembering my inspirations, my own teachers, in whose shadow I am not fit to walk. If there is any complaint, it is that the author of **Canada—A Nation in Motion** glides easily in this work among policy advice and deep thinking about the nature of human migration, and comes all too suddenly to startling intelligent and valuable advice to policy makers based on what makes great civilizations rise and fall. He comes from an ancient civilization with a long perspective and needs to be patient with a young giant, Canada, a country which does not realize its own blessings as the author makes wonderfully clear.

We "boat people", whether we came on Scottish or Irish ships earlier, or later on Jewish, Sikh or Tamil ships escaping dreadful conditions, or else by plane as a professional or investor seeing opportunities for upward mobility or simply a person who came here to breathe clean air and drink clean water, we need, all of us, recognize and show gratitude for that valuable gift we were given when we were allowed to land on

Canada's shores. My own family came to Canada in 1957 on a boat from Rotterdam sailing late in the season. It sank some two years later, one of the great disasters before travel by plane became the first step toward the global village in which my students Tweet before after, and regrettably during class. We were refugees from the Hungarian Revolution, as traumatized as those Tamil people who came decades later also by boat, an event which is explained in the most balanced and intelligent way in this work. Indeed, an admirable quality of **Canada—A Nation in Motion** is precisely its calm, common sense and clear-sightedness, the author's ability to see matters from the most varied perspective. That is especially useful when discussing matters such as immigration which generate passion and cloud judgment.

Samy Appadurai gives especially valuable advice in what has become a troubled area of government policy by which unworthy immigrants crowd out those absolutely needed if Canada is to prosper. My parents arrived in Canada over the objections of my "Jewish Tiger" Dad, an ardent Zionist intent on immigrating to Israel. But no, this was my Mother's "promised land" as she insisted to her last days, and she thrived here from the first playing something of a role Mr. Samy plays helping those who find the transition hard and Canada's social rules unfathomable. In those days, immigration was directed to those born to the British culture, and even in Quebec marked by a British Union Jack in one corner of the classroom, the old Canadian flag with a Union Jack in the other, the singing of British anthem along with the Canadian anthem each morning, and a very pronounced emphasis on "our" culture and heritage which was distinctly and narrowly rooted in the British Isles. Singing Christian hymns was very odd in a classroom largely Jewish, but Quebec's school system was divided according to the design of the original English and French people into a largely

French Catholic and a largely English Protestant system, giving my parents' beloved sons the choice of being altar boys at mass or singing Protestant hymns that I rather liked and sing loudly in the shower to this day. My point is that this was then a wonderful place, but not exactly comfortable with immigrants who did not like their food bland or understand British manners and the rites of the Church of England. Mr. Appadurai is very observant about this period, considering that he would not even have dreamt in those days that he would lead his sunset years in distant Canada.

My parents worked hard from the day we landed till they were no longer able to work. My father was a shoemaker and my mother a dressmaker, neither having much education as Jews in Europe who experienced what Tamil people experience more recently. There was little opportunity and much discrimination even in Canada, but gradually the country changed and became a wonderful land of opportunity. I assure you that we became rich and powerful as people by two factors without which success is not possible for any community. The first is hard work and the second education, but neither is possible without a social framework which eases tension and brings together the creative juices of among diverse cultures. It is "diversity in ethnicity" and Samy Appadurai's main point or "thesis statement", as I earnestly try to convey to my students over decades teaching university level writing skills.

This is not to brag but to underline that excellent thesis on which our future depends as a nation. I have an M.A. from McGill University and was awarded PhD in English from the University of Toronto in its glory days. These are two of the most prestigious universities in Canada, but having restrictions against Jews not long before I entered.

You can find online my publications, but pay special attention to my work on engineering education with Dr. Ahmad Ibrahim, especially our lecture at MIT in 2000. The lecture comes from a lifelong friendship and collaboration between a scholar of modernist literature and a world-famous expert on fuzzy logic, a Jew born a year after the Holocaust in Hungary with an aunt on the famous ship Exodus which carried the traumatized victims of evil racial policies to a new homeland, working with an army officer who fought bravely against my relatives in Israel in 1973. This is then a person presently writing a forward to a work by a gentleman of still another faith. Mr. Samy, who tells us that it is precisely our cultural differences which enrich our collaboration on a personal and professional level, not only within the narrow confines of my circle, but across our very unique nation which has something to teach the world about how people of the most varied ethnicity can live in harmony.

My education has brought and continues to bring me very important clients as a professional writer and editor, but it has been 43 years of teaching university level writing skills which brought me true joy, as it has an increasingly rare breed, a genuine educator, Mr. Samy Appadurai. His all too brief mention of his work as a teacher which most explains this man and endears him to me. One can only hope that Mr. Samy will take the time from his many other commitments to turn his attention next to education, an area in great need of his wise counsel as teacher and principal on three continents before he morphed into his other roles in a busy life where only wimps need sleep, it seems.

Still, I have often comforted parents from immigrant cultures who were alarmed by children like my brother and hero, Peter Linder, who did not heed the eternal plea of immigrant parents to "study, study,

study so you don't have to do what I had to do", and yet became a very successful man through means advocated in the old Horatio Alger stories, "pluck and luck". He rose from our poverty stricken background to become a giant of Canadian commerce, frequently on television and in newspapers as an expert on natural gas and oil prices, often testifying before government panels and owner of a successful hedge-fund in the oil patch. How amused I was at the wedding of my niece in my brothers extraordinary mansion only a little smaller than Casa Loma, a wedding only the Tamil people can throw, lacking only the groom arriving on an elephant dressed like a young rajah. I was standing beside my Mother who prophesied ruin and jail as my brother's future, as have so many Tamil mothers anxious about their children's future when they are not doing well enough to get into elite university programs. My Mother could not understand my brothers enormous success, but Samy Appadurai does when he pays tribute to our system of economic freedom and opportunity, and how important it is to preserve it against the leftist collectivist dream that I once subscribed to like so many people of my generation very accurately evaluated for its shortcomings in *Canada—A Nation in Motion*.

Samy Appadurai insists that the current social and political framework for all its shortcomings builds on Canada's startlingly varied cultures, a source of strength in a world where people are increasingly unwilling to live with each other. We may debate policy. Indeed, we should, as long as we put the interest of our nation first as loyal subjects who gave our oath when we became citizens. Mr. Samy is, it is quite evident, a conservative and I a person on the left, yet we live in a "global village" we are constantly reminded in this work. All around us is negative evidence of what happens when a culture tries to remain pure and shake off those of other cultures as a way to selfishly progress. That path leads precisely to the conditions that brought the majority of immigrants to our shores fleeing war, ethnic cleansing and sundry horrors. Certainly, very few come to enjoy Canada's good climate, but all enjoy benefits too numerous to name, which is why it is good that Samy Appadurai names so many urging us to build on it and show it off with pride before the world.

I was especially moved in this work by a tribute paid to Jack Layton of the Canadian Left whose political testament seemed to have touched Samy Appadurai deeply. While critical of Layton's Quebec policies, political differences stood in no way a barrier to strong praise on a human level for Layton's help as city councilor on matters which engages Mr. Samy daily in serving his community. All this happened decades ago before the Tamil Diaspora brought this hard-working and creative community to our shores. In 1970 when I entered the graduate program in literature at the University of Toronto, I took courses in modernist literature with Marshall McLuhan, the media guru and professor of literature who invented the term "global village" so beloved by Samy Appadurai. This was long before the technical conditions that made it possible were evident. The Toronto of those days was bleak for someone who came from a much more sophisticated Montreal changed by Expo 67, the World's Fair, when a backward, provincial city discovered the world. It is worthwhile in this context to listen to Samy Appadurai's wise counsel in praising the government for its initiative in holding major international political and sporting events for exactly the same reason, that we are always on a world stage on which the varied perspective of our varied cultures are as valuable a resource as oil, iron, corn or minerals.

In any event, I was skeptical of the "global village" argument in 1970 for a good reason. While completing my M.A, at McGill University, I studied with a now very famous novelist called Bharati Mukarjee. In those days, she took her husband's name and called herself Bharati Blaise because Mukarjee brought out a burst of laughter from those unfamiliar with Indian culture in general and her specific Parsee culture from Bombay in particular. She moved to Toronto where the recently arrived Asian immigrants, arriving in large numbers after Trudeau opened the gates, elicited very negative reaction initially. I personally witnessed, and on more than one occasion intervened, when a citizen whose own parents or grandparents fled dreadful conditions by boat berated a new arrival for speaking another language or eating spicy cooking. How things have changed, and yet Samy Appadurai is very attentive to that political and social framework gradually established in Canada which is a wonder allowing immigrants to feel at home and conduct community activities in safety, expecting to be treated with respect and as an equal in dealing with authorities, communities living in relative harmony, in fact a paradise when you look around, even more travel around the world and see conditions which are unthinkable in Canada.

As a scholar, Samy Appadurai substantiates by data the value of immigrants and gives very good advice on how properly structured immigration policy, eliminating the many who take advantage, is of enormous benefit, indeed an indispensable condition for our future success as a nation. Equally important are the wry observations and anecdotes which make abstract thought real, concrete and relevant. How passengers struggling to get on public transport against opposition turn on the less fortunate behind them, for instance, relates directly to how successive wave of immigrant communities behave when they attempt to close the door after them to others who deserve also to get on the bus. Needless to say, not all who arrive on our shores do so in an orderly line, and there is very good advice on immigration policy our decision makers would be wise to listen to. The criticism of the "golden padlock" deserves special scrutiny, for on this fundamental error of pure uncontaminated cultures arose as consequence only ill will, rivalry, a barrier to our development as a people.

To cite one example, Canada lost two great novelists, Bharati Mukarjee and her husband Clark Blaise, an old-time Canadian and a great writer who needed this land as the source of his art, but lovingly followed his wife away from what was in 1970 as far from "global village" as possible. "Cowtown" it was called, the most provincial of the world's large cities. I write this as the Toronto International Film Festival (TIFF) each year brings the world's sophisticates to the most sophisticated of cities, changed from a provincial city of Britain's colonies into a world-class wonder, many times voted the most livable city on earth. That is precisely the thesis Samy Appadurai defends eloquently and intelligently both with hard data, and equally important, personal observations which support the scholarly argument.

There is a long and involved account with many example of how all kind of great civilization arose when through migration different people came together, but instead of conquering and destroying one another to ensure the purity of their culture, they share what was the best and most advanced in philosophy, religion, technology, literature, indeed virtually every measure by which a culture is judged as advanced or backward. It is then with great pleasure that I read Mr. Samy's account of a meeting on community affairs in a Chinese restaurant where he approves of the spicing. That's saying a lot for those who know Tamil cooking, an ancient art of a very high order now available everywhere in Toronto where there was in my youth only the horror of "Canadian-Chinese" food having no perceptible connection to the Orient. Mr. Samy's eyes (and taste buds) always open to the world, he makes inquiries and expresses the most wonderful and innocent delight to find how Chinese cooking long ago migrated to India along with the migration of people and a wonderful example, he takes pains to demonstrate, how such wonders as Mohenjo Daro in Ancient India and a perfectly spiced dish in modern Scarborough arise from the same creative source in the migration of people and the successful blending of cultures, not as conqueror to conquered, but as equals.

My own favourite chapter in a wonderful work is Mr. Samy's account of the horror that rises while he was teaching in Nigeria in a community where some people prey on one another and a school where teachers and authorities are indifferent to their students. No one can read this account of how Mr. Samy saves the life of a westerner at the cost of his own stolen car in getting urgent medical attention without thinking of how horrible it is to live in a community where violence and mistrust is not uncommon. And that's most of the world. We take so much for granted together with all manner of good things we will certainly lose if we do not act wisely in a world hurdling toward disaster where life is "poor, nasty, brutish and short" unless we follow the advice of wise philosophers of the "social contract" like Hume and consider carefully the many recommendations Samy Appadurai makes.

Canada—a Nation in Motion deserves to be studied by our policy makers who make use too often of community leaders while neglecting that unique perspective which is rooted in all the ancient cultures whose wisdom will ease Canada's way in a world "in motion". I look forward to future work by this author who grasps so accurately what makes our country the envy, and sometimes "the meat in the world sandwich".

INTRODUCTION

by
the Author

It is to begin with my love for Canada that prompted me to write my second book entitled "Canada—a Nation in Motion" and also the encouragement and the popular support that I received from readers around the world for my first book on Canada, "Canada—the Meat of the World Sandwich". Along with actively participating in politics, journalism, public affairs, and social events of numerous public office, awards and recognitions I have received, I would like to mention two of them in particular. I have been a council member at the Ontario College of Teachers, appointed by the Lt Governor, and was awarded with the Golden Jubilee of Her Majesty Queen Elizabeth II, Queen of Canada Medal for social service yet, I am a first generation immigrant. My views, opinions and thoughts are multidimensional in nature as a naturalized citizen of Canada and not only as one who has taken the following oath

"I swear (affirm) that I will be faithful and bear true allegiance to her majesty Queen Elizabeth 11, Her Heirs and successors, and I will faithfully observe the laws of Canada and fulfill my duties as a Canadian citizen."

For almost a quarter century, I have committed myself to being and living as a loyal Canadian. However I am also privileged that I was born, raised and completed my university education in Sri Lanka and got associated with Asian affairs and then spent almost two decades in both East and West Africa, actively involved in exploring the rural life, customs and traditions. My active participation and the interest in the public life on three continents are an invaluable asset and a firsthand resource that helped me in analyzing a variety of subjects critically, objectively and comparatively. I have tried my best in this book to balance the material and my opinions, without bias and I believe that you will certainly accept my points after reading my book from the beginning to end. As a freelance journalist, I have written numerous articles and have authored five books and being in Canada, a nation that respects and values freedom of the press and free expression, I have no fear or hesitation in expressing certain critical views.

My intent is not to provoke controversy, but rather to spark discussion and debate for I believe that it is through intelligent discussion that we as Canadians have and will continue to be a nation in motion.

A French journalist was quoted as saying "Canada is the best nation to live in and it is not necessarily refers and limits within the boundary of the province of Quebec, rather widely every part of this great nation. I am so pleased and encouraged to have such comments from a prominent sources from France and it has given a kind reinforcement of the recognition and respect to Canada as a nation in which Quebec is a part of it."

We also have to remember that when the former President of France Mr. Charles de Gaulle was invited as one the most important guests for the centennial celebration of Canadian confederation in 1967, he clearly remarked by saying in French "Vive le Quebec libre" and also considered the Quebecers as brothers and the rest of Canadians as friends as the relationship with Quebec is close and unique. Although there was no intention or motive to promote Quebec sovereignty, it is still a compliment for us. I would also add that Canada is one of the best nations to live in not only because of our stable economic conditions, but also due to its stable government and a clear sense of vision. Through a lot of hard work, the people of Canada from various ethnic backgrounds coexist in a spirit of cooperation and civic pride and we have fairly balanced foreign policies along with a good healthcare and educational system and infrastructure. Whatever changes may occur in the outside world, the relationship between Canada and the Quebec sovereignty movement has not changed drastically nor has Federal government policy been affected.

Let us now see the other side of the assessment of Canada by some of the international organizations such as the United Nations. The UNO recently complained and condemned Canada about certain involvements within and international affairs such as the handing over of suspected war criminals to the Afghanistan government knowing that those people certainly would be tortured. Canada has also been accused of human rights violations by partially depriving the rights and privileges for Native Canadians. These are the two extreme ends of the scale and there are many comments and opinions on the structure, vision and policies of the Canadian government and its people that fit on the extreme right and left sides of the scale and everywhere in between. In this respect, it is the correct thing to do by respecting their concerns about us; but then we must critically analyze the background and the motives behind the criticism.

Canada is a nation that has never expanded its sovereignty beyond its territory and did not fight a bitter war for independence. Furthermore, it developed a new relationship as both an equal partner and as a sovereign state without having to deal with old colonial investments like France and Great Britain. Therefore Canada has no old accounts to be settled, nor does it have old wounds to heal.

Canada has neither interest nor intention to either build a giant military or develop a world class economic power structure to become world dominant. If Canada had such a plan, it would be able to execute it with the abundant natural resources and the steady and consistent political system. The United States of America, after the collapse of the Soviet Union, has been the only super power and dominating force in the international, socio-political and economic sectors of the world and their relationship and every move has certain motives behind it. At times they may proclaim that they want to fight for the freedom of the masses in certain parts of the world. However, in some cases it is clear that the political leaders are aware that the primary concern is to the contrary and these interventions are for their best interests and all other concerns are less of a priority. This is not a brand new approach and it has been used for centuries by the colonial masters and in some cases the advocates for proletariat revolutionists. I do not have to go far and pick some examples such as the involvement of the Chinese and Russian governments in supporting Assad, the President of Syria while the citizens of that country fight against a corrupt dictatorship. However, I do not want to justify the American involvement in Syria and the assertion that their involvement is genuinely for the Syrian people; rather, it is some leftover mistrust from the Cold War against Russia. An enemy of the enemy is always a friend and this idea also applies for the nature of the involvement in the Arab Spring in the Middle East by the United States.

Canada does not have any such plans and moves at the global level, but it has its own agenda in which it is very careful in preserving its identity and maintaining its interest in a very careful and calculated manner. Whenever new challenges are being faced, Canada is very diplomatic and somewhat flexible in overcoming them in a very conservative manner. The recent changes in our immigration policy would be a good example of this. It is very politely and generously designed so that the genuine refugees and the members of the family class sponsorship are welcomed without a long delay and this makes for fewer expenses for the Canadian tax payers and weeds out the bogus claimants and those who attempt to abuse or misuse the system. I believe it is more than what was portrayed. Similar measures have been taken by some other receiving countries, but in a very different approach.

The motion of this nation is so far, fundamentally, on the same track but slight changes in some areas and in some sectors are partially influenced by global changes and challenges while the rest are prompted by the protection of local interests The overall relationship with America after it has been shifted from the United Kingdom continued to be cordial and very unique in nature till recently. When

America was in a shock and morally depressed by the terrorist attack on 11ᵗʰ September 2001, the President was very disturbed and took an aggressive approach to save the American spirit. Naturally, there was the expectation that Canada would take if not a major role at least a significant part in the war against Iraq and Afghanistan. But Prime Minister Jean Chretien somewhat disappointed them by declining their request and in a balanced manner tried to protect long term interests of Canada and clearly informed them that if those wars were sanctioned by the United Nations, then Canada would join. This was not expected and thoroughly disappointed the Americans at their time of critical need and had received great support from some of the members of NATO including the United Kingdom. But Mr. Chretien was very cautious about having too close of a relationship with the U. S. A and it was made clear during his election campaign as leader of the federal Liberal Party against Mr. Brian Mulroney the leader of the Progressive Conservative Party that he would not be influenced by the American government and kept the United States at a safe distance. The deteriorating relationship was somewhat bent by his successor Prime Minister Paul Martin and recovered to a certain extent in the early days of Stephen Harper. However, it is fair to say that our relationship with the United States is cordial but it is deteriorating.

Canada has been trying to keep itself unified; however, there are many blocks that stand in the way. For example there is, the tensions between the rest of Canada and Quebec and the idea of Quebec as a nation, rectifying the economic balance between oil rich Alberta and the manufacturing regions such as Quebec and Ontario and historical blocks such as land claims brought forward by the First Nations. The current Canadian economy is dominated by two major sectors. The first one is the oil sands in Alberta and this sector has created much tension in recent days due to environmental concerns the other concern is the value of the Canadian dollar in contrast to the American dollar. The Canadian dollar at this point in time is at a very high exchange rate globally. This has implications in terms of international trade for countries with which we have had a strong trade relationship can easily wind up choosing other countries to do business with due to the exchange rate being cheaper.

China the rising sun in the east is a growing challenge for the stability of the western economy and many members of the western economic block began to feel the pinch in 2009. It is only the beginning and this is going to alter the overall supremacy of the West. Some economists have predicted that China may take over almighty America and has also already pushed Japan down. The West will not forget the timely assistance given by China to the United States of America and the European Union during the peak of the recession in 2011-12. These days, the nations that once criticized and isolated China before the 1970s have turned around with open arms.

The recent fundamental and in some cases structural changes in global politics, social structure and culture has harkened the beginning of a new era. The collapse of the Soviet Union, followed by the eastern European nations of the former Yugoslavia, Czechoslovakia, Romania, and Hungary among others, is not a sign of the failure of scientific socialism. In fact the establishment of socialism on the soil of the Soviet Union is a historical accident turning the feudal system into socialism without going through the process of capitalism. The revolutionary aspect of socialism was unexpected. Though Socialism as an ideology makes perfect sense on paper, in practice it does not work for there are many interpretations. In fact the collapse of socialism has allowed the people living in these countries to live a better quality of life with the rights and freedoms that many of us take for granted.

In closing, Canada is not an island unto itself. Rather when it comes to the international stage, it plays a supporting rather than a starring role. It does not mean that this country is not important, it means that we do not impose our will on anyone; that we prefer to work by consensus rather than by force. It is this and our quiet quest for excellence that makes Canada a nation among nations.

ACKNOWLEDGEMENTS

I would like to take this opportunity to thank certain individuals who have given me their full support for this project. However, I would first like to thank them for reading this book and providing valuable feedback and also for their patience.

First of all, I would like to thank my family for giving me the liberty to be in my own world. When one is writing a book such as this, it can take one away from spending quality time with their loved ones and so I am grateful for their love and support.

I would also like to thank Andrew Linder, Ph. D for taking time to review my manuscript and for writing the lovely forward to this book. I am also thankful for his helpful suggestions and advice.

Special thanks also go to Ontario International Institute and my friend Suren Sornalingam for their encouragement and moral support.

And finally, I would also like to thank my publisher, Author House for without them this book would not be possible.

Samy Appadurai

CHAPTER ONE

Canada—We Complain,
the World Compliments

I was at the emergency ward at one of the better known hospitals in Toronto at about 7.00 am with a friend of mine who had an emergency health problem. While he was suffering from some sort of respiratory problem, he was shouting loud enough to penetrate all the layers of the atmosphere and hard enough to make a hole in the ozone layer. This scene alerted the attention of other patients who had appeared to be waiting hours for treatment. Some of the patients who thought that they had unbearable pain became noticeably more relaxed seeing him in a much worse condition and realized they themselves were in a relatively better state. The reporting formalities were done in short order and while I was seated in a corner, I listened to some of the patients venting their frustrations. One of them said that "It is a horrible health care system and this not an emergency ward at all. How long we are going to wait?" Another person said "Never mind waiting for a couple of hours, imagine this, my sister had to wait for kidney surgery for years". Still another person said "Look at these politicians,

1

they swallow our money by saying that they want to transfer our files into e-files and then they did nothing fruitful." These complaints never helped in reducing the pain and suffering of the patients, rather they aggravated it. After listening to all of this, "I arrived at two conclusions. The first one that these people are asking whether the glass was half empty. The second one is the assumed mismanagement or misuse of the tax payer's money by the government.

I do not disagree with Canadians who lobby and protest on reasonable grounds. But complaints regarding issues such as inadequate health services, increasing crime rates, school dropout rates, air quality, environmental issues, abuses in the immigration system, discrimination in many sectors, the cost of security for the G8-20 and so forth are unavoidable and should not be ignored or accepted at face value. Sometimes, I wonder if the souls of the forefathers who built this nation get revived and listen to our complaints? If they could speak to us from beyond the grave, they may ask us to look back at their circumstances and at the non—availability of the facilities that we enjoy today. It may serve us well to think about how they survived without pipe born water, without electricity, lacking modern heating equipment for the cold winters, without having industrial strength equipment for building infrastructure on virgin forested land and having to live at the mercy of the weather. At that time as well, we all have to pay for medical treatment and surgery could put our family into debt for years. Quite frankly, I think our forefathers would balk at our lack of courage and forbearance.

First of all let, us get into an Air Canada plane and go around the world and listen to what the world leaders and citizens of countries in all six continents have to say. A recent survey conducted by a reputable institution revealed that over 54 percent of middle aged people from developed nations such as the United Kingdom, U.S.A, France, India, China, Germany, Japan, Australia, Russia to name a few wanted to migrate to Canada and join us in sharing the fruits of our labor. Their reasoning is that that the overall development in Canada which includes better health services, education, transportation, and the peaceful co existence of multi ethnic groups. The survey clearly revels the internal temperature of the world and tells us that the high quality of life coupled with greater maturity in most of the vital aspects of this nation, people and the governing institutions has placed the image of Canada in quite a unique position. I do understand that there are countries in the world that have better strengths in certain respects but lacking behind in many others. For example, China is marching forward as a potential world power having a strong economy. This country has come from a "have not" level to the second largest economy in the world worth 3 trillion dollars. But the denial of fundamental freedoms for the people, freedom of the press, freedom of expression and so on has brought China down in some respects. The world nations that condemned China's deprivation of freedom left it isolation until the early 1970s. It was at that time that Dr. Henry Kissinger; former Secretary of State for President Nixon made a strong political maneuver by recognizing China and establishing a diplomatic relationship. There were a number of reasons for doing this, but the most important one was based on the political philosophy of "The enemy of my enemy is my friend". Although both the former Soviet Union and China practiced the Communist ideology in their economy and politics, they were rivals in their circle. By becoming closer and encouraging China in its development, the strength of Soviet Union would be reduced to a certain extent. Another example is India. India is the most populous democratic nation in the world and a spiritual giant, but India does not have very balanced development and is lags behind in many aspects. Although America is the only super power in the world, American foreign policy is controversial, government debt is in the trillions and that debt itself is more than the GDP of some countries in the world.

Let us now refresh our memory and allow me to capitalize on my years of deep rooted experience on three continents and gauge today's Canada. The unique qualities of Canada certainly supersede its drawbacks. The political maturity of the Canadian masses and active politicians are scoring comparatively high marks. It is pretty clear that Canada has a vision and every move of the government and the voters are very much in synch. Canada acknowledges and values the efforts put forward in building this nation. As a nation we are concerned with diminishing the gap between the main stream and minorities and within the minorities that of the visible and non visible. When it comes to integrating minorities, we are very successful. This is somewhat rooted in the idea of inter—culturalism the idea that all people of all cultures need to work together to support each other while upholding common values. And unlike America's melting pot policy, Canada does not just "tolerate" or dilute other cultures; rather it encourages new immigrants in the preservation of their culture while getting integrated into Canadian life at the same time. Of course, in the due course of time, the third generation of newcomers gets absorbed within the mainstream culture without any outside help. The only drawback is that many show a strong patriotic connection to their ancestral homeland. It began from the father of Canada, Sir John A McDonald, who once said that," I was born as a British subject and live and die as a British subject". It is and will be very important to foster a sense of national pride in new Canadians.

Another excellent example from recent history is that when radical sovereignty members were very active in Quebec and the unity of Canada was at stake, both of the leading Canadian political parties got together, put their party interests aside and brought the national interest to the forefront. They accepted what was the only alternative to safeguard the unity of the nation and that was to strengthen the provincial Liberals of Quebec and create a powerful provincial government, rather than allowing the Party Quebecois to become more dominant. The national Conservative leader was transferred to the position of provincial party leader of the Liberals and even today, the Premier of Quebec Jean Charest acknowledged that he will seek a 4th consecutive victory and not at all rejoin federal politics.

At the Winter Olympics, and the G8 and G20 summits of 2010, the members of the opposition parties disagreed on many things including the spending of almost a billion dollars on security. But when the time of hosting those events came, they all forgot their differences and either cooperated or kept silent. Canadians are smart people; they do not make much noise and watch the situation carefully before making any moves. I can cite a recent example of how Canadians waited until the eleventh hour and approved the way the G8-20 was organized and executed. Canadians take the short term pain for the long term gain. Practicing conservatism in politics brought us away from the Americans. When the thirteen colonies of the new world fought against their colonial ruler the United Kingdom and had the revolution, the Canadians in the north still wanted their independence but without shedding blood or antagonizing their ancestors. The Americans, the sons and daughters of liberty adopted a brand new republic and the presidential system of government, Canada still continues the parliamentary and the constitutional monarchy systems.

In spite of practicing conservatism in many aspects of the government, the structure of the senate follows in the footsteps of the House of Lords with some new Senators appointed by the Prime Minister. It is this idea of "Responsible Government" that makes the new comers who have migrated from over 190 countries around the world feel more at home in Canada.

The whole world was very impressed with the operation and the management of the Canadian banking system when all of the developing nations had been struggling to fight against the worst recession since the Depression of the 1930s. Most of those nations entered the recession earlier and have yet to come out of it whereas Canada entered later and began getting out of it earlier. The conservatism policy in controlling and managing the financial institutions brought in a steady capital formation and a strong real estate market. Though the deficit in the government budget is higher compared to the period of the recessions in the 1980s and 1990s, still compared with countries like the United States of America, United Kingdom, and some other developed nations, the Canadian deficit is still relatively small. The unemployment rate never climbed to double digits and began to come down from 8.1% to 7.9% in the month of May 2010. When it was discovered that there were some new mineral deposits in the northern territories and large amounts of oil sand deposits in Alberta and Newfoundland, Canadians did not get overly excited, rather they carried out their normal routines. The attitude of "stay calm and carry on" has served us well.

My commentary would not be complete if I do not include the stand of Canada on international terrorism. We should appreciate that Canada has not confronted any particular ethnic, religious, or political groups. In fact, Canada never joined as the confronting fighters in the Iraq or Afghanistan wars. In Afghanistan, we are participating due to our obligations to NATO. Internally Canada never deprives the rights of certain groups of people or relaxes its hate crime regulations. There might some small incidents that might have been instigated by certain individuals, and even in those cases Canada has stood firm in protecting the constitutional rights of the victims

Let us now look at the future of Canada. In the future, there is going to be more of a decentralized economy away from Alberta, Ontario, and Quebec to other provinces. There is a concentration of economic activities that have already moved from Ontario to some other provinces due to more of the pulling and pushing forces. The security and protection of the Canadian North is essential. The exports of raw minerals may have to be turned into finished products more than now. Since North American free trade is not moving as had been expected, the extension, search and exploration of new markets are one of the top most priorities. Last but not least, the baby boomers expected that more babies would replace them, but the decline in the natural increase in population does not give us much hope. Therefore, Canadian immigration policies have to meet the challenge of the shortage of man power. I am not worried, we have faced many challenges before and we will do it again.

In closing, allow me to say, this is my country. I love it and I love its people. Let us all be proud to be Canadians.

CHAPTER TWO

The Global Nomads

Any person who drops into the cosmopolitan cities of New York, Toronto, Tokyo, Paris or London may notice that these are not homogeneous cities, but that they truly reflect the world. They might also be convinced that they do not need to go to every inch of the globe to know about various cultures, lifestyles, languages, technological developments and so forth. There are over one hundred and ninety million people on this planet including sixteen million refugees out of seven billion residing outside their countries of origin. These refugees come from over two hundred countries and in 1975 there were only eight million of them. Today, one out of every thirty five people in the world is a migrant and the numbers are consistently increasing. The annual growth rate in migration today is 2.9% and it was 2.1 % between 1965 and 1990. It might appear but a fraction of the entire world population, but the impact of this migration in terms of the general balance of the overall population is rather high, and the volume and the speed is getting faster. The distribution of migrants geographically has shifted drastically since the year 2000 and ten percent of the total population of seventy countries mostly the developed ones are migrants. By contrast thirty years ago, it was only forty five countries. The migrant population in the developed world from 1980 to 2000 has more than doubled from forty eight million to sixty five million. Compared with other developing countries it is fifty two to sixty five million and currently sixty percent of the world's migrants live in the developed world. Their contribution to Europe and North America where the birth rates are declining is largely positive. Between the period of 1980 and 2000, eighty-nine percent of the population growth of Europe and that of North America was seventy-five percent. Twenty percent of Canadians, with the exception of those who were born outside of Canada to non-Canadian parents of which I am proud to include myself.

Today, migrants including refugees from around the world mainly belong to the following categories:

1. Skilled workers. (semi skilled, unskilled and skilled)
2. The investors with their financial resources.
3. Contract basis and later accepted as permanent residents.
4. International students who then eventually get permanent resident status (this is also known as the Canadian experience class).
5. Refugees (government sponsored, sponsored by charitable or nonprofit organizations, government sponsored).
6. Permanent residents admitted on humanitarian and compassionate grounds
7. By marriage and family class sponsorship of spouse
8. Family class sponsorship of extended family members
9. Illegal Immigrants (seasonal and undocumented)
10. The right of return policy of Israel for Jews

Countries	year	Percent age of Foreign born	Total population
USA	2011	11.8%	311, 861 917
United Kingdom	2010	11.3%	62, 008,000
France	2010	11.1%	64,716,300
Canada	2012	20%	33,476,688
Germany	2010	12%	81,802,300
Sweden	2010	14.3%	9,340,7 00

Internal migration from the rural areas to the cities and city to city migration and visits as tourists are also another aspect of the Global Village and in fact this portion of this book was written at the El Fenador Hotel in Cayo Coco, Cuba.

A variety of circumstances push the source countries to supply immigrants and the receiving countries pulled them into their land with mixed feelings around accepting them. No matter what country it is, there may be a point in their immigration history that reveals that at one point in time a sizeable portion of the citizens if not the entire nation was opposed to the emigration of all or certain undesirable ethnic groups. Every nation in the world tries to find all possible means to protect and preserve its homogeneous identity and is reluctant in terms of accepting others permanently or even temporarily. The English Canadians discriminated against the Irish and Scots who arrived from the same groups of islands in Canada. The great Russians pushed down other Russians and the mainland Portuguese discriminated against their own people who had been residing in their colonies and some of them even carried over the same sentiments to Canada. The French and the British in Canada looked down upon the eastern and southern Europeans and were not willing to accept them whole heartily, let alone the Asians, Africans and South Americans.

The fundamental factors for immigration and emigration are more than the imbalance in the global population; rather, the main concern is economic benefits and then humanitarian concerns. For example, the brain drain and gain which has doctors and nurses emigrating to Canada in large numbers to make up for the Canadian trained doctors and nurses who emigrate elsewhere is something many Canadians are familiar with. Immigration is a very complex process, and in this book we will take Canada as an example and examine the evolution Canadian immigration policies, philosophy, structure and implementation.

When the name Canada appears in printed, electronic and visual media, most of the people who have at least heard about the country get a couple of spontaneous images in their minds: phrases such as, 'A land of immigrants", "A land of opportunities', "The land of peace and harmony" and "The country that was built by immigrants" easily come to mind. Some of the First Nations people may say that Canada is "a stolen land" or "North America was invaded by Columbus", but in spite of all these expressions a common idea of Canada is that Canada is "a land of snow".

The political demarcations and the name Canada came into existence very recently. But the history of the original inhabitants of the land dates back to ten thousand years ago. Although the timeline has been determined, there is evidence beyond doubt that of many of the ancestors of the First Nations people migrated from Asia via Alaska and began to spread their settlements from the North West towards the rest of the continent. There is a controversial point of view presented by the natives that there are the only original inhabitants of this land and the rest including the British and French are immigrants and they feel offended when placed in the immigrant basket. This appears to be a simple theoretical conflict but has much sentiment and deeply connected ideas behind it. The natives do not want themselves to be treated differently than the rest of the population, regardless of their economic and social status. They feel that they were invaded, tortured, and massacred and that their identity was destroyed.

Let us assume the natives are the first settlers to Canada and the question of their coming to Canada is a historical accident or due to exploration. The natives did not come from one particular region belonging to a designated tribes, rather their migration might have been from many regions having their own spoken languages, cultures, traditions and their own kinships. They had more differences than commonalities. They had some rival groups and fought among themselves and never got along well. Their nature of life was mainly determined by their occupation and they were mainly hunters and collecting food and other items. They did not expect a constant supply of animals. Since they were wandering from place to place and no designated location of their own and not indulged in making claims and creating any emotional attachments like farmers on their land.

The second major factor is that they endured major physical and climatic changes for thousands of years which in turn affected their lives and forced them to move for their survival. For them crossing the ocean at a narrow point between the eastern tip of Asia to Alaska would have been like crossing a river and at time crossing over in a point of flowing water would have been more of a struggle compared to walking on a solid surface of snow during the winter.

They created settlements and then established a system of living as communities and developed a system of life with customs and traditions for family life and marriage, bringing up children, the type of relationship between the husband and wife, parents and children. They also had very strong spiritual faith in the existence of god, and they made offerings and developed ceremonies to honour the various kinds of spirits. Their system of government though not established like that of the monarchy in Europe still had the elements of legislation, execution and judiciary in an informal, undocumented oral tradition carried on from generation to generation with slight modifications. Over the course of time they lost their roots and no longer have any links with their ancestors and they are now totally the sons and daughters of this land. Though the coastal migration theory is regarded is controversial by some, it is important for it explains that all of us at some point were immigrants to this country.

I celebrated my Thanksgiving last year in a cottage up north almost two and a half hours drive from the city. I was enjoying a cool breeze from the lakeside and was admiring the lovely scenery on the drive back to Toronto, the busiest and most complex city. I had nothing much to discuss with my family because due to being at the cottage, my cell phone was also given a paid vacation and my daughter quickly changed the password and kept it exclusively under her control. What could I do to feed my mind and brain? I saw a few birds flying over in the sky and it caused me to think of the birds in the north and the first thought that came in my mind was their migration routine during the fall season.

After having a beautiful long summer with the experience of day light for months without any break, the idea of facing the bitter cold with darkness all around frightened them and they began to move down south crossing land and water ignoring the political boundaries having neither entry or exit visas. Likewise many birds from Europe migrate to Africa and Asia passing over five thousand kilometers. They are like semi nomads for they do not have to be on the move like the nomads moving around constantly, not only for a season or a particular part of their life and they are on move from the womb to tomb. I had the privilege of being with some nomads when I was in a foreign workers contract position in the State of Sokoto, Nigeria. They raise their livestock (cows and bulls) in the semi desert regions when the annual mean temperature is above 30 degree Celsius and the rain fall is limited for almost three months a year. They carry Lanton, four feet long sticks, a thick plastic tent and a handful of items that comfort them in fulfilling their basic needs. They are in their own world and pay little to no attention to the permanent settlements in a designated area, political operations and disputes between counties, migration restrictions or flexibilities and socialization.

Father Thomas Malthus tried to prove that nature was best left alone and he tried to prove that the balance of the population on the earth would be taken care of by nature by various means and that we did not have worry much about it. Natural calamities such as floods, drought, tsunami, earthquakes, volcanic eruptions in many forms and manmade destructive measures such as wars, conflicts, fights, killings, diseases, and accidents would provide the necessary means to keep the population in check. Though this theory may not be thought purely in practical science, yet it cannot be totally ignored. History provides us with some examples:

A) The Great Irish Potato Famine

B) Drought in the Horn of Africa

C) Earthquakes in various parts of the world

D) Volcanic eruptions

E) Man made factors—WWI-WWII, Korean War, Rwanda

F) Weapons such as the atomic bomb, chemical and biological weapons.

Along with these factors, it is important to consider what happens in the general population in terms of settlement which will we will now discuss.

The Stages of Population Growth I

Should we be happy to hear that the world's population has reached 7 billion? I do have to mention that the accuracy of population figures has an element of doubt. Aerial photography plays a part in calculating the rate of population growth in many developing countries, and there are no records to show if the people living in the virgin jungles and rain forests were counted, if at all. Inaccurate figures were provided by certain countries that were skewed in such a way as to maximize the mainstream population and minimize minorities. That was why when the birth of the 7 millionth child was announced, I thought that it was ridiculous in this highly developed technological word where every second counts; surely, there were better priorities. But then I compromised by rewarding the efforts put forward in terms of the actual counting and the efforts made. Mother Earth has never kept statistics on the number of people who walk on her soil; it is only we who have noticed the tremendous levels of growth and this has given us many messages. In spite of the declining birth rates life expectancy has increased and the quality of human life has improved and it is these contributing factors which lead to the issue of global migration.

Let us now have a look into the demographic patterns. This process is an ongoing phenomenon and some countries have reached the fourth and final stage, while the rest are moving slowly from the first stage.

Ever since man was differentiated from an advanced stage of monkey with his six senses, the only tool making creature has always been on the move. There are many controversial theories regarding the origin of man such as the time, concerning where and if he originated in one particular location and moved around the world or originated at different places at different times. With our modern scientific methods and technology we have discovered that there are areas such as the core of the Amazon rainforest, the equatorial forest in Africa, and underneath the oceans and other bodies of water that though we may obtain some answers regarding the origins of man the outcome that we have reached might not reveal clear—cut answers. In spite of the results that we have gathered from the hard work of the archaeologists, anthropologists and historians thus far reveals that man originated in Eritrea, a country in the horn of Africa which recently gained independence. The research however has been continuing and the conclusions may shift elsewhere as it has in the past from Java, Russia, Uganda and so on. It all depends on the discovery of the oldest remaining human skull. I do not want to go deep into the differences in the shape, color, height and other physical features. According to the research the first man originated around 6.5 million years ago, but the age of the oldest skull that was discovered in Eritrea does not match this time frame. If it is so than man was differentiated at one point in time in one location and migrated to different locations over the course of time.

Migration is not an easy process particularly from a place where he was conditioned to the area. Even if it was economically disadvantaged or had horrible climatic conditions, he would not make the decision to depart. As the old saying goes east or west home is the best and a known devil is better than an unknown angel. It is true even today that in most villages where people are deeply rooted with their culture, traditions and attachments to the land and where agriculture is the main source of income. In spite of this there were manmade and natural causes that pushed and pulled early man to move from their traditional residential areas. The changes in the natural conditions were often the main pushing force. The continent of Lemuria south of the Indian sub content sank into the Indian Ocean and it has been discovered by archaeologists that the first world's civilization existed on that piece of tropical land; the only remaining pieces of evidence are kept in museums as treasures which belong to all of humanity. The glorious Mayan civilization in Mexico is not limited to the remains of the pyramids and some other archaeological discoveries and some have said that this culture existed long before the modern history of North America and certainly before the discovery of America by Columbus. I strongly accept that the modern history of North America began with the entry and settlement of the Europeans. But I do not agree with the idea that the natives of North America were living totally primitive lives. It may be true in some cases; however there is valid research that shows that they had a very advanced civilization compared against some of the European cultures. Sadly one area's civilized society is another one's "barbarians" as was the case with the Romans describing the culture and habits of the people from the British Isles. I believe North America has a wonderful history and that more research has to be made in the study of the migration to this land. The continental drifts which occurred on the earth including the process of the Gonduvana land mainly in the southern hemisphere where South America, Australia and the Southern parts of Asia and Africa were one piece of land even after the development of human beings also had some impact on human migration.

Apart from these factors there are many other natural calamities which caused migration. Just imagine the seriousness of the evacuation of people from the Maldives in the Indian Ocean due to the fact that they are sinking. Volcanic eruptions, tsunamis, earthquakes, and the disappearance of rivers are forces that are very much alive and well and provide due cause for mass migration in the 21st century as they did thousands of years ago.

Climatic changes are another factor that has been contributing to migration as well. When I think about the climate changes, two contradictory incidents come into my mind. I am a critic and commentator on the daily news for my television station (Rogers's channel 686). I really enjoyed it when I analyzed the news about Al Gore, the former Vice president of the United States of America and advocate for fighting against global warming that his mansion was constructed along a lake after the deforestation of the land. The second incident was the summit on global warming held in Copenhagen, Denmark where nations from all over the world actively participated and accused India, China and some other nations of contributing more to the problem of global warming by using cheaper sources of energy. Many of the key members raised their concerns up to the sky and the innocent masses around the world expected some changes to take place like miracles. What happened in the end was that the issue was put on the lowest end of the priority scale for each of the nations involved. Once an important political figure said that global warming was not mainly caused by the industrial sectors and that the over using of sources of exhaustible energy rather than nature's ongoing long term processes was the main problem and that we did not have over emphasize and worry much about it. When Paul Martin organized its summit in Quebec when he was the short term Prime Minister, the nation south of Canada did not adequately participate enough and he was not at all pleased about this.

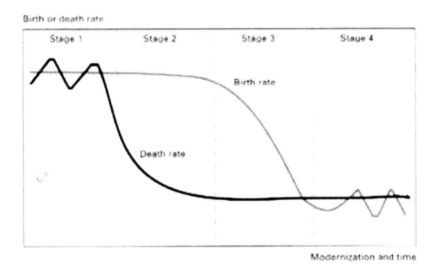

At the rate that world's nations are growing, certainly 14% of the 24 % of the total global land mass will be swallowed by water and we may have to temporarily stop the plans of constructing houses and buildings and focus on the water. I do not think nature will take care of water, plants, and animals. Recently Canada and the other five nations that share the Arctic water body are highly worried about the unexpected speed in the melting of the snow and the effects of the layers of fresh water that come out of the snow on top of the salt water ocean.

The adverse effects of deforestation chased human beings and other creatures in many parts of the world out of their homes. The Sahara desert and the deserts of Iraq are typical examples which show that the land was once a forest and became a desert because of the deforestation that took place due to the need for farmland. The ice age also made drastic changes in the lives of early human civilization and also caused migration and emigration of humans and other creatures.

I do appreciate that researchers and historians have been doing this heavy work and it has brought enlightenment to the issues and I do strongly believe that due to various reasons such as political instability and the deliberate hiding of facts and the blind acceptance of fabricated facts is quite an injustice. I contend that my views are not at all strange and are the unspoken views of many around the world. Let us now come back to the evidence that I have on the migration of human beings by looking at the following chart:

Stage II

Stage one was the primate stage in which man began to use external tools more than totally depending on his physical features like any other creatures on earth. It was at this time that early human beings passed from the Stone Age to the slightly more advanced bow and arrow. It was the stage in which man was just above lower animal kingdom and, being a good partner to nature, was the best practice and there was a lesser need for modification. It was the same man who was wandering around and for whom life was a struggle for food and safety. Early man was always on the move in search for these things and there was not much time allotted to forming a society and using collective actions. This was the pre—arable farming stage and hunting and food collecting there was no need for permanent settlements. It was the stage in which sex was purely an instinct like other mammals and the reaching of puberty was the fully matured stage for sex and reproduction. Sex without having any control naturally or artificially never occurred and no attempt was made in terms of separating sexual desire from concern over reproduction. When we look into the ratio of the population to the reproduction rates of today against this early stage, the rate was much higher than today. But the unfortunate part is that the death rate was also as high as the birth rate. Humans have been given the six senses that are more powerful, provided that they make use of them and even the ultra-modern man on the average uses around 10-15% of his brain capacity. However, primitive man used much less than it does now. Mind, you there are pockets in the world still where we do have people in this stage. For example, in the core of the densely forested areas in the equatorial belts in some areas of the Amazon river, the Congo river, the East Indian Islands and some forest areas in Philippines though some of these groups do accept contact with the outside world. There are also some non—conventional sexual relationships which still exist between human beings and animals as mentioned in the historical mythology in the history of certain nations. I do wonder about this because I believe in the theory of evolution and wonder how it is that these groups can still continue without being assimilated.

Stage III

The nomads particularly in the temperate zones where the climatic conditions were not an extreme of temperatures provided much better conditions. The mild weather provided ample time from struggling and fighting against the weather and it allowed more time to think, invent and discover many things. Even the simple discovery that fire was not only helpful for providing warmth but could also be used to cook and provide light, which in turn gave protection and kept animals away was indeed quite an achievement. The fundamental change was the switch over from hunting and food collection into agriculture. In fact, it was the major turning point in human history by giving them ample opportunity during the growing season to innovate and explore and this made these people use their minds more extensively, which led to a further separation between man and animal. The total outcome of this progress was tremendous. The small groups began to share in the production and process of agriculture, and the distribution of wealth by exchanging goods and services by barter which made life easier. This also allowed the people to connect and share the intellectual resources; they exchanged love and affection along with other good and bad feelings and emotions. This was the stage when man discovered that he is much more capable and different from other creatures. He realized that human beings had the potential of looking forward and going backward and was able to utilize his memory which cannot be done by any other creature in the world. The totality of these developments brought about the great civilizations of Egypt, Mesopotamia, the Indus Valley, Mohenjo-Daro, the Chinese and the Roman and Greek civilizations. It was also the stage in which there was a change in the increase in population. People began to improve their lifestyles and found ways and means in making use of the materials for a better life. They deviated from sex and love being the only pleasure in life to the cultivation of the fine arts and creative pursuits. This resulted in having social conventions such as marriage and this became a part of life which in turn brought stability. These changes also brought certain restrictions and the development of culture fostered the growth of traditions and unwritten laws. Furthermore, the impact of education in health and other areas also improved the early death rates and infant mortality lowered. Here, the slowdown in both the birth rate and the death rate occurred, but the speed of the death rate was much higher than that of the birth rate and this brought on a population explosion. But the mobility rate turned to a different direction. Firstly the wanderers settled down in a designated area and the migration was slowed down. Later, on intercultural and intercommunity trade and other relationship encouraged mobility. When their attempt at the exploration of fertile land proved successful, the move to the new places began.

Stage IV

The sudden increase in the birth rate altered the population demographics drastically. For example, the age groups of those lower than age 25 accounted for almost 50% of the total population and the active population had to earn more in order to feed and support them. This became an additional burden. However, this was not hard and due to the lower standard of living and the cost of supporting expenses was very low and many joined the labor force when they were teenagers. There was no requirement to have a formal education and it was almost considered a luxury. The form of government was almost a dictatorship and the lesser the subjects were educated the better and easier it was to control and exploit them. Religious faith also became a tool of the government and those in power made claims that they were the representatives of god, claimed divine rights and declared that they could not make any mistakes and whatever they did was always correct because god never makes mistakes. It was very convenient for them to exploit the masses in this way to profit from their work.

The primary sources of production were agriculture and then trading. Since the population was low compared with the number of resources that could support them, it was considered under populated. The increase in population was encouraged, and this allowed for the utilization of available land for cultivation and abundant grass land for livestock. Since only manual labor was expected the people began working at a young age and it came to a point where the increase in production depended on the quantity of the labor force.

People began to awaken and used the potential of their brains more than ever before and traditional craftsmanship such as carpentry, blacksmithing, mining, artistry, tool making, shipbuilding, cloth making and pottery making developed faster. The training for this trade pushed the entry into labor market for years later and the stage of being economic independence along with marriage was delayed. The standard of living rose very high and naturally the demand for achieving a high standard of living pushed people to earn extra money. People began to realize that education was not meant only for the rich, but for everyone and that it would lead to a much better quality of life. The improvements in shelter, tools for farming, textiles, self protection and the mode and means of transportation, fetching water and drilling wells, the discovery of roots, leaves and other natural resource for treating illnesses uplifted their overall development. One of the main outcomes was the reduction in infant mortality and the increase in life expectancy.

Most of the developing countries, particularly in Latin America, Asia, and Africa, entered into this stage from the earlier one after they got rid of their colonial rulers in the 1960s and onwards with a few exceptions such as the American Revolution and India just after the

Second World War. In the case of India, participation in the war was a blessing in disguise because the British colonial rulers somehow manipulated their ruling tactics by using softer methods on India rather than the more cruel ways of oppression before the war. The Second World War was more focused on destroying the powerful enemies of the colonial powers in this case Japan, Germany and Italy. The time was running out and the preparation in defeating the enemy was not an easy task. The British used another technique by giving permission to India that if they cooperated and if Britain won the war, more autonomy to India would be granted. It all depended on the level of cooperation that they gave and abstention from supporting the enemy Japan in the east. Over thirty thousand Indians mainly Sikhs, fought with and for the British and thus the British owed a debt to India. Under the leadership of Mahatma Gandhi, India won independence due to the influence of the non violence movement. So far in the world's history he was the only leader who successfully used this method. China and some other countries also won their independence prior to the 1960s.

During the painful war with all sort of destruction, there was a determination within their nations towards the development of patriotism. The United Nations Organization also encouraged and helped them to implement their plans and improved their health, education, and infrastructure. Certain disputes among the former colonies were resolved though some of the former colonies strongly believe that one of the main causes for border disputes and local civil wars was that the British deliberately drew the borders to split the various ethnic groups into different countries so that the different ethnic groups would fight amongst themselves undermining their progress. Since I have worked as a school principal and teacher in Nigeria and Ethiopia for eighteen years, I spent many happy occasions with the various ministers, governors and prominent politicians and local chiefs who have inherited power in ruling the masses of the designated areas. I learned that modern constitutions would not dare to interfere in their regimes. In fact, the issue of border disputes still carries to this day.

How far and deep enough to accept these ideas or not is not my concern here, for the specific reason the influx of refugees and mass killings also alter the migration policies of many countries and I give a few examples below;

i)   The Biafra war in Nigeria
ii) Congo-Zaire
iii) Ugandan war between Ethiopia and Somalia
iv) Rwanda genocide
v)   Vietnam war between the North and South
vi) Cold war between the USA and the former USSR

Stage V—Decline in the Birth rate.

The decline in fertility in the middle income countries and some extent in the higher low income countries has become more diversified and more sophisticated and people began to enjoy the fruits of the Industrial Revolution and modern technology and began to penetrate into the heart of many nations around the world from Europe and North America to Japan in the east. Just imagine rural farms in which the unskilled laborers do not receive free compulsory education and some who have never stepped inside a school have cell phones. These days television, telephones, a constant supply of electricity and pipe born water are no longer considered luxury items. Rather, they are listed as basic needs. The United Nations has also been very successful in implementing the compulsory basic education of children at least until the age of 14.

I have observed other interesting changes that have come from the more materialistic lifestyle we are living. For one thing, it is less concerned about religious and social traditions. These days one's lifestyle is more global than regional or ethnically based particularly in the urban areas and the rural areas are dramatically being urbanized. Marriage is no more holy and noble and sex is now considered a physical need and urge and many of the social and religious restrictions and other laws pertaining to this no longer hold any sway. Although most religions are against abortion, same sex relationships and marriage, premarital sex, divorce and remarriage and adultery there are slight changes that I have observed. One example is that recently Pope Benedict has somewhat reluctantly supported the use of condoms in order to prevent the spread of infectious disease. It is similar to the compromise that Pope John Paul II agreed to with another aspect of theology in South America, namely "Liberation Theology". In the western nations there is the growing tendency that marriage is no more an everlasting bond and in some cases it is not obligated and in other cases it is an unwanted burden. When it comes to sex and reproduction these days they do not go together and it is believed that sex is mainly meant for pleasure, only occasionally a part of reproduction. Also, sexual relationships do not necessarily go along hand in hand with responsibilities of marriage. But in order to get married, the laws can vary and 16 or 18 years of age is the minimum age range though in some countries it used to be 21. Though they are free to have sex it is not encouraged for them to have children at these young ages. These days usually women get married at the age of 26 and men at 28 years of age and they prefer to have children in their early thirties. It appears that today's mother would have been the grandmother in earlier times.

Finally what has happened is that in one point in history the birth and death rates match and if the external migration doors were to be closed there would not be any way to increase the population. Most of the developed nations such as the USA, Canada, United Kingdom, Germany, France, Denmark, Switzerland, Holland, Japan, Portugal, Spain, and Australia are climbing up this ladder.

In 2030 more than a third of population in many western states including Canada and some of the Asian nations such as Japan, Korea will be the seniors and other rapidly developing nations will follow

Stage VI Decrease in population growth

A decrease in the population is the final stage of this cycle. Anyone could postpone or avoid having children, but life expectancy cannot be changed beyond a certain point unless some miracle is invented. The next alternative is inventing sophisticated robots to replace human beings. I also have concerns over the baby boomers at this junction for they are an important treasure.

I am very fond of visiting McDonald's restaurants almost every Saturday before I go for my weekly shopping at No Frills at Brimley and Eglinton Avenue East in Scarborough. It is always crowded with loving senior couples together who are well dressed and particularly the women with their lovely make up with red lipstick featuring prominently. I quietly sit down in a corner and while having my breakfast, my eyes and ears always move towards them without permission. I do not mind this because I am not trying to pry into their business. I admire the intimacy between each couple and their manners and how they enjoy their conversation and their meals. At times, I forget that I have other obligations other than enjoying these beautiful moments!

Whenever I listen to the radio and read the newspapers I am very keen in looking for news concerning the well being of seniors. Most of the so called baby boomers were born between 1946 and 1956, after World War II and account for almost 12 %, (4.3 million) of the current Canadian population of 32 million. It is a high proportion of the age demographic but gradually it will decrease in the due course of time because of the low rate of the natural increase in population. The migration of recent new immigrants fit into the early middle age classification and there is no influx in the number of seniors.

It is my strong belief that we owe them a lot because we are reaping their fruits of their labor, sacrifices, hard work and commitments. If they would not have done such services today, we would not be able to have all these comforts. Once you thank the giver, certainly he will give you more. Seniors are not a burden to us. Rather they are our invaluable treasures.

My close observation and discussions with seniors has brought me to the conclusion that their major and pressing needs are that a kind of recognition is needed. They need to have their concerns addressed well and need their social needs catered to rather than financial supplements. At this point we should thank the provincial and federal government for doing their best in assisting them. Of course, some find it hard to manage their expenses with the pension that they receive from the government.

We citizens have a moral obligation to lend seniors a generous helping hand. Even without spending money or exhausting our financial resources we have to make some sacrifices to help them. We could use some of our leisure time in visiting and helping them. These days they are very careful in welcoming a stranger because of ugly incidents that have victimized some seniors in the hospital and nursing homes such as robbery. However, this should not discourage us from making the effort to reach out.

I am very certain that a little bit of our time will make a big difference for them and in my articles; I share ways and means of how to carry out those assignments. Let us remember that one day sooner or later we will join them too.

The governments of countries where the birth rate is in decline do not want to leave things as they are and have brought forward a lot efforts and initiatives to encourage people to have children. Providing baby bonus allowances and yearlong maternity leave are some examples.

However, countries like China and India which contain almost one third of the population and human resources and from which many immigrants to Canada are from are in an interesting position. These two countries will be able to supply skilled workers for another two to three decades, but then they will experience what we in Canada are going through right now. Once the birth rates in China and India begin to decline, the western world will have to attract more immigrants from South America, Eastern Europe and Africa especially those who are skilled workers.

CHAPTER THREE

Immigration and Emigration in Canada

The evolution of the policies and structure of modern immigration and emigration in Canada since the establishment of the first European settlements till today has gone through dramatic changes in priorities, including race, culturally keeping the homogeneous interests, volume, economic interests and demography.

The British and the French were the dominating colonial forces and controlled the global economy for almost five centuries. They explored and colonized new lands with their subjects and their sovereign states for the colonizer's economic interests unilaterally. Once they captured these areas they claimed that it was their own and did not want anybody else to make any claims. They kept Canada under their control and were determined that their people had the exclusive rights to migrate and settle down in the North American colony as their subjects. There are some fundamental differences in the colonization of North America or the so called northern part of the new continent and Australia. With all due respect to the First Nations, the colonizers treated them very differently. As such, their strength of having an established form of government was not forceful enough or technically capable in challenging the powerful colonial rulers as the Asians and Africans had and it was very convenient for the colonizers to bring the population down to the bare minimum level and to make them dependant for the rest of their lives. Although they inhabited the land thousands of years back and were the only ethnic group who migrated and claimed the ownership of the land, they could not fight against the colonial rulers and were unable regain their position in these lands. This gives the phrase "survival of the fittest" a whole new meaning.

The consequences of the colonization of South and Central America by the Spanish and the Portuguese were similar. The natives who were comparatively weaker in strength and less advanced in terms of their economies and were poor in their protective forces faced the same adverse effects. Their glorious past is dead and buried in the history books and records. Their migration is more a challenge or a major factor that determined the current demography or the immigration policy. Those who have been residing or confined within the reserves are a small island attached to a massive land mass form of the rest of the nation's policies.

Let us now look into the multidimensional aspects of colonization. We should accept the fact without biased opinion that those countries were somewhat more advanced with powerful means to search for new land for their migration. The immigrants who left their countries were the result of the pushing and pulling forces and the ratio of the two was up and down in many cases. The system of government for five hundred years was aristocratic and discriminative which believed that the common masses should be the obedient subjects. They had no right to question authority, though in England the degree was lower and the Magna Charta of 1215 considered and protected some of the fundamental rights of the masses. The struggle for justice, human dignity, and fighting against all sorts of deprivations of their rights including religious rights and the feudalistic structure of the economic distribution came at a price. The vast majority of the subjects were treated as ordinary citizens and they were bound to be ruled and had to obey the monarchy. The Monarchy's claim to power came in two main ways: in some cases it was made by the claim of the monopoly of land with its natural resources by the rulers and therefore the subjects on the land automatically became the unquestionable assets. Another method was achieved in a reverse position in that the subjects living on the land were the property of the rulers and therefore their property also belonged to them. Either way this proved an easy way to justify the deprivation of rights among the people.

A group of subjects who realized the exploitation and undue rights and privileges taken from them realized that they could not fight back and took the risk of emigration. The rulers preferred not to encourage such revolts, but when it got to a stage where it became a challenge they preferred to let them go and some cases even assisted them secretly.

The journey of these immigrants in those voyages with bare minimum facilities including the capacity to preserve their food, medicines and water to an unknown destination was almost a life and death situation. Not all of those ships reached their destinations safely, and there are many pathetic stories in the history books of those who perished. One of the main forces that contributed to the success of some of the adventurous journeys was their determination and courage. The pushing force of deprival contributed to the desire to discover a new land.

We also should not undervalue the contribution made by the respective rulers in facilitating the explorers in making their explorations, taking initiatives and executing the exploration. A good example is Queen Isabella of Spain. She financed the voyage of Christopher Columbus who was the architect in discovering the new world.

The monarchy itself made many efforts in the colonization process to find solutions to economic pressures and for the accumulation of wealth from outside their country. The economy was improving and the population also rapidly grew and the standard of living was slightly getting better and opening a new venue was a pressing issue. The competition in international trade and colonization among these countries pushed them forward in the expansion of their colonization efforts. Without their support and resources, none of those explorers and immigrants would have achieved what they had.

Once they arrived in the lands that belonged to the kingdoms, many of the local people at the early stages totally opposed and fought against them. In due course of time, reality proved that it wouldn't be possible to fight with their traditional tools such as bow and arrow and old-fashioned fire bombs against guns and other more sophisticated firearms. In fact, some were amazed by the power of guns and along with tasting wine and whisky sided and welcomed the colonists. In some other cases, they collaborated with them and negotiated and a came to a deal in which they agreed to have their feet step into the soil voluntarily and sought their help in destroying or weakening their rival kingdoms.

In North America the Thirteen Colonies made a clear and stubborn stand against the British Empire, their colonial rulers, by fighting against them and winning their independence. They had wars against two opposing forces as such with the Natives and the British. They kept their sentiments of being from the same ethnic group, speaking the same language, believing the same Christian faith but another denomination aside. For them, the grievances that they had when they were in their ancestor's land superseded the other. These immigrants uprooted themselves to a certain extant in a homogenous group, but within it there were many variations and sub groupings, and these factors played some influence in their day-to-day life. In spite of all these complexities in the establishment in a strange land a new life, the common goal of leaving their ancestor's land where they had been living for generations and the attachments was not an easy task, and this brought them under one umbrella.

The Americans after the victory in their independence war against the British Empire began to pay more attention to rebuilding their lives and prosperity rather than worrying about the empire or the consequences of the war.

The British Loyalists were the original settlers in the current United States of America. Those who got settled in the northern part of the country took a very different stand and this sparked a clash of interests with the American revolutionists. They generally emigrated from Britain with a similar background, had similar grievances, expectations and hopes and originally did not differentiate themselves from the rest. They had no idea what would happen once they got settled into their new land between their new form of government or any other type of governing institutions and the reaction of and relationship with the British Monarchy. It was a strange experience and there were no tangible historical guidelines to follow. There were two schools of thought which cropped up as major factors as to how to react to the empowerment of British rule. Both of them had one thing in common, that is to be independent but there was some difference in the means such as in a revolutionary or evolutionary method and the approach to achieve the goal.

At the initial stage, it took some time for them to adjust themselves to the strange environment which was new and they faced challenges from the natives and unknown physical and climatic conditions. Although they had migrated from a relatively temperate climate, they were not prepared for the conditions of the northern zones so and the cold winter was a big challenge for them. However, some of these experiences were not unexpected because these people knew that this was the nature of a journey to a strange land and they got themselves prepared for it as best they could. If we examine their background, it will help us gauge their level of satisfaction within the initial stage of their migration. Most of them came from the grass roots level in their society and had the bare minimum for their survival. Some of them were living below the poverty line that was demarked at that period of time and the resources that they had were very few and thus nothing much was left behind. They were not very skillful in terms of craftsmanship nor did they have advanced levels of education and so their value in terms of human resources was limited. The only advantage was that the majority of them belonged to the middle aged population and was able to contribute more in capital investment and in production. In fact nothing more than physical labor was the main expectation during the pre-industrial era.

Their social status and background also mattered during the reestablishment process in Canada. Most them at the early stage came from the bottom levels of society during that time. A fraction of the population was on the top of the ladder as members of the royal family, nobles, lords and land owners and clergymen. The rest of them belonged to the classes of craftsmen and ordinary subjects. They had a very little or no social recognition or status this somewhat established and stable society in an under developed land. There was no well coordinated and established form of centralized government with its own sovereignty. There were pockets of settlements with their chiefs which never had any advanced form of invasion or challenges. Their economic activities were also not very stable and did not have much of a system for obtaining and retaining wealth. Whenever there were intertribal wars, a sizable number of people had to forgo their labor input into their economic activities and joined the warriors. At the end of the war whether they had won or were defeated they had to put extra effort into their occupations. There were no reserves in non perishable goods and no scientific methods of preserving the perishable ones. Human dignity and importance of ordinary people was not well recognized and deaths in whichever the form it took was not accounted for, nor looked upon as a natural thing. Rather, one's death meant the loss of productivity and a loss to the economy.

I do not mean to say that the entire migrant population came from the grass roots of their societies or were the lowest of the low. There was a sizeable portion of them who had an interest in exploration and was seeking new opportunities to uplift their economic status. Others had other reasons that had nothing to with economics such as the quest for more freedom and liberty and these people did not mind it if they had to struggle even for their survival. I do not dispute that there were undesirable elements such as criminals who also got into the mix and there were also those who wanted to induce some forms of radical political change and saw migration as an opportunity to support these activities. There were also those who were brainwashed with false promise that if they discovered gold mines in the new continent they would become fabulously rich almost overnight. To accumulate such wealth, they had to work tirelessly for generations in their traditional homeland and this promise of easy wealth was hard to resist. There were also some sad cases. Among them, there were those who were victimized and felt that they were being punished for crimes that they never committed. During the 14th to 17th centuries, in most of those countries power rested in the judiciary, the legislators and those who enforced the laws. The balance of power was so unfairly balanced that many would not be able to fight for their rights and thus the only alternative was to leave. Along with these people came members of the church with the intention of doing humanitarian services and the desire to spread the gospel while still others were trying to escape forced conscription into the armed forces.

It was during the industrial revolution that the restructuring and overhauling of all economic activities which began first in the United Kingdom and thereafter followed by other western nations. This process of industrialization currently continues to penetrate every corner of the world from the remote primitive societies to developing countries. The invention of machinery brought about the new dynamic sector of manufacturing as a major source of production and this reduced the sole dependency on agriculture and trade though mechanization influenced these two sectors as well. The nature of manufacturing was such that many jobs which had been done by one or two specialized workers were now done by a larger number of lower skilled workers. This was a new experience for many people. In the sector of traditional farming in a land that was sparsely populated the labor force was mostly engaged during certain seasons and it was more or less a slow moving process. Even the production of tools and supplying them and the making of handicrafts was not done throughout the entire year.

In contrast, the industrial revolution brought a new set up in the lives of human beings. Work was no longer influenced by the weather conditions; rain, snow and severe storms were no longer a major concern. Mass scale production in a small area with strong investments first brought a labor force in the hundreds or in some cases by the thousands and their surroundings changed with new larger settlements. The nature of the work itself created a new culture in which the workers who came from many regions and brought heritage and traditional values were somehow unable to continue as they wanted and in some cases their cultures were demonized or diluted. The interesting part of this is that their life style was highly influenced by the nature of the economic sector. For example, those who worked an unchanged shift from Monday to Friday looked forward to Friday as it was the end of the work week. Though they may have been exhausted physically, they loved to enjoy the weekend and after having two days of relaxation, rest and enjoyment on Monday the first day of the week, they would be traveling to work in a gloomy mood. It is how almost all workers, irrespective of their social, cultural, and ethnic backgrounds feels and acts. What is at the core of culture after all is within us and how we feel act and react with external factors both physical and human.

One of the effects of the industrial revolution is the importance of

They were in a very difficult situation and could not go back to the sector of agriculture because there too the penetration of machinery partially closed the door to them. The producers did not care much and they were happy because the machines would not bother to demand better facilities and thus the workplace remained stable. It was also at this time that a portion of the population that was once included as a valuable force for production turned out to be unwanted laborers. There was nothing much to do and realizing the old saying that if there is a will there is way, followed the footsteps of those who left before them for an adventurous journey.

The period between 1896 and 1910 is a very significant period in Canadian immigration history. It was the time that the west and the eastern parts of the country were linked by the railway and the exploitation of the resources of the untapped lands of the Prairie Provinces had begun. Over three million new was in stark contrast with the immigrants who arrived from central and Eastern Europe with their potential skills and experience in the sector of agriculture. They mostly settled down in a very homogeneous group and continued their lives as though it were their land of origin with some modifications to adjust to the physical and human environment. The highest number of immigrants that arrived in Canada was 400,870 in the year 1913. This is the highest number of immigrants in Canadian history. Both domestic and foreign factors contributed for the influx of new immigrants, mostly from the rural areas and some of them from the low income areas of the cities at the time of the start of World War I. Though Canada received millions of new immigrants a sizeable number of them emigrated to United States of America finding jobs in factories. Some went back to their respective countries in Europe and this decline was partially caused by the racist policy reactions against countries such as Germany.

The Immigration act of 1906 brought certain restrictions to the somewhat generous immigration policy in existence since 1862. The immigration act of 1906 brought more restrictions in the entry and also widely opened the gates for unwanted immigrates to depart from Canada. The cabinet was given enhanced powers to exclude any class of immigrants in the best interests of the nation.

The foreign migration pattern was also partially decided by internal migration. There has always been a trend of migrating from region to another based on mainly economic reasons with the exception of the shift from Quebec to Ontario.

Internal migration ratios by province

Provinces	1901-1911	1911-1921	1921-1931
Prince Edward Island	-13.6	-19.4	-11.1
Nova Scotia	-0.6	-7.6	-14.5
New Brunswick	-3.8	-7.3	-11.5
Quebec	4.3	-4.0	0.9
Ontario	9.3	2.3	5.1
Manitoba	41.2	5.1	-1.7
Saskatchewan	125.6	15.1	-0.7
Alberta	123.8	20.9	3.8
British Colombia	69.4	14.8	18.7

Source; Leroy O. Stone Migration in Canada; regional Aspects.

Ottawa government publication, 1969.p.138

There was a mass influx of internal migration from the maritime provinces to the Prairie Provinces for the first three decades of the twentieth century and there was a steady increase of migration from those provinces from 1901-1910 to 1921-1931. In contrast to this, there is a sharp decline in gaining them during the same period. The Maritime Provinces were gradually becoming urbanized and the strength of the pushing forces became slower and the prairies remained predominantly engaged in agriculture and would not accommodate as many as the industrial sector.

During the first decade of the 20th century Canada received 1.8 million immigrants. The Canadian population increased by 34.2% from 1901, to 1913 as 5.4 million to 7.2 million. Effectively from the beginning of World War I, there was a sharp decline in receiving new immigrants to Canada.

The birth of Canada from the British Empire was a slow transitional process, whereas in the Thirteen Colonies a violent revolutionary war took place with the intent to cut off all British influence. Most of the Canadians did not forget the pain of the discriminatory measures taken against them by the British but they buried these feelings in their bottom of their hearts. However these old feelings crop up from time to time and even today. For example the cosmetic changes that have been made by the government by renaming certain parts of the armed forces as the Royal Canadian Navy and the Royal Canadian Air Force along with the display of portraits of her Majesty the Queen of Canada; though these are symbolic actions, it has a very deeply rooted connection towards Britain than our cousins south of border who migrated from under similar conditions. Furthermore Canadians do not hesitate in bearing most of the expenses of the visits by the royal family from tax payer's money.

Although Canada disputed and disagreed it never went against Britain and it is historically evident that Canada is still loyal to Britain to this day. The same sentiment has existed over many years and the variation between feeling closer or far apart is not significant. The migration from Britain or France is like moving from the province of Newfoundland to Ontario or to British Colombia or to Quebec.

The question of how far and how broadly to accept new immigrants was a burning issue among the earlier settlers because of conflicting interests internally as such as whether to have an open immigration policy but with restrictions on selected immigrants or not. Among them the trade unionists, potential employers, and the nationalists had many concerns. The substantial opinion of the rest of the population was that there was no need to make a fuss and that Canada should welcome the new immigrants in an unbiased way because of the national interest and the abundant prosperity. In spite of this there was a sector that was concerned about protecting the homogeneous Anglo society. In the immigration history of Canada that there has been a lingering conflict between the ethnic sentimentalities and the economic superiority and recently economic interests has superseded the other unlike the early stages. I have noticed that the entrepreneurs were interested in having a larger supply of manpower and preferably from new immigrants from whom they could easily and conveniently extract more work in terms of longer hours and they could be paid less. The labor unions were not happy at all in having an open immigration policy because the situation would not be safe and bargaining power would also be adversely affected. The entire mechanism worked on the simple theory of supply and demand; Canada needed workers and new immigrants were a cheap supply.

Migration and emigration processes have been a flourishing business around the world. It began in a very straight forward manner of passing information in two ways to link the source countries the supplier, to the receiving countries, the receiver, as an informal service by individuals including the tradesmen who travelled from region to region. Although their mission was primarily in trade during slow periods, they had ample time to gather and exchange information. The religious missionaries also became another source and they had better and effective contacts in the midst of the people and were able to make links between the two.

The evolutionary growth of this process had taken a new trend of being better organized and formally doing business for making profit. It has reached to the point where they are keeping the information from both sides secret and then physically transporting them and make large sums of money. The business grew wider and expanded to other related businesses. They began to motivate and encourage ordinary people who never dreamt of moving out from their ancestor's village by giving them a rich picture as to the employment opportunities that they were going to have and the big fortune to be had along with the proviso that this chance would never come back. People who never had any chance in their life to make a quick fortune would not mind taking a chance. They portrayed the handful of those people who reached their expectations as the general rule rather than the exception.

Their relationship with the entrepreneurs was also very cordial in terms of convincing them convincing that they had taken all the troubles needed in getting the right supply of manpower and exaggerated their efforts and investments and negotiated for better profits. This reminds me of the origin of banking in Europe when people were using horse carts as the primary means of transportation in the absence of motor vehicles and railways. For common men, travelling was not only difficult but was also time consuming and a single journey took months. They kept their valuables including jewelry, gold coins and money with goldsmiths and paid them for safe keeping. Later on, some other people in the same community in need of money and gave assurances that they would return just after the harvest and asked the goldsmith to lend them the money and told him they were able to pay for it. The goldsmith knew the lender would not be able to return in a short while and repay the money, made income from both the parties by charging interest. Later on, they decided that they wanted more assets and stopped charging money for safekeeping the assets and then when the market became more competitive they had not only forgone the interest but also provided interest in order to get them on their side. This is similar to the early model of immigration services in which the agents made money from both sides of the equation.

Most of those who arrived into the receiving land at the initial stage were not very pleased or happy because the reality that they faced was not to their expectations, for some it shattered their dreams. The reality was that they had to re-set their mind and adjust to an entirely new environment. They also felt homesick or in some cases like a fish out of water. Getting to know new people and developing new relationships and trust was another additional responsibility that they had. For most of them it was the first time experiencing travel by ship on a long journey that lasted for weeks and months. There were times when the ship was shaken by the waves of the sea and some them felt it was the end of their life.

It was too late for them to cry and it was not easy to back out instantly and they had neither the money nor the means. Indeed the quest for prestige and the means to return home and the quest for prestige was better than going back with nothing.

Unlike in the early stages of European migration when the non material values resulted in taking measures in preventing or restricting the entry of others dominated the immigration policies. During this period, utilizing the abundant arable land and other resources was of prime importance. If any additional unskilled supply of manpower was required they were to be limited to the rest of Europe.

CHAPTER FOUR

Broken Padlock—Racial Bias

The ownership of the land of Canada is disputed to a certain extent between the natives and the European settlers, until now this issue has not been fully resolved and I don't believe that there is any chance of this dispute being put to rest in the near future. When we refer to the term "Europeans", it does not include every part of the entire European continent. Though the diversity increased, the initial stage of the settlements was mainly restricted to the English in the United Kingdom and the French in France. Although the Portuguese, Spanish and some other Europeans had some form of contact with Canada in the 15th century, the organized settlements were established by the French and the English. The British were the ones who took the initiative to have settlements built by clearing the forest, constructing roads, bridges and other infrastructure. The expansion of the settlements slowly encouraged more people to utilize the blessed land and make a new life with more comfort. Once they were organized, the settlers came to realize that Canada was a land of golden opportunities though during that period of time they had no idea that from these small communities a nation would be created. In these early days, most of the people settled in small pockets in certain regions. The concept and the boundaries of Canada were so narrowly drawn and they wanted to have the ownership and the access to the land. Within their ethnicity, they were aware that the explosion of the population and the unsustainable economic conditions along with the fact that people from other European nations were looking for fertile land for resettlement fostered a desire to migrate quickly. Though such an urge existed within other ethnic groups around the world, they did not have the means of transportation along with the capabilities and the resources for exploration. It is fair to say that they had the desire but not the means. At that time two countries were becoming powerful in terms of expanding their colonial rule and other countries like Portugal, Holland, Germany and Spain had not reached this point.

Protective measures to ensure priority for certain ethnic groups as opposed to others was a constant battle so the door for migration to Canada was narrowly opened for these two groups of people and it was closed to the rest including the Irish, the Scots and the Welsh from the so called United Kingdom. So the immigration policy during that period of time was based on very narrow ethnic lines. The gates were however open to criminals, prisoners and laymen from the same ethnicity, but they hesitated to accept missionaries, scholars and able men who could make a very positive contribution for building this nation from other ethnicities. We should also not forget that it was a time when these Europeans confronted and faced some threats from the natives and felt that their settlements were not fully secure. Therefore, it was easier for them to spend their energy protecting themselves rather than others from different ethnic though I do not think that this would have been the only reason for this kind of immigration policy.

These settlers were quite ambitious, very hardworking and they made tireless contributions. Not only did they make their lives better, but they made it more comfortable and realized as well that, they themselves would not be able to utilize the abundance and natural resources of the land on their own. Therefore, they began inviting people outside their own ethnicity who had certain skills and who were experts in certain areas such as arable farming and raising livestock. Furthermore, they felt that their precious positions were secure and that they would not be challenged by new immigrants. Furthermore they began to realize that in order to get a higher yield they needed extra manpower and that the resulting benefits from the expansion of the economy would equal more benefits for themselves. It was at this stage that their eyes were opened to the idea of expanding their settlements beyond people of their ethnic group.

Though they were ready come out of their narrow shell and look forward to inviting the new immigrants, still they did want non-Europeans to come and deviate from their similar cultural background. Although they had a lot of differences such as language, culture, the fine arts, habits and living patterns they considered that the root of their cultural civilization was the same. They all had a similar, fundamental way of living and their linguistic inter-relationships and human values were similar so they preferred to pick up some varieties of some apple rather than oranges and pineapples. In the end it was a mixture of rational and economical factors that opened the door for Europeans to come to Canada excluding the rest of the world.

Even though Europe was considered a favorable country with potential immigrants, there were certain groups that were considered undesirable. For example the Scots, the Irish and the Welsh were accepted with some reservations, while other groups were on a "preferred list" or an "inner circle" of sorts. For example, the Germans, the Swiss, the Dutch and the Danish were among the preferred groups. The Scandinavians also got a comfortable place on the list. Then the eastern and southern Europeans were next on the list but they were selected mainly for their skills. The Ukrainians for example, were very talented farmers and were highly preferred for working on the farms particularly in the Prairie Provinces. Their migration to these parts of Canada brought tremendous progress for the nation as well as for themselves. Even today Canada has been benefiting from meeting the growing domestic needs and raising substantial revenue from exporting agricultural products.

The southern Europeans who migrated from Greece, Italy, Portugal and Spain contributed to the progress of this country in more of the non—agriculture sectors, such as mining and construction. In the city of Toronto for example the Bloor Street Viaduct was built by immigrants from these countries in the 1930's.

It is not necessarily the case that the immigration policy and the attitude of the masses go hand in hand. Historically there were sections of the Canadian population that were not pleased about accepting certain groups of people in large numbers and in some cases there were those who were prepared to accept it out of necessity. However there were times that when the economic situation in Canada changed in a negative way the first groups of people to be blamed were the new immigrants. These people having left very difficult situations behind in their home countries found this hard to tolerate. It is quite interesting to witness that the trend of blaming the new comers as an economic burden, the cause of social disorder, the increasing crime rate, and how they consume undue benefits is not a new one. I have seen these types of magnified accusations particularly during the periods of economic recession in the 1980's and 1990's but not much in the 2000s. It reminds me of a time when I was travelling at the peak hours in the morning on the subway on my way to work downtown from my home in Scarborough, Ontario. The train made frequent stops for the passengers to board and leave in order to reach their destinations. The train was almost full at the third station and then the passengers who boarded at the followings stations struggled to get in and then at the next station when others were trying to board the subway. The very passengers who were accommodated at the last station were the ones who tried to block the entry of these new passengers. They seemed to have forgotten that they were all in the same boat and it would have served them to remember that this land never hesitates to accommodate strangers and offered benefits which they received. It is also a land where both the new comers and the nation are in a winning position. I do not think that immigrants have any moral right in harboring negative attitudes towards newcomers as long as the new comers respect law and order and are loyal to this nation.

If Canada had been a country like Germany, Russia, France, England, India, China and Japan that was built by the ancestors for generation after generation and have claims not only to the land but also to all of the historical buildings, cultural and civil institutions and economic means, these would have been the determining factors if newcomers from certain ethnic groups would be allowed into the country. Furthermore, these newcomers would be expected to blend in fully; one example that comes to mind is the necessity to adopt a Japanese version of one's name should one be expected to integrate into Japanese society. I do not mean to underestimate the contributions that have been made by the newcomers in those countries but the degree of their contributions did not alter the well established norms of these societies and the structure of their systems. One example of this is the Greek influence in India. Though the Greeks made many contributions to Indian culture particularly in the realm of art, the cultural norms of India held greater sway over the Greeks especially the religion of Buddhism. The Buddhist teachings made such an impression on the Greek King Menander that he converted to Buddhism and changed his name to Milinda. In contrast to the comparison of these two groups, let us look into most of the South American nations where the Spanish became the dominant culture and where the land was occupied the Spanish descendants. However, these people did not exploit the natural recourses to a high degree with the help of new immigrants and their status of the economic development is still not at the same level as other developed nations with the exception of Brazil.

The approach of the Americans is quite different. The attitude of Americans from the Revolution to the present has remained unique, yet peculiar. The idea of the "melting pot" though it has altered slightly still remains and the idea that one is an American regardless of where one may come from or their ancestral background is still strong. Though it was been said that the melting pot has absorbed and continues to absorb many cultural elements and ingredients, it tastes predominately Anglo-Saxon. I know that German Americans suffered in silence and that African Americans fought against discriminative measures until Barak Obama was elected as the President of America but I am sure that by watching history it will appear in another form.

The overall structure of Canada has been built, maintained and restructured with the materials and the human resources of newcomers who have migrated from across the globe.

Discriminative immigration policies have been in existence from the beginning of the first human settlements to this modern era. The Native people are not considered as a homogeneous entity; rather they are a collection of many ethnic groups having similar patterns of life and following a common path. It is true that there were some commonalities in their ways of living, habits and traditions and the source of economic activities. In spite of it all, they preserved their own identities. Later on, when met with the challenges from the Europeans and with the intent to chase them away it became important to put aside some of their differences and work towards a common goal.

As far as the unresolved disputes between the British monarchies, the government of Canada and the natives who for this piece will be considered as a unified group go, there are two views. The first is that the government has adopted a policy in that they have done economically more than the rest of the citizens of this land and therefore there is no room to complain. The other view is that many Canadians blame the government for providing the native people with more money per capita than anyone else. In contrast it seems that the Natives do not much appreciate the privileges at the expense of forgone rights. My only question is how come at this time where the modernization process would bring these to the 21st century while preserving their identity seems to be impossible considering that that their population is only 1 million out of 34 million Canadians. It is certain that something has gone wrong somewhere and this needs to be resolved. However, it is important perhaps to emphasize that the Native people are not the only ones who have faced discrimination.

It was the continuation of the discriminative actions that was held against the Scots, the Welsh and Irish by the English when they arrived in Canada as immigrants and refugees. Immigrants are mainly pulled by the attractiveness and prosperity of the new country while refugees are pushed by natural calamities or persecution, torture, or discrimination by the rulers.

The Immigration act provided for greater selectivity by the admission process, in order to weed out undesirable Immigrants to some extend from the eastern and southern Europe and mainly from Asia.

Even at the beginning of the twentieth century racially biased Immigration policies were in existence. The Immigration Act of 1910 gave power to the cabinet to prohibit immigration on racial grounds and this continued until the implementation of the new Immigration Act of 1978. The Immigration Act of 1978 though it narrowed down the racial lines, left some room for the cabinet to impose restrictions in a very sweet coated package and this subject will be discussed in a later chapter. Some of the wording in the Act was changed to make the soup milder later on and the basics remained intact.

According to those Immigration Acts it was crystal clear that they were both targeted against non Europeans in particular though it was not spelled out in black and white. It said that:

"Owing to their peculiar customs, habits, modes of life and methods of holding property and because of their prohibit inability to become readily assimilated" This assimilation policy is narrower than the current American melting pot theory. It focused on prohibiting German, Austrian, Hungarian and Bulgarian immigration on 14th March 1914. It was at the time of the First World War and during that time and during the Second World War those considered "enemy aliens" were denied entry and some immigrants from the targeted groups who had arrived earlier and had been accepted were repatriated to their respective nations such as Japan. To this day, some of these Canadians are still wounded from the pain this policy caused and they have not forgiven and forgotten the actions made against them.

Asians were denied entry into Canada from 1923 to 1956 and it was targeted against certain groups such as the Japanese, Indians, Chinese and Koreans but with the exception of farm and domestic workers as well as spouses and under aged children but only if one of the parents was Canadian. Later on, a quota system was introduced, after establishing governmental agreements in 1956, in which 150 Indians, 100 Pakistanis, 50 Sri Lankans, in addition to the migration of the said family members. Consequently the number was increased this remained until 1962.

The continuous passage rule was another form of discrimination. According to the Order in Council of 1914, it was prohibited for anyone to break their journey between his or her native country to Canada. It was possible to migrate from Europe to Canada and they were pretty much aware that it would be possible for Indians to travel on any ship. It was not unknowingly done; rather, it was a deliberate move to prevent the Indians from migrating to Canada on a large scale. Those who came to Canada on the ship called the Komagata Maru which was owned by a Japanese shipping company and hired by Indians is a prime example of how this Order in Council was applied. On this ship there were 376 passengers in which 340 them were Sikhs who were subjects of the British Empire. They began their journey from Calcutta India and reached Vancouver, British Colombia, Canada via Hong Kong, Shanghai and Yokohama in 1914. The ship arrived in the Canadian waters but was not allowed to dock and it was under the strict order of the Premier of B.C. The Indians in Canada organized protests and helped the passengers to disembark but it was all in vain and they had to return to Calcutta on 27 September 1914. At last on August 3rd 08 Prime Minster Stephen Harper made an apology at the 13th annual Ghadri da Mela festival in Surrey, B.C. he formally said that "on behalf of the government of Canada, I am officially conveying as Prime Minister that apology"

The head tax imposed on Chinese immigrants due to the Chinese Immigration Act of 1885 was an act of deliberate discrimination and was meant to discourage the Chinese from entering Canada. It was a pity that after extracting manual labour from Chinese workers to build the Canadian Pacific railway, this policy would have been presented to the world as a decent way of limiting immigrants from non European ethnic groups. It is crystal clear that the Indian and Chinese labourers were conveniently allowed to migrate to Canada to work in demanding and physically dangerous jobs that the European labourers had little or no interest in. Therefore there was no choice other than to recruit the Indians and Chinese and as soon as the project was completed, there was no need for their services. Thus, the head tax was imposed with the intent of discouraging migration. It was evident that among the established Canadians that there was a fear that the Chinese would end up taking over in British Columbia. Therefore this was evidence that in spite of the employment opportunities that were given, there was discrimination in the workplace. There were over 3,000 in the provincial population of 33,586 and that number accounts for 8.93 % and the accumulation of the Chinese was in a very short time. Chinese workers engaged in the construction sites were paid between one third and one half of the wages that their Canadian counterparts made. The hands of the Dominion of the British Empire were not open enough to ban their immigration outright, but were able to restrict them. The tax began with the price of $50.00 and rose to $500.00 in 1903. Although they collected $ 4 23 million which is almost $300.00 today from over eighty thousand Chinese immigrants, the primary concern was to restrict the migration of Chinese. Another method used to prevent permanent settlement plans was to discourage the migration of whole families. This led to many Chinese families being separated for many years only to be reunified when the immigration legislation changed.

When the Canadian immigration policies were modified and welcomed new immigrants without such restrictions, the Canadian Chinese realized that they were the victims of a discriminative immigration policy. Though they became part and parcel of the Canadian culture, they felt that the fee that had been levied on their ancestors had to be redressed and an apology given from the government. Mrs. Margaret Mitchell the Member of Parliament in 1984 raised the issue in the House of Commons at the behest of her constituents. Though it did not bear any fruit spontaneously, it motivated and encouraged the Chinese community across Canada to educate the public about the Head Tax and this also opened the eyes of the Canadian politicians. The negotiations continued and in 1993 Prime Minster Brian Mulroney made an offer and it was rejected by the Chinese community council. Finally, Prime Minister Stephen Harper offered an apology and compensation for the head tax paid by the Chinese immigrants on 22nd June 06 and with that the legacy of the Chinese Exclusion Act of 1923 came to an end.

The discriminative immigration policies also brought restriction for immigrants from desirable countries such as the United Kingdom, United States, France, New Zeeland and Australia with the proviso that they should have the means to support themselves in Canada without being a burden. Highly encouraged were those Europeans who were able to make positive contribution to the economic progress of the country. In spite of these demarcations, the immigrants from the Middle East, although it is geographically a part of Asia, could act as investors and were encouraged to migrate to Canada due to the massive amount of wealth from the petroleum industry. The continuation of economic status as one of the criteria for migration in the Immigration Act of 1906 had a mixed message and as such it was able to restrict migration from the racially undesirable ethnicities. The discrimination was very obvious as it required $25.00 for other immigrants but for Asians the fee was raised in 1914 to $200.00. In the case of Japanese and Chinese immigrants, there was another set of restrictions applied.

In 1914, just after the order was passed by the cabinet, Mr. Munshi Singh, an Indian but a subject of the British colonial government, arrived in Vancouver, British Colombia with less than $ 200.00 dollars and challenged the law in the Supreme court and the court of appeal and the extraction of the long verdict given by the Justice of Appeal is as follows:

The better classes of the races are not given to leave their own countries . . . and those who become Immigrants are . . . undesirables in Canada. Their ways and ideas may well be a menace to the well being of the Canadian people.

The parliament of Canada . . . may well be said to be safeguarding the people of Canada from an influx which it is no chimera to conjure up might annihilate the nation . . . introduce Oriental ways as against Europeans ways . . . and all the results that would naturally flow there from.

In their own interests their proper place of residence is within the confines of their respective countries in the continent of Asia, not in Canada, where their customs are not vogue and their adherence to them here only gives rise to disturbances destructive to the well being of society . . . .

Better that people of non-assimilative . . . . race should not come to Canada, but rather that they shall remain of residence in their country of origin, and do their share, as they have in the past, in the preservation and development of the empire.

As you can probably tell by the tone in the decision, it was clear that it did not matter if a person from an undesirable ethnicity was educated or not or had money or not. It was simply accepted as a fact that these people would not blend into Canadian culture and would cause nothing but trouble. It was also the case that any Indians who wanted to migrate to Canada by ship had to begin their journey in India and reach Canada without any stopovers in between. All were very aware that it was impossible to sail any ship with a large capacity such a long distance without stopping for food or fuel, but that was exactly the point.

Although the government of Mr. Stephen Harper made an apology on behalf of Canada to the Indians for that historical shameful act some of the Indians were not pleased with the way it was made. He also apologized for the inappropriate treatments given to the Native children and for the head tax levied against the Chinese and these two apologies were made in parliament and documented properly. But the apology that was extended to the Indians was in a public platform outside the parliament. Some were trying to justify that the other two incidents took place within Canada and that of the Indians was on the ship. However the discrimination was still there.

It is also true that making the effort to balance the economic benefits with the homogeneous interests was not an easy task. At times, when the advancement of the economic prosperity superseded the protection of the homogeneous interest, the elasticity of the migration policy was as flexible as Malaysian rubber.

The Japanese faced another form of discrimination that was based not on ethnicity, but rather due to the participation in World War II. It was not targeted against common men in particular. During the Second World War, Canada was in the camp of the British allies along with France and the United States against the Nazi regime in Germany and Japanese regime. The restriction was for a smaller period of time during and just after World War II. According to the War Measures Act of 1942 the Japanese citizens were restricted in entry from abroad. Furthermore, the Canadian born citizens of Japanese descent were also subject to deportation. The British subjects of the Japanese race aged 16 and older who were residents of Canada were requested to repatriate.

The Jews were also discriminated against even before the execution of six million Jews within a period of six years during the war. Though there was no such law that restricted the migration of the Asians, in practice there was an element of discriminative measures that were taken against them.

The immigration Act of 1978 almost closed the door on discrimination in immigration policies. It mentions that ""to ensure that any person who seeks admission to land is subject to standards of subject to admission that do not discriminate on the grounds of race, national or ethnic origin, color, religion or sex"

The law made a tremendous change in putting a stop on discrimination in immigration but any law on immigration has some loopholes and there is room for some discriminative measures which may not be obvious. The element of discrimination may be hidden and would not necessarily be easily proven in the justice system but it would linger in the nature of the execution of the laws. It would be also possible in achieving the intended targets by delaying the process, levying taxes to certain areas, imposing strict measures on issuing visas are also some of the technical ways to achieve what has to be done without having any legal challenges.

Anti Discriminative Measures

It is not always true that the government dances according to the tune of the masses. There are times that the pipers of the government impiously play certain tunes and make the people dance accordingly. In certain times the voice of the government has been highly influenced by certain groups of people or regions of the country that helped them by permanently or temporarily supporting the existence of a particular party or winning the election to form the government. The right leader should not always act to satisfy what the people want, rather he should guide and direct them for the long term and it may at times be a bitter pill to swallow but in the long run the people who hate and oppose will turn back and appreciate what has been done. They have to forgo the instant benefits and take short term pain for the long term gain. The regime of a good leader will not be assessed with what they have contributed to the current benefit and well being of the country, rather what kind of foundation that they laid for the future of the nation.

Immigration is one of the main organs of the Canadian government and it is a very sensitive and vital sector that should be planned and dealt with consciously. In immigration, we treat human beings with respect, not in a manner that deals with assets or international trade of services and commodities. It is true that immigrants migrate to Canada more than any other nation in the world and that Canada is in need of new immigrants for the purpose of maintaining the current status and economic activities and progress with abundant natural resources. We shouldn't compare the two aspects as a part of the price mechanism based on demand and supply. I am not inclined or supportive of comparing and contrasting, who needs and gets more benefits from the migration, the immigrants or the receiving nations. Some have the view that new immigrants need Canada more than Canada needs them whereas others have the opinion that Canada needs them more than they need Canada. I rather consider both as two sides of the same coin. Both parties also have the tendency of achieving the best out of the deal as such the receiving nations prefer to have the potential skills or capital for investments, and are not inclined or involved in any terrorist activities or having serious criminal backgrounds. The migration of the new immigrants has various factors that pushed them to leave their native land and choose the migrating country. The predominant pushing factors are as such: poverty, varieties of discrimination, persecution, low income, natural calamity, political instability and lack of employment. There are also the motivational pulling forces that encourage them to migrate to developed nations such as better standards of living with a constant supply of social amenities, better salary and employment, prosperity, safety, stable government, freedom and the ability to have a bright future for their children.

The recent Liberal Party capitalized on the Liberal immigration policy of the late Pierre Elliott Trudeau that opened the gate for unimaginable numbers of immigrants to migrate to Canada including those not having sufficient funds for the initial support or the necessary skills for meeting the scarce demands of the labour market. Even today, after passing the second and third generation of those immigrants that sense of gratitude and sentiment has pushed them to support the Liberal party in the political elections. In order to continue to maintain their support, they are always very supportive of Liberal immigration policies. They always oppose restrictions on any immigration policies, even if the restrictions are in the best interest of the nation in the long run. Still they oppose it when it is brought forward by the Conservative government. A similar trend can also be noticed not only in Canada but in France, England, and the United States of America between the right wing and the Labour or Liberal or Democratic Party in the USA and the UK.

Citizenship and Immigration Canada works with community agencies and also funds and operates projects with the intent of eliminating racism against newcomers. The month of February for example has been declared as Black History Month, the month of May is Asian Heritage Month. Citizenship and Immigration Canada is also dedicated to building bridges between different cultures, Anti racism and human rights outreach projects, racism prevention and Cultural integration training for frontline workers are some of the things that this department has taken on.

Let us have a look at some of their objectives and evaluate how far they have been able to reduce racial discrimination after the arrival of new immigrants. The objectives are as follows:

To reduce the impact of discrimination through the empowerment of new immigrant parents as a result of their active participation in community programs.

- Promote a greater understanding around the concepts of oppression and strategies for stopping racism.
- To increase awareness of racism and discriminatory practices.
- The development of skills in the area of public speaking and communication on issues related to racism.
- Newcomer parents and youth are encouraged to have a dialogue about racism, diversity and human rights in a safe environment.
- Increase youth understanding of the consequences related to prejudice, racism and discrimination in all its forms.
- Increase awareness among Canadian born youth of issues related to racism and discriminatory practices.

These objectives prove that racism has been in existence to a certain extent and in some of the major ethnic groups, racial discrimination in the schools, work place, job market, and in some public places has been an ongoing issue. In some of the private enterprises, there is discrimination against some ethnic groups and it entails more than negative attitudes, it has gone into the scale of salaries and benefits and they are paid less than their counterparts. I appreciate such positive efforts in reducing racial discrimination, but we have gone only a few kilometers on a very long journey. The only consolation that I have is the image that compared with European countries; the degree of racism in Canada is minimal and is fading faster than ever before. In spite of it, it would not be naturally paralyzed and it requires constant treatment, otherwise it may wake up from a dormant state as exemplified by the revival of anti-Semitism in Germany.

There is no harm in being proud of someone's identity, culture, economic superiority and it should be one of the motivating factors for its continuous growth. In fact anyone who forgoes his identity for the sake of a few economic or other privileges would not be trusted and he could jump from where he is now to the superior one later. A broader national outlook and inner determination is highly recommended for Canada, a nation that has been built mainly by new immigrants who migrated from all corners of the globe. The share for the building and developing of this nation by certain groups certainly are the back bone and it has to be acknowledged by the rest. No matter who has made the lion's share of it, it matters that basically every section of the Canadian mosaic has been recognized and has the fundamental rights in terms of preserving and practicing their root culture and traditions without the improvement of the mainstream culture.

CHAPTER FIVE

-Refugees

Other than for economic refugees, for all other refugees it is the last step to flee from the country or land where he or she was born and brought up. Their forefathers had established their lives in their country of origin and these people have deep rooted sentimental attachments though the social amenities may be limited, poor living conditions, a poor economy and lack of employment it does not matter for it is still home. No one on earth is proud to be branded as a refugee. There is no question of being in between the pulling and pushing forces. There is only one force that makes someone a refugee and that is the pushing force to flee. It is the urgent question of the survival from established persecution, torture of all kinds, starvation, extra judicial execution, ill treatment, denial of freedom of expression, jail sentences for innocent civilians, human rights violation and all sorts of inhumane treatments. These factors push them to a strange land where the language, culture, lifestyle, climate, food, religion and the norms of the society are different and where it is hard to reestablish their life.

The persecution could be based on religion, race, ethnicity, language, political views, gender, or a combination of these factors and the method and the degree may vary but the established danger to life remains the center of focus. These experiences are not easily wiped away from the heart and in some cases the pain is passed onto subsequent generations. The physiological injuries can be easy assessed, but the invisible injuries such as psychological and emotional damage might not be completely cured and totally erased. Most of these refugees were punished for no crime committed by them. They suffer at times because being a member of a designated group. Refugees who were victimized badly, but have no means of fleeing remain and continue to suffer whereas those were victims to a lesser degree would be able to flee and gain refugee status. Of course, economic refugees who can continue to survive in their home land have not experienced established persecution and take the mean advantage and undue privileges and occupy the seat meant for the true refugees. These economic refugees portray themselves as real victims and abuse the system to have economic benefits. It is very hard for the refugee system to screen them. Although many receiving countries are aware and improved the system and minimized the loopholes, no system was able to wipe out this problem.

There are over 25 million refugees and 70 million displaced people, internally and externally around the world. The number has been going up and the refugee accepting countries cannot take all of them. The interesting part of it is that the country which create refugees sometimes grant asylum to the refugees created by another country. An example is during the Khalistan war in the 1980's. Indian Sikhs fled India as refugees and countries like Canada, Germany, Britain, and France accepted them as refugees. Refugees from Afghanistan and Pakistan received asylum in India during this same time period.

The refugee policy of most of the accepting countries is based on the 1951 UN Convention on the Protection of Refugees. It defines a refugee as someone who has a well founded fear of persecution because of race, religion, nationality, membership in a social group, or political opinion. In the 1990's in Canada some groups of people advocated to include persecution based on gender. It has been the section stating that being a part of the social group that is very flexible and covers all types of persecution in general for it refers to the suffering from individualized persecution, not generalized persecution. The violence or persecution must be directed to the refugee claimant not in general. Refugees fleeing from generalized violence would not be accepted as refugees. The victim of a bomb blast targeted not to him in particular, but to a rebel controlled area may not sufficient for him to be qualified to be a refugee and the claim may be refused. Canada is the only major refugee receiving country that accept refugees in permanent exile, the rest accept them temporarily until the situation is determined to be safe. The bottom-line of the Canadian refugee exercise is aimed at resettlement whereas most of other receiving nations give protection until they are able to return back to their respective countries sooner or later depending on the circumstances. In Canada, if a refugee claimant is accepted as conventional refugee the next step will be permanent resident status and in two or three years time then there will the move to apply for naturalized citizenship within five years or a little longer. Those who do not meet the refugee criteria but are not a burden to Canada, are economically independent, have a valid reason for being unable to return would be able to be absorbed as permanent residents under humanitarian and compassionate grounds. A similar system being practiced as Refugee 'A' and 'B' the second group comes under refugee 'B'.

Though the definition of what makes a person a refugee is roughly the same for all countries, the interpretation varies with each government. A rejected refugee claim of a person with the same or similar evidence might gain refugee status in another country. That is one of the reasons that many refugees enter through the land border between the USA and Canada and claim refugee status. But many prefer to come to Canada for various reasons such as free health services, most of their relatives reside in Canada and so forth. The fundamental reason is that they feel the accepting ratio is higher in Canada and is a safe haven for refugee. A refugee who wants to escape from a dangerous situation and save his life should not pick and choose. If someone flees from Somalia to Canada by flight and it was in transit in Paris France, he should break his journey and claim refugee status in Paris, not in Canada.

Internal flight alternative is another concept that limits the influx of refugees. A particular part of a nation might be dangerous, but he could survive in another corner of the nation. This person's refugee claim would not be accepted either for his life must be in danger no matter where in the country they may be.

In practice, asylum counties are reluctant to condemn a source country that is also friend or ally, but a refugee is more likely to receive protection in an enemy country. Most of the asylum countries are Western Europe, USA, Canada and Australia. They are biased against communist countries. Refugee claimants who fled from Communist countries had a better chance than from the anti communist bloc.

After the Second World War until the collapse of communist regimes in Eastern Europe, Vietnam, China, North Korea and Cuba this policy was more or less used to stop the expansion of communist ideology to the Third World countries by discrediting them. There is no doubt that most of the fundamental freedoms such as freedom of expression, press, has been denied in those countries. In some cases people who should be included were excluded and excluded were included. In many cases of the refugees who were fleeing from communist countries, they were accepted mainly not because of personalized persecution but generalized persecution whereas refugees from non communist countries had to go through the bottle neck of the system. The ratio from the asylum seekers from those countries was higher than the rest. I do not think the application of the refugee system is fair to the deserving cases. The political ideology should not interfere or dominate the refugee system. When a government officer flees his country he is being treated as a defector, whereas recently the sportsmen from Cuba disappeared and eventually claimed refugee status. It was clear that they were treated slightly differently. It should be justified, no matter who he is, everybody is equal in front of the law and I do not think there should be an exception or preferential treatment. The decision for admission should be justified.

Some economic refugees and others who do not meet the entry criteria abuse the system and join the crowd of refugees as a short cut and eventually gain a permanent resident visa. The USA has an alternative system for those who want to be green card holders by joining the immigration lottery system that has lesser qualification to get in than the others. But Canada does not have such a lottery.

Every receiving country has a quota for refugees. Among those countries, Canada comparatively accepts more refugees than many others. Is it an obligation for a nation to accept a certain number of refugees or optional to the sovereign state? It is hard to define how it should work. The world's refugees total number, and destination is not easily predictable, though, it is an issue that is being created by fellow human beings

There are some practical difficulties that receiving nations have to face and resolve in the best interest of the nation. A good example is when Bill Clinton, the former present of the USA, wanted to get rid of most of the illegal immigrants, the bordering country Canada made itself alert because many of those illegal immigrants would make a mass exodus to Canada under the pretext as refugees. Fortunately, the idea was given up possibly not to lose the Spanish American vote. When one receiving country makes it difficult other receiving countries are loaded with an influx of refugees.

There is a big back log in processing the refugee applications. For example, in Canada in the year 1981 the back log was 81, 000. It was not only caused by the lack of insufficient facilities and the man power, the influx of a high number of refugee claimants. The delaying tactics of the refugees case handlers as well. They did make it clear that at point in time the processing would be faster and easier, so that many positive results could be delivered or a general amnesty would be given as was done in May 1986.

Another important group to consider is those who arrive on shore by boat. The Jews on the board the ship fleeing Nazi Germany were refused by country after country, each refusal made it easier for each subsequent country to refuse as well. Canada was no exception to this and refused this ship as well. However, the so called boat people who came to Canada from Vietnam were accepted as refugees, where 174 Sikhs from India who arrived in a Chilean registered freighter The Amelia on the shore of Nova Scotia from West Germany, Belgium, and Netherlands were turned back.

After the September 11, 2001 terrorist attacks in the United States the chances of refugees who arrive on our shores being accepted as refugees is harder. The refugees cannot be expected to comply with the immigration regulations at the time of their leaving to safeguard their life from established persecution. They are counting every minute and they would not be able to have the proper legal documents prepared beforehand. If he can get those documents from his government, at times he can be considered as a refugee. Forging travel documents in order to flee was somewhat accepted but these days most of the western countries do not entertain the forging of travel documents of the receiving country. It is because through past experience, some terrorist disguised as refugees entered Canada and somehow sneaked into the USA and got involved in destructive activities against USA. There are also those who got engaged in illegal business such as smuggling drugs, weapons, and people.

Refugees arrive in three categories, the refugees who enter into the border by land, ocean and the rest by air, illegally in the sense with having no entry visa; they account for almost one third of the total refugee population of Canada. After signing the safe third country agreement it has been reduced drastically. The second group is selected from abroad and the responsibilities of their resettlement are shouldered by non profit and charitable organizations.

The third one is the government sponsored refugees. The government is directly involved in selecting refugees abroad and helps them resettle in Canada. They are able to gain permanent resident status immediately or sooner than the refugee claimant who arrived or reached the border and knocked at the gates and since all of them are already selected as refugees there is no room for reselection and returned some of them.

The increasing number of refugee around world cannot totally be resolved, but can be helped if accepting nations allocate more resources, develop a better way of identifying real refugees and hiring well trained skillful workers. Along with timely processing, the situation of refugees in Canada would be better. This is not a cure but these preventative methods would very much reduce the number of false claims and ensure that true refugees are allowed into this country.

Do Not Panic—Tamil Refugees

"Do not be panicky "stated the head line of the editorial written by the chief editor of the Toronto Star, newspaper on 14th August 2010, a day after the arrival of 492 Tamil refugees at the sea port of Vancouver after being on the cargo ship called the Sun Sea for more than three months; the journey having started from Thailand through the Indian ocean to the Pacific. Though they arrived in the Canadian section of the international waters in the Pacific Ocean on 13th August, the cat was out of the bag a couple of weeks earlier. The ship originally set sail to reach an island near Australia, somehow their entry was denied and the course was changed to Canada where the highest numbers of Tamils have been residing. Canada would not have been the first choice on the list if not for its generosity and the gate for immigration being wide open. The Refugee Claimant process in Canada is much easier and the refugee policy itself is quite different from other refugee receiving countries. All of the other receiving countries accept refugees from various countries where they are being persecuted and allow them to temporarily reside until the situation in their country of origin returns to normal and safety is assured. In Canada, refugees have been welcome to make their claims and along with certain conditions applicable to all new immigrants, such as medical exams, eventually they become members of our family.

Such a privilege is one of the main factors that attract many refugees from around the world and once someone has been accepted as a convention refugee and maintains law and order and all that is expected of them, their permanent residency and naturalized citizenship is almost guaranteed. The generosity of our refugee policy and its implementation in particular and Immigration in general have been considered a weaker part of the process. Of course, there are some loopholes in any system. Although more restrictions, modifications and new criteria have been evolving in the family class sponsorship and independent class immigration policies and processes; the case of the refugee system since Canada accepted the Refugee Act of 1951 of the UNO, has not been fundamentally changed, rather, the genuine refugees have been welcomed. Comparatively, the percentage of the acceptance of refugees from the claimants and the ratio of accepting refugees in Canada is pretty high. The recent statistics (1984-2008) of the annually granted permanent resident status from the category of refugees reveal that just over ten percent of the total immigrants with the exception of as high as 19.9% in 1985 and as low as 8.8 % in 2008 were accepted. As you can see by these numbers, Canada is not stingy.

Though America and Canada follow the same immigration policy of the UNO, many refugees are very much inclined towards claiming refugee status in Canada due to various reasons, including better treatment and the possible notion on their part that if the case is prolonged long enough eventually the claimants are allowed to stay. Both Canada and America however encourage safer means of reaching their borders, such as land and air and discourage any potential refugee claimants from taking unnecessary risks that could lead to danger.

The Hon. Jason Kenny, Minister of Citizenship and Immigration Canada, brought a shift of emphasis in the refugee policy by encouraging the acceptance of refugees from the land where they are persecuted and discourage those who reach our border illegally to claim refugee status. Those who come into Canada illegally and claim refugee status are in a sense jumping the queue compared with other potential refugees.

The government has no reservation in accommodating genuine refugees but is careful in weeding out the bogus refugees. before September 11, 2001 the focus on bogus refugees was centered on economic refugees who pretended to be refugees, but their primary concern was to gain economic benefits. Since the terrorist attacks in the states in 2001, the focus has shifted towards terrorists. The Canadian government does not want Canada to be a fertile ground for terrorists who can then export their activities to other countries.

The right honorable Prime Minister Stephen Harper said about the recent arrival of the 492 boat people at a press conference on 17th August 2010 in Mississauga that "Canada is a land of refuge" . . . We are responsible for the security of our borders, and the ability to welcome people, or not welcome people, when they come" . . ." Canadians are pretty concerned when a whole boat of people comes-not through any normal application process, not through any normal arrival channel—just simply lands"

Now the primary concern is not on the mass exodus of refugees arriving in Canada. Rather it is the suspected involvement in this case by a banned terrorist organization. Either some of the refugees might have come in disguise as ordinary citizens or operated the entire journey or had financial commitments in this operation. It is a matter of security and the concerned departments may have something to back up these concerns and communicated these with government. The two letters written by the refugees and some of the evidence given by some of them suggests that they came on their own as citizens and have no involvements with any groups. There is a tug of war between the supportive forces of the Sri Lankan government and the sympathizers of the Tamil refugees who are concerned about regaining and preserving their fundamental rights. There are views by some Canadian lawyers and media analysts that if the Tamils have not been granted their basic human rights even a year after the war ended on May 18, 2009, human rights violations are still happening. If such problems had indeed been solved, the root cause of fleeing refugees would have stopped. It would not be easy for other nations to unilaterally interfere in the matters of a sovereign state but the international organizations would be able to do so. The United Nations Organization has praised the Canadian government in allowing those refugees to enter into Canada and processing their papers. The government is looking at this case through many lenses. For example, the rumors that those refugees might have paid between $40,000.00 and $50,000.00 per head, that a portion of it might have gone from Canada to finance an illegal project, and human trafficking are all being considered. Furthermore, the next concern of the government might be that if these factors are true, where does the profit of this business go and will it be to the business entity or any other organization?

There is another concern that some Canadians think that there is potential link between the so called boat Tamils numbering 76 who arrived last October and the current refugees. There is also another rumor circulating in some pockets of the atmosphere that in conjunction with the current ship another two of these ships will be arriving sooner or later. Though this cannot be verified, I believe that these accounts may have been fabricated to a certain extent.

Canada has been one of the few countries that give more weight to the refugees from all continents, irrespective of their socio-ethnic and other elements of their backgrounds. Even after receiving them, they have been looked after pretty well. I have met a couple of Canadians who are the second and third generations of refugees in Canada and some of them do not want to recall all of the persecution, atrocities, tortures and all sort of abuses and victimizations that they underwent in their respective countries. In spite of it, to almost all of them, this land was viewed as a strange and foreign place but eventually they felt that they were very fortunate and some said lucky to become citizens of this country. A few others said that even though they had been residing in Canada over the last two decades, they love their ancestral nation and they do not want to forgo their citizenship and become Canadians. Canada accepted 37,500 Hungarian refugees in 1956-1957. When there was political turmoil in the former Czechoslovakia, Canada accepted 11,000 refugees in 1968/69 and when the Asians who had been residing for a few generations in Uganda, some holding British passports were sent out in a very abrupt way, Canada acted quickly and received 6175 of them in 1972. In 1973 Canada accepted over 6,000 Chileans and welcomed 9,000 Indochinese and then over 60,000 of the Vietnamese in 1979/80, after the end of the Vietnam War. 155 Tamils, who came from Germany under the pretense of coming from Sri Lanka, were given Ministers Permits while they were on the Canadian shores of the Atlantic Ocean. When the earthquake, one of the worst natural calamities affected Haiti, Canada was generous enough in accepting a couple hundred of the victims.

Generally, Canadians have very high hopes and are confident that the Canadian government will not let these refugees down. Some of them became offended at the remarks made that implied the boat people were associated with terrorism and money laundering. They believe that these comments bring about negative feelings towards refugees. In some cases the means are justified by linking the fact that if it were not for the troubles back home, these people would not be in this position of having to flee on a cargo ship. They also feel that the gravity of the entire situation is not clearly understood by many western nations.

The Canadian government would not single out the Tamil boat people from the global asylum seekers. The location of the refugees fleeing has been shifting from time to time due to natural calamities and manmade wars, but certain formulas are similar and a common solution is required. Mostly all of the major opposition political parties have remained silent to an extent and would not want to utter any serious comments. But one of the candidates for mayor of Toronto opposes the arrival of those refugees to Toronto. According to him, the income against the expenses for the Torontonians of 2.5 million is insufficient and if another one million new comers, particularly the refugees come, and then there will not be enough money to go around. This candidate has since said that they will not withdraw the comment.

In the end, we should all wait and see the truth and proceed from there. I think that we do not have to panic because Canada has handled many other serious issues in our own quiet way. I believe what the Prime Minister has said is true. Canada is a land of refuge and to that I add, let's give these people a chance.

CHAPTER SIX

Immigration: An Overhaul is Overdue

The Immigration sector in the overall content of today's Canada has taken a central position more than ever before and its impact has deeply penetrated into not only the demographic growth, but also in other areas. A short list would include in the healthy economic development with exploration of minerals, safe and reputed foreign policy, education with technology and research, effective maintenance of law and order, preservation of Canadian values while accommodating the heritage values of the new Immigrants, protecting the human rights of every Canadian irrespective of his/her socio-ethnic, linguistic, religious, color and regional backgrounds, fighting against infiltration of the international terrorism and preserving democratic values. There has been a drastic changes in a tremendous speed is all of these sectors globally and internally and that too with the effects of the revolutionary changes in the technology.

It is very frustrating and disappointing to see the current structure of immigration that was laid out in 1976. It has since had some cosmetic changes from time to time to address timely issues that have cropped up but it is kind of like the renovation of an old building; it is insufficient and fails to address the fundamental restructuring of the immigration system as a whole. It appears to me, the changes that have been brought about so far are almost like an elephant giving birth to a mouse. I do acknowledge that other developed nations who are in a similar situation facing a lack of sufficient manpower to replace the growth in the number of baby boomers and the decline in the birth rates are not cited as role models. It is not the concern of how the rest of those nations handle this issue, it is very pressing concern for us and we have to handle it in our own way no matter what others may do. The average Canadian is sick and tired to read, watch and hearing about how we are addressing the problem and mending it for the time being without taking bold steps. It is not a question of how far the loopholes are being pitched up and how to overcome these problems for the time being. Rather, the surgery for the system is overdue. The solution is beyond limiting or tightening or restricting a certain group of new immigrants or encouraging others to come to Canada en mass such as skilled workers. The areas where Canadians and the government are concerned are as follows:

1. The acceptance of the number of immigrants annually
2. Encouraging and willingness in accepting certain types of immigrants
3. Tolerating of discouraging certain types of migrations
4. Drawing a line between the current challenges in accepting the refugees and UNO regulations.
5. The existing discrimination against new immigrants
6. The acceptance and dilution of the culture brought by new immigrants
7. Blame and share for certain crimes on new immigrants

8. The global shifting source countries and their impact
9. Distribution of immigrants in the Canadian regions
10. Brain drain and gain
11. Elimination and repatriation of unwanted or unaccepted new immigrants
12. Canadian citizenship in regards to citizenship rights by birth and revocation of citizenship
13. Humanitarian and compassionate considerations
14. The influences of the U.S on our immigration policies
15. Temporary foreign contract workers
16. Foreign students
17. Temporary resident visa regulations
18. Free trade and immigration policy
19. Awarding Honorary citizenship
20. Linguistic skills in Canadian official languages.

The acceptance of the number of Immigrants annually

Immigration Overview: Permanent and Temporary Residents
Permanent residents
Canada—Permanent residents 1986 to 2010

Category	1986	1987	1988	1989	1990	1991	1992	1993	1994	1995	1996	1997
Family class	42,381	53,798	51,389	60,943	74,667	87,949	101,109	112,641	94,188	77,378	68,317	59,927
Economic immigrants	35,797	74,077	80,201	90,130	97,924	86,493	95,788	105,645	102,305	106,624	125,368	128,349
Refugees	19,187	21,456	26,760	36,852	40,216	54,074	52,338	30,593	20,433	28,093	28,474	24,307
Other immigrants	1,835	2,666	3,170	3,567	3,601	4,248	5,544	7,751	7,453	761	3,865	3,400
Category not stated	0	0	0	2	0	0	0	0	0	0	1	0
Gender not stated	154	81	64	53	44	44	13	11	8	9	46	52
Total	**99,354**	**152,078**	**161,584**	**191,547**	**216,452**	**232,808**	**254,792**	**256,641**	**224,387**	**212,865**	**226,071**	**216,035**

Category	1998	1999	2000	2001	2002	2003	2004	2005	2006	2007	2008	2009	2010
Number													
Family class	50,865	55,260	60,613	66,787	62,288	65,120	62,272	63,374	70,515	66,240	65,582	65,204	60,220
Economic immigrants	97,909	109,245	136,282	155,716	137,863	121,046	133,747	156,312	138,250	131,245	149,070	153,491	186,913
Refugees	22,842	24,397	30,091	27,916	25,113	25,983	32,686	35,775	32,500	27,954	21,858	22,850	24,696
Other immigrants	2,547	1,031	460	206	3,780	9,197	7,115	6,777	10,373	11,312	10,735	10,626	8,845
Category not stated	0	0	0	1	0	1	0	2	2	1	2	1	7
Gender not stated	32	18	9	12	4	2	4	1	2	2	1	0	0
Total	**174,195**	**189,951**	**227,455**	**250,638**	**229,048**	**221,349**	**235,824**	**262,241**	**251,642**	**236,754**	**247,248**	**252,172**	**280,681**

Percentage distribution

Category	1986	1987	1988	1989	1990	1991	1992	1993	1994	1995	1996	1997
Family class	42.7	35.4	31.8	31.8	34.5	37.8	39.7	43.9	42.0	36.4	30.2	27.7
Economic immigrants	36.0	48.7	49.6	47.1	45.2	37.2	37.6	41.2	45.6	50.1	55.5	59.4
Refugees	19.3	14.1	16.6	19.2	18.6	23.2	20.5	11.9	9.1	13.2	12.6	11.3
Other immigrants	1.8	1.8	2.0	1.9	1.7	1.8	2.2	3.0	3.3	0.4	1.7	1.6
Gender not stated	0.2	0.1	0.0	0.0	0.0	0.0	0.0	0.0	0.0	0.0	0.0	0.0
Total	**100.0**	**100.0**	**100.0**	**100.0**	**100.0**	**100.0**	**100.0**	**100.0**	**100.0**	**100.0**	**100.0**	**100.0**

Percentage distribution

Category	1998	1999	2000	2001	2002	2003	2004	2005	2006	2007	2008	2009	2010
Family class	29.2	29.1	26.6	26.6	27.2	29.4	26.4	24.2	28.0	28.0	26.5	25.9	21.5
Economic immigrants	56.2	57.5	59.9	62.1	60.2	54.7	56.7	59.6	54.9	55.4	60.3	60.9	66.6
Refugees	13.1	12.8	13.2	11.1	11.0	11.7	13.9	13.6	12.9	11.8	8.8	9.1	8.8
Other immigrants	1.5	0.5	0.2	0.1	1.7	4.2	3.0	2.6	4.1	4.8	4.3	4.2	3.2
Gender not stated	0.0	0.0	0.0	0.0	0.0	0.0	0.0	0.0	0.0	0.0	0.0	0.0	0.0
Total	100.0	100.0	100.0	100.0	100.0	100.0	100.0	100.0	100.0	100.0	100.0	100.0	100.0

It is very obvious and evident from the immigration statistics that there is a careful shift in encouraging and inviting more immigrants who are economically beneficial to this country. The number of family class immigrants has declined as can be seen in the rate of 42.7% in 1986, to 30.2% in 1996, 28% in 2006 and 21.5% in 2010. Also, the number of immigrants accepted as refugees as permanent residents has also gone down as can be seen in 1986 19.3%, in 1996, 12.6%, in 2006, 8.8% and in 2010 8.8%. In contrast to the Independent Class Immigrants, the rate has gone up as in 1986-36% in 1996—55.5% in 2006—54.9% and in 2010—66.6%

Canada—Permanent Residents by Category (principal applicants)

Number Category	2001	2002	2003	2004	2005	2006	2007	2008	2009	2010
Spouses and partners	34,273	29,434	33,859	38,312	39,766	39,455	39,760	39,634	39,082	36,338
Sons and daughters	3,523	3,215	3,260	2,855	3,082	3,011	3,209	3,111	2,911	2,865
Parents and grandparents	11,076	11,439	9,927	6,706	5,729	9,588	8,011	8,520	9,022	8,253
Others	2,047	2,136	2,392	2,220	2,160	1,932	2,082	1,461	1,061	1,126
Family class	50,919	46,224	49,438	50,093	50,737	53,986	53,062	52,726	52,076	48,582
Skilled workers	58,910	52,974	45,377	47,894	52,269	44,161	41,251	43,361	40,733	48,821
Canadian experience class									1,775	2,532
Entrepreneurs	1,608	1,176	781	668	750	820	580	446	370	291
Self-employed	705	636	446	366	302	320	204	164	181	174

Investors	1,768	1,234	972	1,671	2,591	2,201	2,025	2,832	2,872	3,223
Provincial/territorial nominees	410	680	1,417	2,086	2,643	4,672	6,329	8,343	11,801	13,856
Live-in caregivers	1,874	1,521	2,230	2,496	3,063	3,547	3,433	6,157	6,273	7,664
Economic immigrants	65,275	58,221	51,223	55,181	61,618	55,721	53,822	61,303	64,005	76,561
Government-assisted refugees	3,392	3,021	3,007	2,813	2,683	2,762	2,789	2,770	2,883	2,820
Privately sponsored refugees	1,654	1,343	1,611	1,436	1,449	1,545	1,627	1,560	2,194	2,109
Refugees landed in Canada	8,391	7,483	8,412	11,181	13,776	10,646	8,023	4,880	5,206	6,309
Refugee dependants	1,405	1,535	1,650	2,630	2,179	2,444	2,262	1,894	1,467	1,403
Refugees	14,842	13,382	14,680	18,060	20,087	17,397	14,701	11,104	11,750	12,641
Retirees, DROC and PDRCC*	109	—	50	34	13	11	7	2	4	0
Temporary resident permit holders	0	—	73	114	88	96	80	90	92	87

H and C** cases	0	463	1,691	2,062	2,046	2,462	2,546	2,022	1,907	1,827
Other H and C cases outside the family class / Public Policy	0	2,929	6,284	3,468	3,179	5,374	6,287	6,611	6,693	5,215
Other immigrants	109	3,476	8,098	5,678	5,326	7,943	8,920	8,725	8,696	7,129
Category not stated	1	0	1	0	0	1	0	1	0	5
Total	**131,146**	**121,303**	**123,440**	**129,012**	**137,768**	**135,048**	**130,505**	**133,859**	**136,527**	**144,918**

Percentage distribution

Category	2001	2002	2003	2004	2005	2006	2007	2008	2009	2010
Spouses and partners	26.1	24.3	27.4	29.7	28.9	29.2	30.5	29.6	28.6	25.1
Sons and daughters	2.7	2.7	2.6	2.2	2.2	2.2	2.5	2.3	2.1	2.0
Parents and grandparents	8.4	9.4	8.0	5.2	4.2	7.1	6.1	6.4	6.6	5.7
Others	1.6	1.8	1.9	1.7	1.6	1.4	1.6	1.1	0.8	0.8
Family class	38.8	38.1	40.1	38.8	36.8	40.0	40.7	39.4	38.1	33.5
Skilled workers	44.9	43.7	36.8	37.1	37.9	32.7	31.6	32.4	29.8	33.7
Canadian experience class									1.3	1.7
Entrepreneurs	1.2	1.0	0.6	0.5	0.5	0.6	0.4	0.3	0.3	0.2
Self-employed	0.5	0.5	0.4	0.3	0.2	0.2	0.2	0.1	0.1	0.1

	C1	C2	C3	C4	C5	C6	C7	C8	C9	C10
Investors	1.3	1.0	0.8	1.3	1.9	1.6	1.6	2.1	2.1	2.2
Provincial/territorial nominees	0.3	0.6	1.1	1.6	1.9	3.5	4.8	6.2	8.6	9.6
Live-in caregivers	1.4	1.3	1.8	1.9	2.2	2.6	2.6	4.6	4.6	5.3
Economic immigrants	49.8	48.0	41.5	42.8	44.7	41.3	41.2	45.8	46.9	52.8
Government-assisted refugees	2.6	2.5	2.4	2.2	1.9	2.0	2.1	2.1	2.1	1.9
Privately sponsored refugees	1.3	1.1	1.3	1.1	1.1	1.1	1.2	1.2	1.6	1.5
Refugees landed in Canada	6.4	6.2	6.8	8.7	10.0	7.9	6.1	3.6	3.8	4.4
Refugee dependants	1.1	1.3	1.3	2.0	1.6	1.8	1.7	1.4	1.1	1.0
Refugees	11.3	11.0	11.9	14.0	14.6	12.9	11.3	8.3	8.6	8.7
Retirees, DROC and PDRCC*	0.1	—	0	0.0	0.0	0.0	0.0	0.0	0.0	0.0
Temporary resident permit holders	0.0	—	0	0.1	0.1	0.1	0.1	0.1	0.1	0.1
H and C** cases	0.0	0.4	1.4	1.6	1.5	1.8	2.0	1.5	1.4	1.3

Other H and C cases outside the family class / Public Policy	0.0	2.4	5.1	2.7	2.3	4.0	4.8	4.9	4.9	3.6
Other immigrants	**0.1**	**2.9**	**6.6**	**4.4**	**3.9**	**5.9**	**6.8**	**6.5**	**6.4**	**4.9**
Category not stated	0.0	0.0	0.0	0.0	0.0	0.0	0.0	0.0	0.0	0.0
Total	**100.0**	**100.0**	**100.0**	**100.0**	**100.0**	**100.0**	**100.0**	**100.0**	**100.0**	**100.0**

* Deferred removal orders class and post-determination refugee claimants in Canada

**Humanitarian and Compassionate Grounds

These days, the Independent Class Immigrants are on the top of the list of preferred class immigrants while pushing the ethnic and regional preferences down to an extent. Still, there is concern over the number of skilled workers and investors among the overall number of independent class immigrants. For example in 2001, the principle applicants from the family class were at 38.8%, in the refugee class it was 11.3% and 49.8% in the independent class. Among all these three categories, almost half of the total immigrants in the independent class are the principle applicants and has outnumbered the rest. In spite of it, if we look closely, 62.1 % of the total number of immigrants was granted permanent resident status in 2001. This is a great percentage in the overall immigrant categories. Still 50.2% of them are dependants such as spouses and children and it is not necessary for them to be skilled workers. This could be a financial burden or the expenses could be seen as par for the course when sponsoring dependants.

There is also another argument that new immigrants are ready to work for less pay and more hours and that the employers are aware of this and try their best to exploit the situation in their favour Consequently this has an adverse effect on the local labour force. In fact, this is really a question of the distribution of wealth from the income generated from business and it has not contributed much to the negative side on the national economy as a whole. One Statistics Canada's study concluded that if the labor supply increased by 10% then wages would decline by 3%-5% and this would affect young Canadians in particular.

Should we really worry about the number of immigrants that Canada should have in relation with checking and balancing the flow with the natural birth, death and emigration rates? Or are we to assess the potentiality of the natural resources and other economic factors and its contribution to the overall economy?

Recent immigrants, earlier immigrants and the Canadian-born collectively express high levels of positive identification as citizens of Canada and there is a significant variation in sharing between their sense of belonging to their ancestral heritage and that of being a Canadian who belongs to the categories of recent immigrants, earlier immigrants and the Canadian-born. Although there is a certain degree of positive identification as citizens of Canada, there is an element of being attached to the homogeneous ethnic group in their local communities. There is a war among all ethnic groups in these three categories in terms of drawing a demarcation line between Canadian values and that of their own that they brought from their home country. This issue has many faces and some values are compatible to Canadian values, some are similar and can be easily bent and manipulated, whereas others can be held rigidly. Usually the third generation of new immigrants absorbs the main values of Canadians in their day to day life to the greatest extent. But none of the ethnic groups including the First Nations, the Quebecois, the English, Irish, and Scots, though they have been residing in this country over the last five hundred years are proud and determined to maintain their cultural values. Their primary concern is that the cores of Canadian values are those of their root heritages. There was a silent message passed when there was an influx of new immigrants from Southern and Eastern Europe and Asia. In the history of immigration to Canada it was challenged when measures were brought forward in limiting the influx of certain ethnic groups entering into Canada. However, when looking at the differences between the three groups, there is an increased tendency in absorbing Canadian values. It also depends on how they distinguish the importance of it. Some of the ethnic groups who have mainly arrived in this country are primarily attracted to the high standard living, the economy, political stability, and the high level of peace and harmony in society. They would also make a positive conclusion that the Canadian culture and way of life are also superior to theirs and in the psychological war, the Canadian values win.

It also depends on how far each ethnic group identifies the economic superiority and impact of it on their culture. Some of them are still strongly convinced that though they are in a disadvantaged economic condition, still their culture is always superior. I have for example, met a couple of Greek Canadians who have similar beliefs even at a time of economic instability. Earlier immigrants and recent immigrant respondents who strongly identify with their community are significantly more likely to identify as citizens of Canada. This suggests that micro-community identification may play a significant role in influencing macro-community identification. For recent immigrants, ethnicity is a significant variable which appears to have an impact upon response patterns.

I believe that there is not much contradiction between identifying as a citizen of the world and identifying as a citizen of Canada. And those who have accepted the concept of a global citizen are significantly more likely to positively identify as a citizen of Canada.

The tremendous increase in the ethno-cultural and linguistic diversity of immigrants to Canada over the past forty years also provides insight into feelings of belonging, perceptions of settlement as psychological security, self-esteem and feelings of being at home in the world. A very strong or somewhat strong sense of community implies that identities are generally understood to be constructed, multiple, dynamic and relational as opposed to being essential or predetermined. Some fear that globalization will continue to blur national boundaries, further directing identities away from a strict focus on national affiliation.

We are quite concerned about the rapidly growing number of baby boomers and the challenges that the Canadian economy is going to encounter but we also have to deeply consider the next generation. The children of the baby boomers who were born between the periods of the 1980's onwards are another rising economic force. Although their growth rate is generally declining, they are a vital part of the human resources in the future of this nation.

We also have to take into consideration the we cannot be picky all the time and the supplier nations with qualitative man power will not remain static in their current surplus of educated and skilful man power and their fast economic growth as such the Chinese at 8-9% and Indians at a 7-8% growth rate will be able to absorb their local manpower and the increase in local employment opportunities and the improving standard of living would discourage them from looking for a venue where they could utilize their potential. When the local demand increases and supply of local man power slows down by the decrease in the birth rate, certainly there will be a slowdown in supply and the receiving nations have to go back and encourage and improve the incentives. But should there be a more aggressive approach in terms of restricting the immigration policy? Or should we look over the whole future of this nation taking into consideration future plans, size of the demographic patterns, age distribution, limitation of local migration, current and future economic plans of the historically preferred nations, cultural globalization and the shift from the ridged cultural practices among other factors?

This is not a matter that is mainly confined to the immigration policy makers and the inclinations of the government towards one particular direction. Canada has historically depended on immigrants and it is not fair to act drastically on the matter of the migration of certain group of people and then making an apology. It does not mean that I do not give due respect to Prime Minister Harper for making an apology for the Chinese Head Tax and the Komogata Maru incident where a ship full of Indian immigrants was not allowed to dock in Vancouver in the early 20th century. As far as Canada is concerned, immigration is a vital part of the country and is in a constant state of change. Some of these changes both now and in the future might not necessarily be comfortable or pleasant but will hopefully respond to the growing needs and changes in this nation and we as Canadians will be able to handle them.

Stage—1902-1910
Historical Highlights

1896 to 1905: the settlement of the West with an offer of free land results in large numbers of immigrants from the United Kingdom, Europe and the United States

1906: *Immigration Act*

1910: *Immigration Act*

1913: 400,000 immigrants arrive in Canada

1914 to 1918: immigration slump during World War I

1928: opening of Halifax's Pier 21, the Atlantic gateway to Canada

1930s: extremely low levels of immigration during the Depression years

1940s: during and after World War II, approximately 48,000 war brides and their 22,000 children arrive in Canada

1950s: Canada receives about one and a half million immigrants from Europe

1952: *Immigration Act*

1956 and 1957: Canada accepts 37,500 Hungarian refugees

1962: new immigration regulations are tabled to eliminate all discrimination based on race, religion and national origin

1967: the government amends Canada's immigration policy and introduces the point system for the selection of skilled workers and business immigrants

1968 and 1969: Canada takes in 11,000 Czechoslovakian refugees

1972: Canada resettles more than 6,175 Ugandan Asians

1973: Canada accepts more than 6,000 Chileans

1975 to 1978: Canada resettles almost 9,000 Indochinese

1978: *Immigration Act* (1976) came into effect April 10, 1978

1979 and 1980: 60,000 Vietnamese, Cambodian and Laotian "boat people" arrive in Canada

1999: Canada accepts more than 7,000 Kosovo Albanians

2002: *Immigration and Refugee Protection Act* (IRPA) comes into effect June 28, 2002

Canada—Permanent residents as a percentage of Canada's population, 1860 to 2009

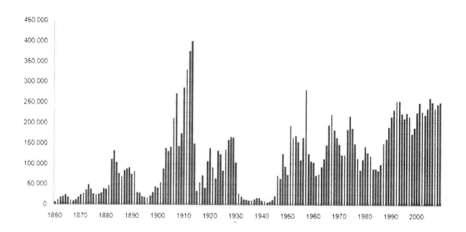

Year	1860	1861	1862	1863	1864	1865	1866	1867	1868	1869
Number	6,276	13,589	18,294	21,000	24,779	18,958	11,427	10,666	12,765	18,630
% of Population	0.2	0.4	0.6	0.6	0.7	0.6	0.3	0.3	0.4	0.5

Year	1870	1871	1872	1873	1874	1875	1876	1877	1878	1879
Number	24,706	27,773	36,578	50,050	39,373	27,382	25,633	27,082	29,807	40,492
% of Population	0.7	0.8	1.0	1.3	1.0	0.7	0.6	0.7	0.7	1.0

Year	1880	1881	1882	1883	1884	1885	1886	1887	1888	1889
Number	38,505	47,991	112,458	133,624	103,824	76,169	69,152	84,526	88,766	91,600
% of Population	0.9	1.1	2.6	3.0	2.3	1.7	1.5	1.8	1.9	1.9

Year	1890	1891	1892	1893	1894	1895	1896	1897	1898	1899
Number	75,067	82,165	30,996	29,633	20,829	18,790	16,835	21,716	31,900	44,543
% of Population	1.6	1.7	0.6	0.6	0.4	0.4	0.3	0.4	0.6	0.9

Year	1900	1901	1902	1903	1904	1905	1906	1907	1908	1909
Number	41,681	55,747	89,102	138,660	131,252	141,465	211,653	272,409	143,326	173,694
% of Population	0.8	1.0	1.6	2.5	2.3	2.4	3.5	4.2	2.2	2.6

Year	1910	1911	1912	1913	1914	1915	1916	1917	1918	1919
Number	286,839	331,288	375,756	400,870	150,484	33,665	55,914	72,910	41,845	107,698
% of Population	4.1	4.6	5.1	5.3	1.9	0.4	0.7	0.9	0.5	1.3

Year	1920	1921	1922	1923	1924	1925	1926	1927	1928	1929
Number	138,824	91,728	64,224	133,729	124,164	84,907	135,982	158,886	166,783	164,993
% of Population	1.6	1.0	0.7	1.5	1.4	0.9	1.4	1.6	1.7	1.6

Year	1930	1931	1932	1933	1934	1935	1936	1937	1938	1939
Number	104,806	27,530	20,591	14,382	12,476	11,277	11,643	15,101	17,244	16,994
% of Population	1.0	0.3	0.2	0.1	0.1	0.1	0.1	0.1	0.2	0.2

Year	1940	1941	1942	1943	1944	1945	1946	1947	1948	1949
Number	11,324	9,329	7,576	8,504	12,801	22,722	71,719	64,127	125,414	95,217
% of Population	0.1	0.1	0.1	0.1	0.1	0.2	0.6	0.5	1.0	0.7

Year	1950	1951	1952	1953	1954	1955	1956	1957	1958	1959
Number	73,912	194,391	164,498	168,868	154,227	109,946	164,857	282,164	124,851	106,928
% of Population	0.5	1.4	1.1	1.1	1.0	0.7	1.0	1.7	0.7	0.6

Year	1960	1961	1962	1963	1964	1965	1966	1967	1968	1969
Number	104,111	71,698	74,856	93,151	112,606	146,758	194,743	222,876	183,974	164,531
% of Population	0.6	0.4	0.4	0.5	0.6	0.7	1.0	1.1	0.9	0.8

Year	1970	1971	1972	1973	1974	1975	1976	1977	1978	1979
Number	147,713	121,900	122,006	184,200	218,465	187,881	149,429	114,914	86,313	112,093
% of Population	0.7	0.6	0.6	0.8	1.0	0.8	0.6	0.5	0.4	0.5

Year	1980	1981	1982	1983	1984	1985	1986	1987	1988	1989
Number	143,140	128,642	121,179	89,192	88,276	84,345	99,355	152,083	161,583	191,553
% of Population	0.6	0.5	0.5	0.4	0.3	0.3	0.4	0.6	0.6	0.7
Year	1990	1991	1992	1993	1994	1995	1996	1997	1998	1999
Number	216,454	232,815	254,809	256,678	224,394	212,869	226,073	216,038	174,198	189,952
% of Population	0.8	0.8	0.9	0.9	0.8	0.7	0.8	0.7	0.6	0.6
Year	2000	2001	2002	2003	2004	2005	2006	2007	2008	2009
Number	227,455	250,640	229,049	221,348	235,825	262,241	251,642	236,754	247,247	252,179
% of Population	0.7	0.8	0.7	0.7	0.7	0.8	0.8	0.7	0.7	0.7

CHAPTER SEVEN

The Rising Sun Never Set in the West

The multiple colors of the Canadian Rainbow shine beautifully and some stand out more than the rest for a while and later give an opportunity to others. Right now, the color of Asia is getting sharper and brighter and is gradually replacing that of Europe. The modern technological world has made the globe a small village and it resonates with a common culture and lifestyle and has melted away the residue of age old rigid forms of culture. The tendency of the modern man leans more towards accepting people with their skills and the richness of their potential, rather than their ethnic identity. This preference is the norm to a certain extent but has not been adopted totally by others due to a sense of pride and superiority. Asia is no exception.

Though Asia is diverse within its regions in terms of its ethnicities, cultures, religions, political philosophies, and economic structures, there are certain commonalities among them as the western nations have. Asia being highly diverse culturally is more homogeneous in its vital elements of ethnic composition.

Asians still maintain their root heritage values from their historical times even when they were forced directly and indirectly to give up and absorb the values of the colonial rulers as such the Portuguese, Dutch, British, French and Spanish for a period of over five centuries. It was a very systematic way of undermining their values and destroying them. The psychological war that the colonizers waged had a very high negative impact on Asians and brought down their heritage values and convinced some of them that their own heritage values were barbaric or uncivil and that the faster they adopted the values and beliefs of the colonial rulers, the better off they would be. I do agree that in some areas they were advanced at that period of time but, it was not perfect.

The discriminative methods of the colonial rulers deprived certain rights and privileges to those who continued to follow their way of life and had to undergo a lot of pressure, and this pushed them into an underprivileged class of people in their own land. Those who surrendered their values also were not treated equally but put them in a more privileged class. After the independence war of India fought with the weapon of non violence against the British Empire was won by Mahatma Gandhi, it opened the eyes of the world wider and brought recognition not only to India and but to the entire Asian continent further it paved the way for the struggle towards independence for the rest of the colonies in Asia and Africa.

Let us now examine the ancient world civilizations and see where Asia stands in the continuum. Though it has not been fully proven, the existence of the Lemurian civilization in the Indian ocean is considered by some archeologists and historians to be the first world civilization and some of those elements have been in existence among the Dravidians who have been residing in the southern part of India.

The Chinese and the Indians still continue their root culture and civilizations even in the modern world. They do acknowledge and accept the technological progress and the contributions made by the western world particularly since the industrial development of Britain and they had no other choice other than to accept it. But when I look at other parts of the world where ancient civilizations disappeared, I feel proud of the Asian civilizations for having survived the test of time. I also noticed that it has become unavoidable that when the rural areas became and continue to become urbanized, the culture of the urban dwellers has a stronger influence and this process has and continues to move at a tremendous speed and deep into the virgin lands.

Whether or not religion still plays an important role in many people's lives is an important question and personal spiritual beliefs can take on many forms. For example, one may have faith in god but not practice within any religious boundaries whereas another person may belong to a strict faith community. There are Atheists who do not believe in god and Marxists who believe that the life of the material world is final and that idealism cannot supersede materialism. However, it is important to note that the world's major religions have their roots in Asia. The Middle East in Asia is the birth place of Judaism, Christianity and Islam. Hinduism which is considered to be the oldest religion, Buddhism, and Sikhism were founded on the Indian subcontinent. The entire world is enveloped with Asian religious beliefs, except for South America, Africa and in some remote areas of Australia.

The first and direct link between the North American continent and Asia dates back to the so called pre-historical period and it has been almost accepted the first human wave came from Asia, particularly from Mongolia and they are the First Nations of Canada and Asians are also concerned about the well being of the natives as well. There is historical evidence that Chinese fishermen touched the Pacific coastal line of the North American continent centuries before Columbus discovered the so called new world. While history provides some interesting accounts, our immigration numbers also tell a fascinating story as you can see in the chart below:

Immigrants to Canada from the top ten countries

#	Year; 1970		2000		2010	
01	United Kingdom	26,497	China	36,715	Philippines	36,578
02	United States	24,424	India	26,086	India	30,252
03	West Indies	12,456	Pakistan	14,182	China	30,197
04	Italy	8,533	Philippines	10,086	United Kingdom	9,499
05	Portugal	7,902	South Korea	7,626	United States	9,243
06	Greece	6,327	Sri Lanka	5,841	France	6,934
07	Yugoslavia	5,672	United States	5,814	Iran	6,815
08	India	5,670	Iran	5,608	United Arab Emirates	6,796
09	China	5,377	Yugoslavia	4,723	Morocco	5,946
10	France	4,410	United Kingdom	4,647	South Korea	5,539
11	Other Counties	10,445	Other Counties	105,985	Other Counties	132,882
	Total	117,713		227,313		280,681

The drastic shift in the migration from its traditional and preferred European nations to Asia is a drastic change when compared to earlier periods in Canadian history when there were specific policies in place to either limit the number of Asians coming into Canada or stop them outright. But the slowdown in the rate of natural increase in population and the economic growth that was able to cater to the employment needs back in Europe had very little influence in terms of pushing forces but Canada was very much in need of migration of more human resources and willingly or reluctantly accepted skilled workers. And the favorable among the non favorable groups were the Asians and it is evident in the demographic patterns of the top ten source countries. In 1970, among the top ten countries that provided immigrants, the Europeans countries had taken the lion's share with the first two leading countries being the United Kingdom with 26,497 and the USA with 24,424. Immigrants arrived from Asia, India ranked first whereas in the year 2000 the leading source countries supplying new immigrants were China 36,715, India 26,086, Pakistan 14,182, Philippines 10,086, South Korea 7,626 and Sri Lanka 5,841 and in 2010, the Philippines 36578, India 30,252, and China 30,196. There is a significant increase from the Philippines from 10,086 to 36,578 and some increase from the United Kingdom, France and the United States and a downward trend in the Chinese migration from 36,715 in 2000 to 30,197 in 2010. The economic slowdown and the heat of the recession in Europe and the USA pushed more immigrants to Canada where the attack by the recession is comparatively mild and Canada is a pulling factor. The decrease in Chinese migration is certainly influenced by the high rate of economic growth and the improved standard of living among the business and skilled workers and also a minor shift in the ridged state monopoly system of enterprise and in spite of all the restrictions of the migration policies of the Chinese government.

The enthusiasm of skilled immigrants was and is often dampened when the reality of settling into Canada sets in. Often, their high hopes do not materialize in the first four years in general for skilled workers who have perseverance and are determined to find jobs in their field. Most of them struggle to find such jobs for almost four years and during the gap they have to take odd jobs and are often not being paid equally with their Canadian born counterparts. In some cases, these are less skilled jobs and this adds fuel to the fire of frustrations that they undergo in a strange land.

Let us take taxi driving as an example of a profession in which new immigrants mostly from Asia work at the initial stage and out of the total number of 50,110 taxi drivers 50.1% of them are immigrants.

Immigrant taxi drivers by country of birth

Country	Drivers	%
India	6,220	24.8
Pakistan	2,960	11.8
Lebanon	1,790	7.1
Haiti	1,455	5.8
Iran	1,040	4.1
Britain	830	3.3
Somalia	775	3.1
Ethiopia	765	3.0
Other	9,295	37.0
Total	25,125	100

The evolving economic stability and strength is deeply rooted in China and India and eventually in a decade or two they becomes the two main superpowers next to America and hopefully Brazil will follow them. It has taken them a little more than a half a century to get out of the economic dependency from their colonial rulers and reorient their values and restructure the force of the economy to their independent and self motivated system of profit making. Furthermore it has taken some time to address local issues based on their regional, ethnic, or religious grievances that were ignored because of the suppressive rule of the colonizers who were considered a common enemy for all. Once they were chased out, they began to settle their old accounts.

CHAPTER EIGHT

Changes on Immigration—2012

The dark clouds formed by the migration to Canada in different categories by the world nations have been cleared up to a certain extent as far as the Immigration Ministry is concerned. It allows the sun to rise with hope for the general immigrants to migrate to Canada by making it easier, faster and less costly for the processing of immigration papers. There has been much criticism of the immigration law Bill C31 which was passed in parliament in June 2012 such as it being more restricted and depriving of privileges and not very helpful to new immigrants. I do advocate for the overhauling of the policy and the remaking of the system of immigration to Canada is overdue. I remarked on this in my one of my earlier books entitled "Canada-The Meat of the World Sandwich" The structure and the policy of the current immigration system was laid in 1976-78 and there were changes made from time to time which helped overcome certain present issues but was not examined and thoroughly changed for a few decades.

There has been a fundamental change in the economy, the effects of the technological revolution, internal migration and international migrations and the foreign policies in the last 35 years. But in the sector of immigration there were some cosmetic changes, but the fundamental structure has remained.

Immigration is an ongoing and vital part of this nation. It does not necessary mainly confine to the shortage of human resources or in considering the economic stability and optimizing the economic growth in order to maintain a high standard of living locally and overcome the global challenges.

The honorable, Jim Flaherty, the Minister of Finance once commented in his federal budget for 2012-2013 that Canada is not an Island in the world economy. That is equally true in the sector of immigration as well.

The current immigration sector has left no stone unturned and it has its own impact on the demography, manpower, communication, social amenities, taxation and the maintaining of law of order in this country.

Whatever has been said and done the current demographic pattern of Canada with the distribution of population by age, ethnicity, and linguistic skills matters more than counting the number of immigrants and scaling it up or down to maintain the current number for the immediate future. It is inevitable that in the present and in the future Canada will not be able to manage without the migration of immigrants constantly and periodically. There are two main factors that contribute to the welcoming and acceptance of new immigrants. The decline in the natural birth rate in Canada continues to get deeper and there is no sign of any drastic change. In spite of all the efforts that are put forward by the government of Canada the citizens of Canada have limited the birth rate significantly. The alternative that has been advocated is replacing some of the services of the human beings by the products of technology. But this has its own limitations and it can only replace a smaller portion of the services that been provided by people and I don't think robots will be created to work in factories and offices and replace human power. Unless there is a miracle, under normal circumstances there are no chances in taking a u-turn in the decline of the natural increase in population.

The impact of the growing rate of seniors on Canadian human resources and economy has been felt by the government and, whether they like it or not, it is a moral obligation of the tax payers and the government to provide the services and the meet the finical obligations according to the current Census of 2011. The data it reveals is that seniors account for 14.8% of the total population whereas children under the age of 14 account for 17.6%. These numbers reflect that the active population of Canada is around 68% of the population. Compared to India, one of the fastest growing economic powers in the world, the seniors account for 5.5% and children under the age of 14 counts for 13% and this shows only the slightest difference in the percentage of the active population compared with Canada. In India, there is also a decline in the birth rate and not much of an increase in the senior population and this will eventually increase the ratio of the active population.

In recent times, some research works has been made to gauge the numbers of new immigrants in Canada, American and in some European counties. Some of the research done has suggested that it would be better to accept a lower number of immigrants based on the import by the immigrants to this nation and expenses paid by the tax payers for them. These researchers have come out with the controversial figure by averaging the number of current immigrants by half. In contrast, some researchers in demography and immigration have given consideration to the natural wealth and resources of this country and Canadian economic law suggests that Canada should always have 10% of its own population as new immigrants. This is healthy in terms of production and in marketing and this would not be a burden on the Canadian economy or to Canadian society. These researchers do have their own backing for their findings and there was another study recently suggesting that Canada would be able to accommodate 100 million people. In the immigration history of Canada it was in 1913 that Canada accepted 400870 new immigrants. Since the year 2000 until now, Canada has accepted between 225, 000-250,000 new immigrants. If Canada would have accepted one percent of the population it would have been around 335,000 per year. The capability and capacity of having a certain amount of immigrants does not necessarily depend on the size of the land and the total number of people. It mainly depends on the capability of the economy to cater to the population. As far as Canada is concerned, it is not only having the largest size of land next to Russia, but also has over 60 different types of minerals such as uranium, gold, diamond, natural gas and oil sands. These are very rich in economic value; therefore after assessing all of the important factors including the wealth of this nation, Canada is certainly able to accept at least 1% of its own population if not more. I do not mean to say by accepting 1% of new immigrants that this will lead Canada to become an over populated country because with the current population of just over 30 million people, Canada is under populated.

I do agree the number of accepting new immigrant's matters to the Canadian economy but we should also analyze the type of immigrants that we have been accepting. Currently over 66% of them are skilled workers and investors and refugees account for 8.8%. The rest belong to the family class sponsored immigrants. Almost two-thirds of new immigrants are rich in their skills, education and experiences and if we cannot make a system that can utilize their talent and optimize their productivity I would say a major part of the blame goes to our system, not on the immigrants. I do acknowledge that new immigrants undergo certain training that is required to get themselves updated with the fast changing modern academic and profession developments in their field. And due to the nature of the Canadian economy, none of the skill workers would prefer to leave their field of expertise and engage themselves by performing duties where their skills and wisdom are not required and they obtain little to no satisfaction on the job.

Let us also throw some light on the age distribution of immigrants. The statistics in Canada reveal that the highest percentage of skilled workers are in the middle aged group and their contributions and productivity are more of an asset than a burden to this nation. There are also screened as a part of the process of their immigration to show that they are free from criminal records and that they are not a white elephant in terms of consuming the lion's share of the health care expenses.

We also need to look into the other side of immigration. The source countries that many immigrants to Canada come from invested in social amenities, health, education and their overall development and it is very unfortunate that they would not be able to get the outcome from the invest that they have made This may be due to certain reasons such as the sector of education trained many students but their current economy would not be able to utilize them due to the lack of investment or in proper management or corruption. So the receiving countries achieve a major gain out of these skilled immigrants without making a great investment in their human capital and this junction I would say "who derives more benefits in this migration process, those source countries for the immigrants or the receiving counties at the other end?" Some of the new immigrants in spite of these unfavorable circumstances in their countries of origin where the unemployment rate is high or even after being able to find jobs in their field of expertise live on a lower income and in poor living conditions due to political instability, and discriminative measures, they would not mind migrating to the developed nations and do whatever is required to live a better life. Usually, an active and motivated type of immigrant initially spends almost 4 years to get adjusted, undergo certain training and obtain certification to work in the field of their expertise. However, sometimes a new immigrants cannot make the proper effort and achieve success in this initial stage in getting themselves prepared and usually will settle for working in a job outside their field in order to survive.

I do acknowledge that there are successful entrepreneurs and businessmen who migrated to Canada or arrived as refugees with little or no money that have become successful and have accumulated millions of dollars. Would it be justifiable to ask they are examples or exceptional?

I don't dispute what some immigrants say in that they believe that there is some sort of hidden agenda when it comes to immigration. According to them, the selection of immigrants is not purely based on their merits or in the best interests of this nation. Of course the term "best interests" is conveniently expressed by all groups concerned about this issue. The interpretation of what is in the best interests of the nation is a very vague idea that can be manipulated to suit the ideas of any particular group. In order to justify the changes, they magnify the areas which are convenient to them. This is what happened during the Cold War between the Soviet Union and the United States of America. Both parties mainly defended their system of government and their own economic theories and decried the opposing view and demonized those inside and outside the system. This was a tactic with the intention of preventing their own people from getting influenced by the other side and hence why they portrayed the negativities and the problems of the people who are in the opposite camp. There have also been certain hidden elements and interests in preventing large scale migration from certain regions or by certain ethnic groups. This has been done by sugar coating the truth and the use of attractive wording so that in the eyes of the outside world, the intent is not to discriminate against certain people or groups.

In the immigration history of Canada there have been elements of discrimination against the mass migration of certain ethnic groups. For example, historically there was discrimination against the mass migration of Asians to this country. There are certain immigration critics and human rights advocates who want to express their dissatisfaction with certain policies and want to see amendments which suit their points of view. There have always been two types of immigrants, the favored and unfavored and the favored are encouraged and warmly welcomed. The unfavorable immigrants are tolerated but not necessarily accepted. Sometimes those from unfavorable groups were needed only for certain things such as the building of the Canadian Pacific Railway because not enough local people were able or were willing to do the work. It was fully expected that these people would leave the country once the work was finished. There are elements of this attitude when it comes to certain immigrants today. For example when it comes to refugees, we seem to get excited when a large group of migrants comes to our shores on a rusty old ship rather than by airplane. Why do we call these people cue jumpers?

I have recently been approached some community leaders and ethnic journalists who outright asked me about Bill C31. They believed that this bill was targeting people of certain ethnic groups. I told them that this might have been the immediate cause for this bill to be created but the general purpose of this bill is much broader and encompasses different elements.

Are the Current New Immigrants Assets or a Burden?

"I have two degrees and strong work experience, but I spent a year underemployed in Toronto and over a year unemployed in Vancouver . . . . I have since moved to Calgary, where opportunity is everywhere."
Brendan Baines, 28—The Globe and Mail, 29th May 2012

Although the above statement is partly a reflection of the current economic recession in Canada and the adverse effects from the deep recession in the United States of America and in Europe, there are other contributing factors to consider when it comes to underemployment or unemployment. The outstanding of baby boomers in the job market by new immigrants to Canada is another important factor.

In spite of what some politicians, academics, and immigration critics may say, it is acknowledged that this nation has been built by the sweat of immigrants and that Canada is a land of immigrants. However, in contrast, there is some research that has done by certain academics which considers new immigrants both in the recent past and now, as burdens or liabilities to the nation and the work force.

Their conclusions are mainly based on economic input and its returns by new immigrants to Canada. Professor Herbert Grubel of Simon Fraser University mentioned in his research piece entitled

"The Fiscal Burden of Recent Canadian Immigrants" that in the year 2002 alone, the costs and benefits received by the 2.5 million new immigrants who arrived between 1990 and 2002 exceeded the taxes they paid by 18.3 billion. Another critical author on immigration, Daniel Stoffman was not in favor of accepting the current level of immigration and concluded that if it continues as it is, it will have a very negative impact on those who were born in 1980-1995 in terms of their future job prospects.

A similar study was made by Mr. George Borjas of Harvard University, himself an immigrant to the USA and a world renowned immigration economist, clearly states that immigrants do not benefit the economy. He also recommended in his book entitled 'Heavens Door" that the United States should reduce its intake of new immigrants by half. In Britain, a report produced by the House of Lords in 2008 and presented to the government recommended the reduction in the intake of new immigrants to below 190,000 from what had been originally planned. The report also mentioned the side effects of allowing such a large number of new immigrants in terms of social amenities and housing.

In most cases, the private enterprises would prefer to have more immigrants so that they will have an ample supply of workers. Based on the theory of supply and demand, the higher the supply in comparison to the normal demand it would be easier and cheaper to have new immigrants in the labour force for there will be less demand for better working conditions and higher wages. Whereas on the opposite side the labor force as a whole would prefer that there be fewer immigrants in order to preserve local jobs and the benefits that go along with them.

CHAPTER NINE

Experience of an Expatriate in Africa

I had a wonderful opportunity in Africa while I was engaged in teaching in Ethiopia and Nigeria. I spent most of my time studying their life customs, language and their heritage values. Being a foreign worker, my assignments did not require much time. The teaching itself was not like what we have in Canada where there is lots of preparation and follow up required. I was considered one of the best teachers for my excellent work. But I considered that I did much less than what I should have done. I satisfied the Ministry of Education and the societies' so called educated elites, but not my conscience. I had been teaching in a government school in the city of Lagos, Nigeria and I had been doing a lot of extracurricular activates. I was organizing seminars, workshops, developed the debating club and preparing news summaries and analyzing news and so on. The unit leader of the school is third in rank next to the Vice Principal. In fact the given assignment of the unit leader is to have overall supervision and work alongside the administration. But he also acted as a spy for the Principal. He is in the good books of the Principal and it was an open secret that he had absolute freedom. He could come any time and leave the campus at any time. No one even dared to question him, for questioning him was like questioning the authorities. He went and reported to the Principal that I had been doing such work. The remark made by the Principal was "Let him play like a boy playing with toys. As long as he does not interfere with our execution of administrative work you do not have to worry. Let him play. Leave him and do not worry about him." The comment that was given failed to appreciate my work, but I did not bother because I knew that it had been appreciated by the students and the society. I also do not mean to discuss this as though it is a common practice in Nigeria.

Part 2

I was in a college known as Aisgba Community College in the state of Ondo, Nigeria as head of the social science department and as hostel master of the boarding school. I spent most of my spare time working with school children and their immediate community and I was very active. I began a project of having the students build concrete blocks to build a church on the college grounds. It was a missionary school supported and financed by the Ondo State government. We made over five thousand of these bricks and did the labor work and made it possible to build a church the size of almost ten thousand square feet. The school appreciated my efforts and I was given a token gift and many other awards by the Kings of the local regions.

The area where I was working was a thick tropical forest region. It is not easy to penetrate the forest; it was a swampy area with almost daily rain in the afternoon. It is pitch dark even in broad daylight. There is no path. Mosquito's bite you and snakes move around as they wish. We were advised to take the vegetable ladies finger and bite it now and then because some of the poisonous snakes are allergic to it and change their direction when they smell this vegetable. It would not be a problem for me because I am a vegetarian by birth on my Hindu religious grounds. There are very poisonous snakes with a bite that can kill instantly and there are no hard dry places to lie down. I got the interest in exploring this area and developed my courage after reading books about the European explorers in Africa. The feeling that I got at the initial stage was that I was entering into a bloody war zone; that life and death were side by side. However, after remembering an earlier incident, I changed my mind.

It was on 7th January 1981. I went with my friend, Physician Thanikasam, an expatriate, to Ado Ekiti, a small city to spend some time in bars having fun and to purchase spices and other groceries for the week. It was a normal pattern. It was in the evening at about five o clock that someone from the community stopped his vehicle and told me that an expatriate man crashed his car on a bridge and both the husband and wife fell into the river. I rushed to the scene and picked them up. My friend being a medical doctor gave first aid and told me that the condition of the lady was critical. We took them to the nearby hospital and had them admitted. We were informed that if immediate surgery was not performed, her right leg would have to be amputated. I was not aware of the medical complications and the terminology that they used, but I knew the situation was urgent. They told us that they did not have the facilities to do the surgery there. I had no other choice other than request the taxi driver to take us to Ibadan where there was a hospital where the surgery could be done immediately and more professionally. He declined our request. In Nigeria particularly in the south, armed robberies are very common and the law enforcement bodies could do very little. I had heard that in some cases the criminals collaborated with the police force and that a portion of the proceeds of the crimes was given to the police. I risked my life and got hold of a friend of mine and I proceeded to drive to the Ibadan hospital which was located almost 70 km away. We started at about 8 pm and reached the Hospital at about 9.30 pm. I did not want to drive faster, though it would be better to be without any delay. The vehicle was a not a comfortable one for someone to lie down on the seat for, it was the vehicle of my friend who was an engineer. He did not need a luxury car, though he earned a very high salary being employed by a British company. In fact, Nigeria is an oil rich country. I very well remember after the oil prices shot up in the 1970's the former ruler of the military government General Yacob Gowon said "Our problem is not the money; our problem is how to spend the wealth". Recently, the Premier of Alberta made mentioned a similar view. Having very high oil revenues, it would be possible. The British and America construction companies made a big income similarly from oil rich Nigeria.

We reached the hospital safely and made the proper arrangements. I had the long leg and used my influence for the woman to get into surgery. We were advised by the Doctors and others not to return home during the night and to stay the night and leave early in the morning. We appreciated their concern. I thought for a while that we might have saved the woman's leg and that we would lose our precious lives. We did not have any other alternative other than to leave right away because my friend had to be at his work site early in the morning. The cementing of the bridge which was a multimillion dollar project was the most important task. Since he was in charge of the project and the chief engineer he had to be on site. I thanked the concerned people and left. We passed safely for almost fifty kilometers. It was during the very short dry season. Except for the months of November—February all the rest of the year daily rain fall is common. We were passing through a dense forest area. I was negotiating a curve. I was tired and sleepy as well. The visibility was poor. I saw a big tree that had been placed across the road and blocked the way. There was no possibility that the tree had fallen because of wind because it was not the windy season and the rest of the areas where we had been traveling did not have any signs of this. I suspected that we were caught in the hands of armed robbers. I slowed down and put the lights on high beams and flicked them on and off. I did see someone. I stopped the car. In a fraction of a second from both sides of this road a couple of robbers rushed to us. They had covered their faces with black masks. We opened our door and raised our hands up. They came closer and got our wallets and other belongings and searched for weapons. The only weapon that we had was our active brains. We were practically carried like logs of wood and thrown into the dense forest. I could hear the movement of my car. I was pretty sure that our car had been stolen and moved to a hidden location but I did not know where it was. Car theft and robbery was very common in the southern part of Nigeria than that of the north where the more passive Muslim population is predominant. Ibadan and Adi Eiti are in the south and are the biggest cities in West Africa. We were warned not to make any noise nor make attempts to move even an inch.

It was a very dense tropical forest. There was hardly any space to lie down. I had to stand on my knees as if I was worshiping the trees around me. Usually robbers kill and then flee for the value of life is very cheap to them. It was not an isolated incident. A month before, a foreign doctor was robbed in the night, was killed and the body was left in the forest. I was aware of this. I was determined to keep quiet and stay there and wait for the bullet to penetrate. I had a very strange feeling within myself. My mind was firm that I had no other choice other than to accept whatever was going to happen to me. But my body could not accept my command; it began to act by itself. My whole body was shaking. Since it was the dry season the ground was filled with fallen leaves like a carpeted floor. It was like a very sensitive sound studio. Every slight movement or noise was well noticed. It was a very secret operation. The robbers did not want oncoming vehicles to have the slightest suspicion. My friend was suffering from a bad cold and at times he could not control his sneezing. I was praying to all gods I could think of irrespective of the religious boundaries. Even at the critical stage my body refused to listen to me. One of the robbers might have thought that I was a brave person and was trying to escape. He began to warn me by counting. He said if I did not stop when he counted up to three, he would fire a bullet. He started to count. One, still my body did not listen to me. I was helpless. My body continued to act the way that it wanted. When he said two my body stopped shaking.

I then got the courage to face any situation. I escaped from the first step but it was not yet over. Usually criminals killed hostages or leave them and run away when the dawn approaches. There was a possibility of getting shot. My mind was getting ready for it because there was no other way of escape from the scene. I lifted my head a bit and began looking at the road. I saw a car come at a tremendous speed and slow down at a distance of approximately 300 meters and alternatively turn the light into a high and low wink. I could guess that they began to suspect something. They were approached by the robbers. The car was forcefully stopped. The robbers went and beat them up and scared them. They did not want to remain on the road for long and took them into the forest. I could not see what had happened to them. But

I am pretty sure that they were tortured and made so scared so that they would not retaliate or make any move to escape. It was going on till dawn. It was at about 5.30 am. I did not see any one on the road. I was not sure whether they left the scene or were hiding in the forest and waiting for another vehicle to rob. I asked my friend to follow me. He hesitated and did not want to take the chance. He told me it was a matter of life and death. I was worried when the public in the morning begin to look for the culprits, that they would suspect that we were the ones who robbed the others and punish us. Either way there was an element of risk involved. I decided to walk onto the road. I saw a truck stopped beside the log of wood that was kept across the road. In a split second, I thought that the robbers were still around and that if I had made a mistake; I would have listened to him. I had the only consolation was that my friend was in a safe position and that I would be killed. The driver and two other people who came with him approached me and asked what was going on. I was relieved from the tension and told him the whole story. They removed the log of hard wood and cleared the way. I was sure that the robbers left. I went into the forest and brought my friend and got into the truck and came back to our residence. We reported the incident to the police, but we knew very well that they would not do anything about it.

Part 3

A few months later I attended a wedding party. We were drinking and dancing and I was a very good dancer then. A gentleman approached me and introduced himself as a business person. We exchanged greetings and then for the sake of courtesy he asked me how I liked the country of Nigeria. I gave him my honest opinion. I said that the people were in general very cordial and friendly and relayed the incident that had happened to me. It was a surprise for me to hear that he was one of the gang leaders who engaged in similar operations. He was kind enough to apologize and told me that in the future if any such incidents happened to me again that I should meet with him. He then gave me his address. I thanked him and continued dancing.

Part 4

Four months later a good friend of mine had his car stolen. On a beautiful sunny Sunday morning, we ate our breakfast and played cards for a little while inside the quarters of a single male friend of ours. We had eaten a light lunch because we had plans to go to another friend's home for dinner later that day. We continued our card game and watched a movie and then at about 7:30 in the evening, we went to our friend's place and had a very delicious dinner. After dinner our friend's wives felt a little bit bored and wanted to play cards with us because at that time foreign workers did not usually intermingle socially with the local population and thus going out would have been awkward. We accepted their offer to play cards and continued well into the night. We then spread out some floor mats so that we could settle down and sleep for the night.

The following morning we had some tea and travelled back to our respective quarters. I began preparing my agenda for the upcoming work week and, about half an hour later, my friend in whose home we had eaten lunch the day before came to our place by taxi. Now this was unusual because my friend had a car, a French model to be exact. My friend was in a panic and I could not make any sense of what he was trying to tell me. If he was a married man with a family I could have guessed that maybe his child was ill or had been in an accident—but this was not the case. He told me that his car was missing and he had no hope of getting it back because usually stolen cars in Nigeria could not be easily recovered.

I then prepared a cup of tea for my friend and tried to get him settled down. But then I suddenly remembered something. I remembered the gentleman that I had met at the wedding party a few months previous. He had told me to come to him if there were any problems around the issue of stolen vehicles. Unfortunately, I had forgotten where I had placed his business card. So I told my friend about this man, but he did not exactly take me at my word. Of course, I can't exactly blame him for feeling that way because it is a bit strange. Undeterred, I went back into my room and somehow managed to find the business card.

My friend and I made our way to this man's house because back then, telephones were not very common. He welcomed us into his home and we saw a group of people inside playing cards and drinking whiskey and beer. I then told him what exactly happened to my friend's car. He asked me the location and the date and time that my friend had lost the car. He then shifted a sliding door across the wall and I could see a collection of file folders that took up the entire space. He picked up the file for the particular location and studied through the pages until he found the correct one. It was quite a surprise because he mentioned that brand name of the car and the contents of the inside right down to the glove compartment! We were completely shocked and my friend almost stopped breathing. Even the Ministry of Transportation would not have such details! Then the gentleman took a piece of blue paper and wrote something down which I didn't recognize because it was in his language and then ripped it in half and gave the half with the writing to us. He then explained that we had to go to a particular location at a certain time. We thanked him for his time and then left.

Two days later, my friend and I went to the location that we had been told about. It was about 50 kilometers away from our home. A large trailer was coming in our direction and we waved the piece of blue paper three times. The trailer stopped and the driver checked my half of the blue paper alongside his half. They matched perfectly at the center and we were asked to meet the driver at another location 10 kilometers away after 2 hours. When the time had come, we arrived at the said location and we found the car and the trailer. There was no sign that the car had been kept in the jungle but rather inside the trailer—could it be that this car was going to be shipped out of the country? It's hard to say. We thanked the driver and took the car. One thing that we noticed was that all of the contents in the car had been left untouched and nothing was out of place. It appeared that among these thieves, there seemed to be some honor.

The following afternoon at about 4 o'clock the same gentleman who had arranged the pickup of my friend's car came to our home. He wanted to go to my friend's home in order to check out something in the car. Though he spoke of this in a very polite way, I was feeling rather uneasy. We went to my friend's house and though this gentleman was extremely polite to him my friend was also very nervous and bordering on scared. He was afraid that his life was in danger. The gentleman asked my friend to open the car door and my friend was in a panic. The man was looking for something underneath the driver's seat and my friend and I were terrified—was he looking for a weapon? He then found what he needed. It was some kind of clip board that had some papers attached to it. What the papers contained I did not know but I could make out a few license plate numbers. The gentleman apologized for the inconvenience and went on his way.

Now you're probably wondering what this story has to do with Canada. First of all, crime is an issue no matter where you live and Canada is no exception. Also, many people who immigrate to Canada have been victims of crime, some worse than what I experienced in Nigeria. What I am trying to say in this story is that despite what happened to me, I was able to recover and move to Canada to start a new life. In fact for over 10 years I have worked with the Metro Toronto Police as a Community Liaison. In Canada crime is taken very seriously and we are fortunate to have the law enforcement bodies that we do. If a similar incident happened to me here, the car thieves would be brought to justice, even though I would probably not see my car again!

It is easy to criticize Canadian law enforcement and it is true that the system is not perfect. But to those of us who come from places where justice is a bargain across a counter. Indeed, we are very lucky to be living in Canada where justice and respect for the law are core values.

CHAPTER TEN

Canada: Nations within a Nation

The Canadian Constitution is such that it has given more than a fair share to the provincial governments and it might be interpreted that the concerns of the provinces are better addressed. Their rights and freedoms are more protected, their identities are well maintained, they are given the opportunity to develop their regions with enthusiasm with the hope of obtaining the lion's share in the revenue, and they concentrate intensively in their overall development and the preservation of their values. On the point of overall Canadian national interest, the progress and the development of each and every inch of all of the provinces sum up the gains for the nation. But when it comes to the national share versus the provincial, it is very critical. I am quite certain that most of us maintain the view of keeping the current share from the national wealth for the provinces as it is and would also prefer to keep the rights and privileges that go along with it should. By contrast there are others who are not satisfied with this arrangement and advocate for a larger share. It is also hard find anyone who says that the provincial governments enjoy with undue right.

In the recent provincial government election in Alberta, my views regarding the fair share between the federal and provincial governments were prompted by the concerns voiced by the Wild Rose Alliance Party. It accused the provincial governments of Ontario and Quebec of having a share of the employment and other benefits from the sale of the oil sands and when certain forces around the world made very negative criticisms on buying and using the oil sands by mentioning that it pollutes the air and contributes more to global warming. This statement was made by South Africa and some other member nations at the 2012 summit on global warming in the city of Durban, South Africa. The European Union itself blamed us in exporting more of the oil sands and exporting to China, United States of America and some other countries. Even U.S President Barak Obama was reluctant to sign the Keystone XL agreement, not out of the best interests for America; rather, his motive was primarily to not to lose votes from Americans who demonstrated their negative view of constructing the pipeline for the potential environmental damage it may cause. Apart from the external opposition, even within Canada there was some opposition against the construction of this pipeline which was intended to supply oil from the oil sands in Alberta to China from the west coast of British Colombia by local First Nations groups. As far as the Native people are concerned this has nothing to do with the inconvenience caused by the construction of the pipe line, rather it is the delays surrounding long overdue land claims.

It is not limited these projects and there many more projects related to oil sand refinery and export such as Bakken Access Program, Westward, Texas pipeline, Bakken Marketlink, Alberta Clipper pipeline expansion, Mid –Continent expansion, Bakken North Project, basin Pipeline expansion, Rainbow pipeline 11, Athabasca pipeline Twining project, Bakken expansion program, Northern gateway, Keystone Cushing Gulf coast link and gulf coast access.

Energy resources in Alberta, along with those recently discovered in Newfoundland and many more to be discovered in some other provinces and territories and other minerals and its local consumptions and export markets in the USA, China and the rest of the world pose unique challenges. Finding such minerals in other parts of the world and alternative sources for them will certainly alter the dependency on other resource exporting countries and this is another area where we need to have an alternative plan.

At this point, I am also somewhat concerned about the nature of the export commodities such as the exporting of the oil sands and other minerals at a cheaper rate to provide an opportunity to boost the economy and employment rates of those importing nations in which some are our economic rivals, instead of refining the crude oil sand and make use of those minerals in our manufacturing industries more than what we have been absorbing and generate more revenue and supply more employment opportunities for the unemployed Canadians. The current unemployment rate compared with other developed nations is not in the bottom range. We should also take into consideration that these are exhaustible resources. The silent investments in the mining industries in Africa and South America by Canadian companies generate substantial revenue and help us maintain better relationships that will help us in many ways in the long run.

The level of generating wealth by each province is not consistent and the ups-and—downs are also inevitable. As such the Eastern provinces were pretty much subsiding on generating income from the fisheries in the past and when there was a decline they were forced to become a have not province. With the exception of the province of Newfoundland with the recent discovery of oil, the rest remained in the same position. Alberta has been pushed to the top of the ladder by the discovery of the oil sands and the almighty Ontario, the long time backbone of the Canadian economy is on the verge of tumbling from its prestigious stage and this has mainly been caused by external and internal factors in combination. Since the province of Ontario has a diversified economy, it does not have to worry like some other provinces such as Alberta, and the eastern provinces that are mainly depending on a single commodity in generating revenue.

Both have and have not provinces rarely come to a clear cut solution of what they get in return for what they give to the federal government. The provincial premiers have met several times by themselves and then collectively with the federal government and exhausted all avenues to come to an agreement that brings satisfaction between the have and have not provinces and the federal government. The formula of equalization that was mainly advocated by Dalton McGuinty Premier of Ontario was more centralized in balancing the share than what a province contributed in exchange for what they are entitled to and this was more of a proportional proposal. But the federal government is more inclined in helping the have not provinces more than in terms of their contribution to the federal government and this has come partially at the expense of the have provinces. Extending more help to the have not provinces by the federal government is not at all a controversial issue or a disputable one but sharing from the collection of wealth from the provincial government is a major concern from the provinces that contribute the lion's share to the federal government.

The provincial governments also learned an unpleasant lesson from the federal government when Prime Minister Jean Chrétien downloaded some of the responsibilities to the provincial government from the federal government. All the provinces welcomed and accepted this without any hesitation or reservations, hoping that transfers for the due expenditures would be made to the provincial governments. However, the reality hit hard and the provinces did not get the desired cash. The chain reaction also extended to the municipalities when the provinces downloaded some of their responsibilities to the municipal governments. Mr. David Miller, former mayor of Toronto, complained that the provincial government had not paid in proportion to the downloaded responsibilities that had been transferred to the municipal level.

Healthcare is another area that the provincial governments are not pleased with. The transfers of money for the health care services and the transfer agreement that was created by the former Prime Minister Paul Martin was somewhat accepted by the provincial premiers and it is on the verge of expiring. I do not think the new deal will have enough revenue from the federal government to meet the growing health care expenses due to the increase in the number of baby boomers from today's 12.3%. The provincial funding would not be able to meet the expenses and Canadians do not want to tamper with the basic structure of the health care system by introducing a two tier system or private health insurance as it is practiced in the United States. Though some researches came out with some statistics that seniors do not consume more than the proportional percentage of health care expenditures, still overall expenditure is growing tremendously high. The growth of the population due to the natural increase in the birth rate and immigration also contribute to the cost of healthcare and this is one aspect that needs to be kept in mind as well.

Though it is not always necessary, the position of the economy has a direct influence on political power and the rights and responsibilities of the provinces in sharing with the federal government. Still the economy has a vital role in influencing it. It has been said by some of the politicians that the federal government treats the provincial government of Quebec in a very distinct manner in many ways including the allocation of more money than what it deserves compared with other provinces. An example of this is the allocation for the settlement of newcomers. Per capita wise Quebec receives more than that of Ontario. Is this favoritism or is it justified by the political distinction? Although Quebec has been considered as a nation within a united Canada, it is also to be considered as one of the provinces and there should be some sort of parallels between the two. Quebecers historically claim that they have certain rights on this land and that they were the first European settlers and established their own government and ruled themselves as a colony of the French until the British conquered it in 1774. Canada was declared as an independent nation under the British North America Act of 1867. The French descendants and their next generations in Canada continue to have their close and unique relationship with France which cannot be underestimated there are even French Canadians who prefer to be a part of Canadian national identity. But the descendants of the British in Canada would like to continue their ties with United Kingdom, they too developed a close and intensive relationship with the USA and shifted their economic, political, social and other relationships. This kind of shift from one sovereign nation to the other made some significant alterations in the relationship but t all three of these nations have roughly the same ethnic origin. There is always a conflict in the interest of Canadian sovereignty and the attempts to be closer to the USA has pushed us to compromise and become more elastic in terms of forgoing some rights in order to make some gains. The burning issue is where to draw the line between the economic security and dependency of the U.S and maintaining our sovereignty and an arm's length relationship. It was noticed that when Brian Mulroney was the Prime Minister of Canada, he was more inclined towards the USA and when Chrétien was in power he maintained more of an independent stand on the relationship. One example of this was that when U.S President George W. Bush with the help of NATO forces initiated a war against Iraq and Afghanistan the USA expected the direct involvement of Canada in the war, but Chrétien was strong in his stance that Canada would get involved in the war, provided it received sanction from the United Nations.

The French Canadians are in three camps and the first is the strongest and most consistent in keeping the dream concept of Quebec as a separate independent nation alive. The second group is to remain within the federal government with better rights and privileges and the third one is to remain within Canada until the ripe time comes for separation. The support from the swinging Quebecers has been moving from one to another but the strong supporters of sovereignty are solid and strong for their cause. The federalists particularly those who were born after the Quiet Revolution are also firm in their stand and the deciding force is the swinging group.

The average Canadians of non French origin could not even dream of a Canada without Quebec. But they do not have much say or voice in it and they can only advocate and encourage them to remain in

Canada. Brian Mulroney put his all possible effort in the best interest of keeping this nation undivided and his Meech Lake agreement that was brought forward on 30 April 1987 did not win and then the Quebec referendum of 1995 was almost in a winning position and with less than a percentage it was defeated. In the 2003 Federal election, the late Jack Layton won many seats in the province of Quebec and defeated the Bloc Quebecois and acknowledged and appreciated their support and tried to be more favorable to them. Once he said that if the Quebecers were able to get 51% of the vote in a referendum for a separate state, it could be accepted. Recently, former Liberal leader Michael Ignatief said Quebec eventually will become an independent country and that a victory for Scottish separatists in an expected 2014 referendum will launch a new effort by Quebec nationalists to fulfill their dreams of sovereignty. He further said in an interview with the BBC in April that "Quebec and Canada have little to say to each other and that the two already are almost separate countries . . . Scotland that devolution of central powers, whether from London to Edinburgh or from Ottawa to Quebec City, likely will be only temporary. Now effectively . . . we're almost two separate countries. Although Quebec does not have sovereignty it acts domestically almost as if it did, and that I think has produced this strange reality that I don't think most Canadians I'm thinking of are happy about". Although later on he said that what he meant was different, he did not deny what he has said. The question of Quebec independence was also asked by a member of the Bloc Quebecois to the Dalai Lama on a recent visit to Ottawa. He said that "Canada it's a democratic country so if the majority of Quebec people decide to say yes for the independence. I'm sure in Canada it's going to be accepted"

In closing, it has become increasingly clear to me that this country is going from nationalism to regionalism and it is important that national unity be maintained for like it or not we depend on each other. We are one country but we have many faces and this is what gives Canada a challenging beauty.

CHAPTER ELEVEN

Diversity in Ethnicity

Ethnicity and race at times cross their boundaries. There is no separation like water tide compartments. It overlaps. It gets interpreted differently by many ethnic groups around the world. In South Africa, where racial segregation was in existence there was no room for ethnic differences. Irrespective of where they were from, the British, the Dutch, the Germans and all other Europeans and the Jews were placed in one superior basket. The Asians, regardless of their ethnic backgrounds were left in the second basket. The third one was the interracial population between the whites and non whites and the last one was the Blacks, the bulk of the population of 80%. But within each group there were ethnic differences. The Blacks had many ethnic groups within the segregated race. In the modern era the genocide of Adolf Hitler based on the supremacy of the Aryan race and the systematic elimination of Jews left a black mark in the history of mankind.

Ethnicity versus nationality

The concept of ethnicity and nationality should be conceptualized differently than that between ethnicity and race. Nation is not some what a well—defined terms in Canada. The recent recommendation made by the conservative government of Prime Minister Stephen Harper on the Quebec issue that "Quebec is a nation within united Canada "Already the natives have been given recognition as the First Nations therefore the usage of the word nation is not a new phenomenon in the Canadian context. The province of Quebec has been considered as a distinguished society. Society is more in terms of the territory of culture and language whereas nation is more of political recognition. Though the Prime Minister eliminated the fear of giving a step ahead for the sovereignty advocators, there is doubt that an element of promotion is there. It could be a step that might have delayed or temporarily subdued the potential threat of the sovereignty issue and at this important time the issue has not been aggravated. The sound economic condition of Canada, the unemployment rate in the single digits and the consecutive surplus budgets of the federal government have made the separatists not push the sovereignty issue. Mr. Harper might have thought that the last referendum of 1995 was defeated by a very narrow margin but at that time the Prime Minister Jean Chretien won his election in a riding in the province of Québec,

The so called Wild West has been complaining that they do not get their proportional share of the national cake. The Reform Party in which he was an active member and leader has held grievances against the Liberal party and their focus on central Canada and has dominated Canadian politics. They have been more of inclined towards getting justice or otherwise finding alternatives. The marriage of the Canadian

Alliance with the Progressive Conservative Party might have been based on the mistrust on central Canada. I do not know how long this marriage will last. Furthermore Mr. Stephen Harper a westerner was for the first time elected as the prime minister of Canada. The excessive revenue from oil boom and having abundant oil reserve, the second largest in the world of the province of Alberta made some of the elites in dreaming for a nation by itself. Alberta. Mr. Harper might have had in his mind that by giving a small fish that will deny the big one.

There is a room for to think in a very different dimension it is more of political than patriotic move. Mr. Michael Ignatief the defeated candidate for the leadership of the Liberal Party made a proposition that Quebec is a nation. A few weeks before the Prime Minister announced that Quebec is a nation within a united Canada. It might have prompted Mr. Harper to get the support in the parliamentary election by getting more votes in the province of Quebec. Already, in the last election 0f 2006 conservative Party

Cultural Mosaic
Assimilation/ Multi culturalism/Melting pot/ Bicultural

In the American vision of diversity, the whole is perceived as greater than the sum of its parts. All ethnic groups have unified into the national identity. There are various interpretations of culture, language, religion, arts and music, color, and other aspects of ethnic values. Some of them are deep rooted in history. Karl Marx claims to be more scientific in his theory of human life and developed the idea that the economy is the basis of all human behavior. The whole exercise of human activities has been revolving around materialistic interests and that would be the only and final goal of life. It is the survival of the fittest. The identification of nationality, ethnicity, and race are meaningless. Capitalism will certainly have two opposite forces. The capitalists will continue exploiting the laborers. The so called free enterprise system will eventually lead to a monopoly system. The small industries will be swallowed by the big fish. Therefore the monopoly controlling the resources and the wealth will be in the hands of a few capitalists. It is not necessary for them to look into the well being of the common masses. They do have some concern because they have to market their products and services. The size of the market does not necessarily depend on the size of the population. It depends on the purchasing power. Therefore the system of capitalism would not allow the masses to be too poor.

He classified the people into two camps, the exploiters and proletariats regardless of their backgrounds. At the final stage of Communism there will be one system of government, one policy of the government and the world will be reaching an everlasting system of economic plans. The global concept has taken a different path. According to Marxism, all those ethnic, religious groups and languages will eventually disappear. Accordingly, the worker is a worker. The nature and the interest of the capitalist is only one and that is to exploit the laborer. In economics, there are four main factors of production. They are land, labor, capital and entrepreneur. In a state monopoly, the government has the overall control and the ownership. The government is formed by the masses. The masses would not go against themselves. Therefore, the producers and the consumers are on both sides of the same coin.

In America, nationalism and statehood have taken the utmost priority. There is no question of German American, Irish American, Native Indians, Latino American, Asian American and African Americans. No matter where your roots are, you are an American. That's it. Be a fully fledged American or be a foreigner. There is no question of coexistence of many ethnic groups. There is no mid—way.

In contrast, there are no homogenous people in any nation on the globe. The national boundaries have been altered from time to time. Nations have been merged, separated and so no. There are non Jews in Israel and non Catholics in Vatican City and non Muslims in Saudi Arabia. Their numbers may be insignificant but there is no restriction by their constitution for other ethnic or religious people to be there. Even among the Native Indians there are a lot of tribal groups have been in existence. Though the Americans claims the Native Indians are Americans, the natives do not totally agree on the concept. Some of the natives have the very strong conviction that Columbus did not discover America, rather he invaded it.

There is another aspect that is very interesting. The Blacks who were brought to the Caribbean from Africa and the East Indians and the Chinese as labourers were addressed by the term coolies, a word that might be derived from the Tamil language that is spoken mainly in South India and Sri Lanka. The word "coolie" generally speaking means labourer. Their categories of work and social status put them together as one class. Eventually, their roots were cut and they formed distinctive groups, namely West Indians and African Americans in the case of the United States but the recent migration from those areas still maintains this tribal identity. Multiple tribal or multi ethnicity migration is a common phenomenon.

The North American continent has always been a land of immigrants. Even the Native Indians migrated from Asia via Alaska. It is the most accepted theory of the early inhabitants of America over fifty thousand years ago. The land of America was discovered by the Europeans and through their colonization around the world the rest of the world came to know it. Christopher Columbus landed in America in 1492 even though his group intended to visit India. It was a time when agriculture and trade was the two main sources of generating wealth. The countries that had abundant natural resources for agriculture engaged in it. Those who do not have much of it got involved in trading. It was mostly trade by barter. The Europeans in many countries had a big problem in preserving meat and other items that for the cold season. In the absence of the refrigerator, canned food, and other modern facilities that would brought by the industrial revolution in England later on, preserving meat and other foods was a big problem. There was no way of importing fruits, meats and vegetable easily from the tropical zones or from the temperate zones in the southern hemisphere. Spain and Portugal did not do very well in terms of agriculture. They were forced to sail their ships and do business around the world. At that time exporting spices from the Indian sub continent was a very successful business. Those spices were mainly used for preserving meat and other times for the winter season. Though there were spices available in North Africa, this was not well known to the European for the exploration of Africa was not in full swing.

Portugal and Spain were located beside each other and they came to an unwritten agreement that was more or less an understanding that the Earth was round rather than flat, and therefore it would be healthier if one group moved west and the other east. They would of course meet in India but on opposite sides. The Spanish sailed their ship and landed in the New World. Those who landed on the islands in the Caribbean Sea concluded that they landed in Western India on islands and named it the West Indies. When crew of Columbus met the native people they called the inhabitants of North America "Indians" in an extension of the misapprehension that they landed in India. Even today they are called Native Indians. The interesting part of it that that inhabitance has no idea about India and there is no cultural or any other relationship with them. The Native Indians belonged to hundreds of different tribes, speaking over one thousand languages in which many of them disappeared, their culture, norms of society and traditions are different. They settled down from the northern polar reign to South America. Their languages have not developed written script and almost all of them have been spoken languages. They were originally hunters and collectors of food. At the early stage they did not confine themselves to one particular area. Later on these people got settled in places and began to engage in farming. They had a system of local governance but not national. After their colonization they lost their freedom and a systematic elimination took place. Many of them began to learn European languages and many of their languages went into extinction.

Melting Snow of the Multiculturalism Policy and Practice

I really enjoyed being the Mayor in one of the pavilions at the Caravan International Festival in Toronto; festival with entertaining shows and a variety of cultural displays exhibiting traditional cultural treasures of over twenty five ethnicities from many corners of the world which took us around the world in less than eight days. Since it was a pleasant program held in the evening for a week during the early summer, the turnout was rather encouraging with a more diversified audience in attendance. Much to my pleasant surprise some of them had arrived from the United States and from Europe with much of the entertainment dedicated to exploring the roots of and the struggle to preserve the cultures of those nations. I am still searching for the answer to a question that arose in my mind during this event and that is: Is this celebration a reflection of the survival of multiculturalism in the long run or just a symbolic gesture?

I do appreciate the current principle of multiculturalism and the current multiculturalism policy with its focus on acceptance rather than merely tolerating people of other cultures by the Canadian government and the people. So far Canada is one of the leading nations, if not the leading nation in providing accommodation for the cultures of Canadians who have migrated from over two hundred countries. In this piece I wish to compare the existence and survival of multiculturalism in Canada with other countries that practice multiculturalism and with nations that have alternative cultural policies.

Multiculturalism transcends national boundaries while preserving and getting integrated with the predominant culture. The interesting part of the origin and growth of many cultures derived from the unique human wants and the ending target remains uniform and unchanged from the primitive man to modern man. Hunger, self protection, self esteem, sex, love, union, shelter and recognition are some of the emotional, psychological and physical needs common to everyone.

The physical features and climatic conditions are the basic factors that regulated the fundamental and structural establishments. The physical features can be classified into four main groups:

(1) High elevated features such as Mountain Gangers and Plateaus—the Rockies, the Andes, Himalayas,

(2) The grass lands,—the Prairies, Pampas, the Savannas

(3) The coastal regions—The Pacific, the Atlantic regions in North America, The Mediterranean, The Indian and the Arctic regions.

(4) The deserts—The Sahara the tropical desert, the Siberian desert, Australian desert

(5) The Forest Zones—The Amazon forest, The Congo

Canada is the first country to adopt multiculturalism as an official policy in 1971, by the initiative of Pierre Elliott Trudeau and it has been taken care of by the consecutive governments of both the Conservatives and Liberals, though their approaches, focus and priorities have had some slight variations. I would do an injustice, if I do not mention some of the initiatives and implementations made by our governments. They channel quite a lot of money for these activities and policy implementations for Heritage enhancement, Heritage Language Education, promotion, and designated the 27th June as Multiculturalism Day in 2002.

.

UNICEF of the United Nations Organization in 2003 has acknowledged that children in Canada are less likely to fall behind in schools than similar children in the twenty—two other industrialized nations as one of the achievements.

Since the beginning of time, human beings have been differentiated from apes in the process of evolution. Even though they share a similar biology, psychologically human beings are shaped by the rhythms' of life and all cultures move through the process in a similar way from the womb to the tomb. This process has remained unchanged from the time of primitive man to the modern man who has been highly influenced by modern technology. Though the means and the pattern in deriving the ends may have changed, the single goal of living happily on this earth has remained constant and all cultures move towards the same direction. To put it in another way every individual, including twins born by the same mother have certain differences in biology and psychology. In spite of these differences, as Aristotle once said "Man is a social animal "and he is bound to share with fellow human beings and form a society. The established patterns of the ways of living are shared by the members of the group and these norms become unwritten laws and the members of the society are expected to abide by these norms. Along with this, the gravity of the punishment given to those who disobey depends on how the society values their norms and how flexible they are.

In the United States of America, there is the concept of the "melting pot" and no room for multiculturalism, though some may say this idea is changing,. Mean while, in countries like Germany, France, Spain, Portugal, Italy and Greece the preference is given to a mono—culture. In Switzerland, there is a confined form of multiculturalism which is similar to Germany; it is very difficult to become a citizen in these two countries and one must show such a strong amount of integration into the mainstream culture to the point of almost erasing their own cultural identity. Contrast this with France in that though there is an all encompassing idea of "being French" one can still maintain ones cultural practices provided that they do not go against the French identity. For example, the attempt to make the wearing of the niqab, the face covering worn by some Muslim women illegal in France illustrates this idea. France was founded on the principle of equality between the genders, and the mask drops to reversal goes this French value.

Canadian cultural background was more European based in the middle stage of its history followed by the biculturalism of French and English. When there was slow down of migration from those two countries, Canada opened the gates wider for the mass flow of emigration for eastern and then southern Europeans.Canada was full of Europeans, as the majority and the rest were minorities. The Asians who had mainly migrated to Canada as laborers underwent discriminative measures such as head taxes for Chinese along with the Exclusion Act. There was also the unrealistic restriction when traveling on ships that there was to not be any break from the origin of the journey and the ships were not allowed to dock on Canadian waters. A prime example of this was the Komagata Maru incident in which a ship full of migrants from India was forced to turn back from the west coast of Canada.

Finally Pierre Trudeau made multiculturalism as a policy of government and opened the door wide for people from all continents. It had a dual purpose, Trudeau understood pretty well that there was a slowdown in population expansion and the economies of Europe had reached a substantial stage of development. The economy was able to provide employment but the internal exploration of arable lands and improvements in the manufacturing industries and new construction of roads, bridges, buildings and other infrastructure was needed. There were no other alternatives other than welcoming and encouraging others to migrate to Canada particularly visible minorities. The second reason for Trudeau's policy was to weaken strengthened sovereignty movements by diluting the Canadian biculturalism policy into multiculturalism. He once said that there were two official languages but not biculturalism.

The end results of the implementation of multiculturalism have not been very successful in many European countries and France and Germany have reluctantly acknowledged their difficulties. Regardless of how one may feel about multiculturalism, it is very clear that no matter what you try to do in terms of preserving one's own culture and traditions gradually over time they will fade away due to a number of pushing and pulling forces. The second and third generations who are born and raised in Canada and have intermingled with other communities have become absorbed into the main stream culture and they do expose or inherit the symbolic gestures of their native cultures. Having annual cultural shows, displays, dressing up in traditional outfits have not gotten into the core of their respective cultures. Culture begins internally in the mind and heart and reflects in their way of living. The pulling forces of the main stream culture are very powerful. Their inherited identity and languages are not being duly encouraged and motivated by the respective communities. Language is one the main vehicles of transferring from generation to generation and these people of the second generation learn French or English as their first language and less than 30% of them learn their heritage languages and too few reach up to a functional literacy level.

One of the main forces that have influenced multiculturalism is technology. It has penetrated from the public life to the personal life so deeply and most of us have been influenced by it universally. In most parts of the world, the cellophane, television, radio, internet, cable, satellite, airplane, bullet trains services and washing machine, are common in life for all irrespective of their language, culture and ethnicity. People have been losing the essence that is their cultural values traditional cultural values and the urban and technical culture brought many of us together as members of the global family. The immigration pattern also has shifted its locations. These days many skilled immigrants are migrating to Saskatchewan, Manitoba and Alberta whereas in the past many immigrants settled into the urban centers. Regardless, they are bound to inherit the culture and values of where they are living and thus become a part of the mainstream culture. The impact of these immigrants to rural parts of Canada has also had an impact on the culture of those areas as well for these areas have a long history of being heavily influenced by European immigrants and immigrants from other cultures are bringing a lot of changes to these regions.

The outlook of our fellow human beings and the relationships between them has become broader and more open. The Americans would not have even dreamt of having a fellow American of African American heritage as President, but it happened as a result of the evolving consciousness of the people. I do acknowledge that several of the factors behind his victory that go beyond his personal background.

Multiculturalism is more than a matter of cultural preservation and promotion; rather, it is a tool used to maintain the identity of each and every ethnicity. This can pose some very real problems in that it can prevent the full integration of immigrants into mainstream Canadian society. Sometimes in the name of respecting other cultures, we end up silently allowing practices that go against our values to occur. One of the beautiful things about culture is that over the course of time it changes and these changes can often lead to better things. I am not saying that having cultural events and keeping ones language and foods etc are wrong. The problem is when one hangs onto these things with an iron fist—these traditions can become like a cage.

The acceptances of the policy of globalization also made it easier for the developed world to penetrate into the heart of the conservative and rigid minded people and broke the ice in their backyard. These days the opening for many opportunities in economic activities, government operation and the private sectors and having participants from other groups has given wider room for openness in their minds and the hearts in terms of accepting them as a part of society.

Most parts in the world have become liberated from rigid cultural—centered attitudes, not only in their day-to-day life but also in other aspects such as inter-marriage with other ethnic, linguistic, and religious groups had made us more liberal than ever before in the civilized world.

One of the revolutionary impacts of technological development is that it has created and opened new venues in employment pools. Thousands of semi-skilled and unskilled laborers are employed in the manufacturing sector, financial and investments, operation and marketing, communication and transportation, government sectors, defense and maintaining law and order, tourist industries, hospitality. The development of an occupational environmental culture penetrates into their own culture and forms an entity all of its own.

The growth of the trade unions, mostly in the socialist countries and other developing nations which have established trade unions gather with their members not only in the workplace, but also in community and social events and this again forms another cultural entity.

Finally, what I would like to say is that we can do very little in terms of preserving cultures. Given the advances of technology and the progression of time, preserving cultures is like trying to stop snow from melting. If we allow the snow to melt and allow it mix with the waters of the ocean—it can become a thing of beauty.

The modern modes of communication and transportations are faster, have lower risks, are better and affordable for the masses and, brought identical forms of cultures into a massive main land and they slowly shared, interacted, and interchanged some of their cultural values. People who had not traveled out of their own region are flying out to countries far away for thousands of kilometers for various reasons, such as on pilgrimage, family, employment purposes, sports, business, tourists, social functions, and education and family get-togethers.

The new venue was opened in the Middle East in the early seventies when the Oil exporting Arab nations began to use oil as a weapon against the western world that was supporting Israel. The Goddess of the Black Gold all of a sudden blessed with abundant wealth and for some those countries money is not a problem but how to spend it is the problem, I can also remember in 1973 Jacob Gowon, the president of Nigeria and the Premier of Alberta also made similar remarks. They began to expand their structure and many unskilled and semi and skilled workers arrived as foreign temporary contract workers from the Philippines, Pakistan, Bangladesh, Sri Lanka, Malaysia, Indonesia and some of the investors from Canada, the U.S.A, and from Europe. Their life pattern more or less brought them under another umbrella.

The birth of indirect democracy has also been an important development. The popular saying in this process is one man, one vote, irrespective of his color, religion, and ethnicity, economic, social, and educational and other differences. Though in many countries, particularly in the African and Asian countries the tribalism, caste concerns, religion and linguistic barriers are still a determining factor when it comes to victory or defeat.

One of the chief achievements in the process of democracy is the establishment of human dignity which was ignored or exploited by other forms of government from the historical period to today. By respecting one's own sense of self respect, the same can be extended to others. These developments helped bring people under the umbrella of political parties which in turn brought forward the concept of globalization on the grass roots level.

These days the strong command of the name of god and the influence of many religions in politics has gotten weaker. But the rise of Islam demolished main barriers in their denominations such as Hamas, Ismailia, Shiite and Sunni and brought together most of their over one billion followers as a strong force. The realization that all of us are sons and daughters of God, regardless of religious denominations helps us in mobilizing the masses together.

CHAPTER TWELVE

Multiculturalism and Globalization

There are certain eye catching terms like multiculturalism in the public and private sectors that are frequently used with prowess and pride and have become more of a means to get recognition from the masses or higher ranking officials. In a democratic country such as Canada, it is the masses that have been targeted while in a dictatorship the higher ranking officials get the attention. Some of the words have become heavier and more important due to socio–economic changes and political influences. These words have been sleeping in the dictionaries for many years. People have rarely used them. Some of the words in literature used by Shakespeare, Milton and many other poets were used only in the literary circles. Some of these words carry different meanings depending on the community in which the word is used. For example the world spinster in the United Kingdom is used as a respectable term in addressing an unmarried woman but in North America it carries a very different meaning. In this case it means that that the woman in question is a person who is unable to find a partner.

Another example I can think of comes from the time when communism came into practice after the formation of the Soviet Union. During that era, the term "master" was synonymous with exploitation. I have witnessed in south East Asian and some African nations the use of this term as well, but it did not convey the same meaning as in the former Soviet Union. The word master was also used in some of the South American countries in the 1870s and during the colonial period words such as master and lord were frequently used. In South Africa the coal miners referred to the white man as master and even today, fine art teachers in India and Sri Lanka, who are males, are addressed as master.

I have also noticed that there are two terms that are popular among religious groups of various denominations and those terms are brother and sister. The use of this word has nothing to with the biological relationship among people but refers more to a relationship based on faith. In some cases these terms have been linked with racially segregated and groups of people who faced systemic discrimination. For example, during the American civil rights movement it was very common for African Americans to refer to each other as brothers and sisters as a sign of solidarity; members of trade unions have also done this. The purpose of using these terms is to foster a sense of unity among the people and to provide support.

There are several popular terms that have captured the minds of scholars and the masses and these are: as follows; globalization, the global family, multiculturalism, terrorism, fundamentalism, famine, and gay rights. But like the words "master" and "spinster", these words take on different meanings depending on where they are used. Karl Marx, for example, advocated for globalization in the form of the political system of communism. The concept of being under one umbrella made workers around the world feel united regardless of their color, race religion and language. I can remember that I had been invited to deliver a speech on African socialism along with other scholars at the Jimma teachers college in Kaffa, Ethiopia. It is fair to say, that I am not a fan of Marxism; I do not agree with the concept of idealism versus materialism and the idea that the ultimate goal of life is to be rid of the materialistic world. Previous commentators battled within themselves in promoting their brand of socialism. It was in the middle of 1972 that I read the book titled Juna Socialism written by Julius Nyere, the president of Tanzania, a former British East Africa colony. Julius Nyere was one of the leaders who fought for the liberation of Tanzania. He mentioned in his book that the culture and the traditions of the country along with their economic and political systems could help create and establish a form of socialism without the need to import a brand new system from the outside world. What he was referring to was Marxism. There are also some Islamic writers and leaders that have developed another concept based on their interpretations of the teachings of Islam and this are referred to as Islamic socialism.

We are people of two worlds. Man was born with neither culture, nor race, nor language, nor religious practice. There is a distinct deference between human beings and other living creatures in the sense that human beings are more socially linked. It does not mean that the animals have been living as individuals. Birds when they fly in a group have a leader and a pattern of flying. The bees have a well organized kingdom. There are designated duties and rights from the queen bee to the worker bees on the bottom. I have noticed in tropical countries that crows when one of them discovers food, it will invite other crows by making a particular noise. I had seen a wonderful sight in the school compound of the Jimma Secondary school in Ethiopia

167

where I had been working as the principal. Usually the first shift at the school starts at 8.00 am and the second shift starts at 1pm. I usually reported for work much earlier and in fact I was the one who entered early and left late. There are tall trees in the school compound. There was a family of monkeys living in the branches of those trees. There were three in the family the male and its female and their son. I had seen them for more than five years. It was on a Thursday in the evening when the male monkey fell from the tree and died. I saw that the rest of the family was hanging in the tree branches and weeping. Once they saw us passing in their direction, they moved up the tree and pretended that they had nothing to do with the situation.

Even plants at times communicate amongst themselves. In a particular area in Japan, deforestation had been taking place on a mass scale for a period of time. Some kinds of trees in that dense forest made some kind of reaction and it was noticed by the workers and they notified a zoologist who performed some research and concluded that these trees had indeed communicated with each other. The communication of the members of the same species is one thing and that of with other creatures is also another wonderful thing. Of course man communicates with domestic animals such as cats, dogs, parrots, bulls, cows, horses, rabbits and so on. There are a lot of true stories about how domestic animals reacted when their master was in danger or killed in a plane crash, killed by someone or when danger is ahead.

Socialists such as Ulrich Beck and Zymunt Bauman have used the term 'Globalization' in their publications.

Man is a social animal. He cannot survive by himself. He has the need for directly or indirectly communicating with fellow human beings, no matter who he is and what type of person he is. Isolation is the worst punishment, it is harder than torture. Man has been moving around the world ever since he was differentiated from the apes. Anthropologists and historians have been trying to find the origin of the first man. It has been going on like a hide and seeks game. The remains of the oldest skulls were found recently in Eritrea and Ethiopia. Dr. Leaky and his son spent a major part of their lives in the horn of Africa around the Olduvai Gorge in the east African rift valley. They discovered human remains from time to time in various locations such as Java and Russia and many other parts of the world. Now the unanswered question is that whether man was differentiated from apes only in one place or in more than one place at various times or at the same time. If man was differentiated in more than one place he would have remained wherever he was differentiated. If not he might have started migrating around the area. But it is established that man had been continuously living in the same place. There are various factors that have contributed for migration and immigration. The two main factors are the natural calamities and that of the man made. In some cases it is the combination of the two. Let's look at the birds in the northern polar region. They could not bear the severe cold during the winter season and made their seasonal migration toward the southern temperate zone and northern parts of the tropical zone passing over thousands of kilometers and back in the spring. The only difference is that they do not have to obtain visas to enter a territory and there are no restrictions or boundaries where other birds claim ownership. The fishes migrate in the oceans at times with the cold and warm ocean currents. We are in an advanced era when man has been trying to migrate to other planets. It is not hard for man to migrate from one location to another.

What do these factors explain?

There are two opposite forces behind the migration of people and these are the pushing forces and the pulling forces. Usually most immigrants give the issue of migration much though and consideration. They have some sort of attachment to the land where they were born and brought up. The attachment to the land, rivers, trees, lakes, the birds and animals is very strong. But so are the memories of the games they played as children, the arts, culture, and the pride in their history, traditions, customs, the places of worship, and the resting places of their ancestors along with the stories of how their people fought against invaders of all kinds. These memories are not easily forgotten and it is very difficult to leave forever and move to a strange land where the customs, culture, language, art, traditions and food habits are totally or partially different from those of their own. It is always said that a known devil is better than an unknown angel. I do not mean to say that the land that they left is a devil. But the pushing forces might have been devilish in a sense. In most of the cases of migration, there is a deep rooted unpleasant threat to their life and some other negative forces are also involved. The interesting part of it is that people migrate from different countries at various times having many reasons and they follow similar procedures and encounter identical problems. On the other hand the ones who were at the grass roots level and were at the bottom of the society in economic resources would not have been able to know the ways and means of migrating. Only the ones who know the ways and have some means are able to migrate successfully. It was evident when I interviewed an Immigration officer in 1991 at the provincial immigration office that he mentioned similar concerns.

Historically, the pushing forces have played a major role in migration. In the days when people were living in the Stone Age, they were not confined to the nation having a well organized political system. It was the time when most of the people were not civilized and enlightened by wisdom. When I mention the word civilization I do not mean to define it in the same way as Mr. George W Bush, the President of America did after the terrorist attacks on September 11, 2001 in New York City and Washington.

There are many examples of civilized nations around the ancient world. The Egyptians, the Etruscans, Indus valley, the Chinese, the Mohenjo Daro, Lemurian, the Greek and Roman, and the Mayans are all great examples of ancient civilizations which made many contributions to the world. The beauty of human beings is that there are people living in different stages of civilization around the world. We can also see that there are people in the tropical forests in South America around the Amazon River valley, around the Congo River and in the forests of the Philippines who have little to no contact with modern civilization. There are some primitive societies in the Polar Regions as well. By "primitive", I do not mean uncivilized, I am referring to people who are still living their traditional lifestyles before contact with modern civilization and technology.

CHAPTER THIRTEEN

Canada Under the regime of the Right Honorable Prime Minister Stephen Harper

Is Harper—A Living Legend

"I can tell you this; We have made Canada more united, stronger, more prosperous and a safer country" said by the Right Honorable Prime Minister Stephen Harper at the rally organized by the Conservative supporters in Ottawa in marking the 5th anniversary of their reign on 23rd January 2011. Let me begin my review of these comments by analyzing the circumstances and the challenges that the Prime Minister has faced in leading a minority government along with the achievements he has made along the way.

At the time when Harper defeated the minority Liberal government led by Paul Martin in the election of 2006 and was declared as Prime Minister on January 23rd 2006 by the Governor General, Canada did not go into recession that greatly. However, the rich nations began to enter into a recession and very gloomy economic clouds covered the bright sun. The international economic waters had to go through the violent storms and waves. A year after Harper began to reign; most of the economic ships of the rich nations got into the troubled waters and shed jobs which slowed down the speed of navigation, moving back and forth. The ship steered by Greece hit the monetary rocks and like the Titanic was about to sink and collapse. But the European Union, United States of America and Canada came to its rescue and saved it. Other neighboring nations of Greece, such as Portugal, Spain, and Italy were also on the verge of collapsing. Even the almighty American ship was in trouble after experiencing the breakdown of some of the financial institutions, corporate bankruptcies and sufferings of the real estate market by the consequences of subprime mortgages.

There was another moderate ship sailed by a dynamic Captain that moved smoothly without any major disturbances and attracted the attention of the other captains of the rest of the ships. It was witnessed at the G8 and G20 summits respectively held in Belleville and Toronto in 2010. The financial management and handling of the overall economy which placed us comparatively in a leading position left Canada as a role model. It was not my intention of underestimating your intelligence by saying the ship belongs to Canada and the captain is Stephen Harper. In fact, Canada was the last country to enter into recession and first to move out of it and currently it is in the stage of recovery. Canada comparatively suffered with mild waves, whereas some of the developed nations which had entered earlier are still deeply suffering the adverse effects. Of course Canada suffered in having lost many jobs, some of which have disappeared completely, deficit balance of trade, increase in government debts, budget deficits and the reduction of some of the social services. Let's compare this situation with the past, particularly with the recession of the 80s and 90s in Canada and the current one with other industrialized nations. In the past the cuts in social services were deep and sharp and left people in a miserable state. The unemployment rates were in the double digits and when compared with the United States were higher. Now it is the reverse. The interest rates were not as low as 0.25%-1%, it was very high. The credit ratings of certain provinces like Ontario was very low and it led to difficulties in borrowing money. The Liberals knocked down Brian Mulroney in the election having the big punch of eliminating the Goods and Services Tax of 7%. In the end what happened? In 13 years rule they broke the promise and kept the GST in place. But Harper reduced it to 5% from 7%, respectively by 1% on 1st July 2006 and 1st January 2008 by 1%.

Other important factors that influenced the Canadian economy are the gaining strength of the Canadian dollar along with a higher foreign exchange rate. These two main factors have kept the Canadian economy going. When it came to selecting a country for his first state visit US President Barrack Obama chose Canada believing that it would be the better choice. He met with Harper and discussed economic stimulus measures in terms of encouraging and boosting the economy and how these measures could boost the consumer confidence of both nations. Harper realistically said to Mr. Obama that the boosting of the Canadian economy does not totally depend on the stimulus programs within Canada but also on the strength of the US economy. The rising Canadian dollar and weakening purchasing power of America has not encouraged the import of products from Canada. There is the exception of the oil sand which is a hot commodity right now and America prefers to purchase from Canada at this time of political turmoil in the Middle East.

Harper keeps our economic relationship away from political matters and independently acts accordingly to the best interest of Canada. He was very smart in moving the issue of trade restrictions on softwood lumber exports with George W. Bush and was quite successful in reducing the barriers and managed to receive back a portion of the taxes and import duties levied by the States. Harper has realized that depending solely on the American market is not safe and has travelled around the world establishing stronger markets with the European Union, India, China, and Pacific Nations. In spite of all of this however, the value of exporting services and goods to America cannot be underestimated.

When Obama was adamant in implementing the protectionist economic policy and did not give Canada considerable status as its traditional trade partner, Harper quickly established trade relationships with other nations ensuring that the Canadian economy did not suffer.

Harper is a very smart leader in keeping the sovereignty of Canada in a prominent place by not dancing according to the tune played by the American piper. He did not want to please them at the expense of Canadians and acted very independently. When the request was made by America for Canadian airspace for the purpose of protecting America from Russian targets, Harper flatly refused. Canada unilaterally decided and informed the NATO countries that it will withdraw its forces from Afghanistan in July 2011 and was not bothered by the criticisms made by those countries. In spite of it when Canada was asked to keep or send some of our forces for training the Afghanistan army in Kabul he reluctantly accepted this request. But now the NATO nations have brought in a deviated plan in which Canadian soldiers will be giving training not in Kabul, but in Kandahar which is a dangerous area. Already Canada has lost 154 soldiers. Harper has to be in power to resolve this matter in a very diplomatic way.

Harper has also brought a meaningful unity in the bottom of the hearts of many ethnic groups and I would like cite a few of them. The Chinese immigrants were very much offended by the racially biased act of levying a head tax on them in the late 19th and early 20th centuries and no leader was bold enough to make an apology but he did it on 23 June 06. But on another occasion, when he was invited to attend the Olympic Games in China along with many of the world leaders, including the ones who made loud noises against the human right violations in China, most of them went and participated, not because of love of the games but because China is a fast booming nation and pretty soon will become a super power and is going to sit next the USA. But Harper did not show any interest and though he did not mention directly the reason for not participating, it is obvious that the human rights violations could have been one of the reasons if not the only one. He extended apologies to Indian immigrants for Canada them not allowing themto disembark in Vancouver, Canada on the Komogata Maru in the early 20th century. He also extended a big apology on 3rd August 2008 to the children of the First Nations who were abused in the residential schools. It may appear to be just a formality in trying to console them for the punishment given for a crime that has not been committed but it is a very high concern, and it is a psychological and emotional relief for an unhealed old wound.

The sovereignty of Quebec is a thorn in the flesh that is hard but not impossible to remove. I am very glad that the morale of Quebec has been elevated by its recognition as a nation from the distinct society, on November 22nd, 2006 though the Bloc Quebecois is still complaining that it has not been blessed constitutionally. I am very worried about the unity of this nation because of the corruption and the less effective rule of Premier Jean Charest who was at one time the National Conservative leader and was brought into the role of the Liberal leader of Quebec in order to keep the nation strong and united from the growing forces of the Party Quebecois.

The great success in conducting the G8 Summit on 26-27 June 2010 in Huntsville and the G20 in Toronto pushed the best image of Canada forward in the global scene and boosted the Canadian economy and its strength. The great success of the Winter Olympics 2010 in Vancouver is very much comparable with the Summer Olympics in Montreal

The timely and effective humanitarian services for the victims of the earthquake in Haiti without attaching any strings was really cited as an example to other concerned developed nations. The spontaneous reaction of the Governor General by pouring out her hidden sentimentality by weeping and exposing it publicly can be interpreted in many ways. Her concern for the people of her home country was genuine. However one may ask if a similar disaster had occurred in another country would that have provoked the same reaction? Harper quietly and sharply handled the situation and did not make it an issue and when the time came, he appointed Mr. David Johnson the president of Waterloo University and a well read educator without any party bias.

Harper also kept the party interests aside when it came to national integrity and he would not bend down. I can cite a good example of this; when it was said that former Prime Minister Brian Mulroney was involved in inappropriate business dealings pertaining to the purchasing of air busses, Harper called for an independent enquiry and washed his hands of the matter even though he had consulted Mulroney on many occasions and made use of his wisdom and wonderful experience.

Harper has acknowledged that this nation has been built by immigrants and the doors for new immigrants have to be widely opened and encouraged. To make it more comfortable the right of landing fee was reduced from $ 975.00 to $ 490.00 and allowing internationally adopted children to be granted Canadian citizenship instantly rather than going through the hurdle of permanent residency. The new bill that has been in discussion recently is directed towards handling those who bypass the queue (human smuggling to be exact) but not the denial of entry of any refugees as a whole based on race or any other demarcations. The Canadian Charter of Rights also protects the cases of refugees who arrive in Canada illegally.

In closing I would quote what Harper said on 28th June 04 "until someone someday achieves a majority the fight is not won or lost" His dream will become reality in the next election by forming a majority government by whom, not by anybody other than Harper.

II. Conservative Government on Probation

The marriage of convenience between the opposition parties was broken even before the honeymoon started and the NDP and Bloc Québécois are now in tears. Do not worry babies. Mr. Jack Layton was having a sweet dream during the election campaign of occupying the seat of Prime Minster and replacing Mr. Harper. The election results woke him up with a start and the dream quickly disappeared. His second dream was to defeat the Harper government by any means and become a member of the cabinet in the expected coalition government. This dream has vanished and it is hoped that he will snap into reality and come down to earth. He should have learned that the current Liberal party is not headed by Mr. Paul Martin or Stephan Dion. This selfish and revengeful attitude was revealed well before the budget was presented to parliament. He said that he would certainly vote against the budget and defeat the Harper government. It appears that he does not care about the national interest and cares more about the party's interest at the expense of the country and the tax payers. How dare a long time city councilor and leader of a left wing political party backed by union workers in the middle of a global recession, switch over the government for the sole reason of getting rid of Mr. Harper's government and ignoring the consequences! Furthermore, it is surprising to me that without even having the slightest idea or clue about the contents of the budget firmly made the decision not to support it. This clearly shows that the true motive was something other than the best interests of the nation. At least he should have given some weight on the visit of Mr. Barrack Obama President of the United States; America being the biggest importer of our exports. What will the nature of his visit be? Will it be a formal visit and limited to having some superficial discussions with the Prime Minster and then return back to the States? Will they mainly discuss their interests in Afghanistan or just discuss climate change and global warming? Maybe they will discuss pressing Canadian issues, such as Canada's sovereignty in the north and The North American Free Trade Agreement and the relaxing of the restrictions on border crossings. Whatever the case may be, his visit at this time of change in politics and economic recession, is much more important for us than the United States.

The Bloc was not an inclusive partner of the coalition but a conditional supporter in planning to defeat the Harper government and I do not believe that their extension of support was based on the best interest of the nation. This party has a clear mandate of serving the best interests of Quebec and when it comes to priorities, Quebec sovereignty reigns supreme. If this is challenged by the Canadian national interest, certainly the line would be drawn on their side. Every voter knows that the sudden 'U' turn was made by these parties not on economic stimulation as they like to portray, but something related to the parties interests. I am sure in the long run Canadians will forgive but not forget the way these parties acted at this critical moment.

The Liberals did not care much about the coalition but recognized the current situation and acted wisely. They know very well that in the middle of a deep recession it is not easy to handle it with a party that has a brand new leader though he has extensive academic skills. They would not be able to handle this situation against an experienced and balanced leader and the failure of which would lead the party from bad to worse in the next election. They might have allowed the Harper government to sail on the rough part of the ocean and when the economy reached the recovery stage, push for an election by finding some excuse and paint the picture that if they had been in power they would have handled it wonderfully, there would have been no job losses and no deficit and they would try to gain more voters. Their calculation in reading the heart beat of the voters is wrong because voters know very well the capabilities of handling critical situations from having a minority government in the past. Voters also know that most of the election promises were fulfilled in a short period of time by the Conservative government.

The second reason is that whatever is said and done, they are to be aware that voters in the last election had given a clear mandate for Harper's party to govern, not permission for the opposition parties to form an alliance and a coalition government. If they try to defeat the government again, they will have to face very serious consequences in the next election whenever it is going to be held. The bottom line is not to antagonize the voters and in the last election, the Liberals performed very badly and the process of getting back their reputation is not that easy and every move has to be well planed and wisely calculated.

Mr. Ignatief has to do a lot of homework to clean up the mess and bring party members from internal camps to a unified front. That could be done starting at the party convention that is scheduled for early May of this year when he will be elected as the full fledged leader of the party. He would then be able to build a solid foundation to rebuild the party and repair the damage. But until then, it is better to cooperate with the government. Mr. Stephan Dion did not want to bring down the last government for many reasons; the main reason was that he wanted some time to rebuild his party and quite cleverly at the time of voting, abstained. This assured the survival of the Harper government and by doing that, the credit of those bills would not directly go to Harper's government.

Last, if not least the Liberals might have the national interest at heart in giving probation and support to the government and I do not think this was the only reason for supporting the budget. The conditional support to the budget by placing the government "on probation" is a very diplomatic and political move. As the Liberals are holding the remote control of this government in their hand, whenever they are not pleased with the move they presume that they will be able to gain the support of the rest of the opposition parties and bring down the government. They have taken it for granted that they have been given the mandate by the voters to be the boss of the government and give probation. At this junction, the rest of the opposition parties have no hope of forming a government by themselves in the near future. They should consider their agenda and act accordingly and not always be so adamant in bringing Harper's government down at any cost.

I believe that some of the Liberals have foreseen that for a stronger and better future of their party, it would be advisable to keep a distance from the NDP and Bloc Québécois. This will result in having more votes in the future so that Liberals will have a better chance in defeating the Conservatives. The left wing Liberal supporters at times cross over to the NDP and cast their votes and wise reverse and in the province of Quebec, the Liberals have been fighting against the Bloc in getting non hard line sovereignty votes. If it is a favorable time for the Liberals they would not mind collaborating with the rest of the opposition to defeat this government. Bringing down Harper's government should not be a hindrance in building up the Liberals in the future. Voters have not forgotten the election promise of not having a coalition government with the NDP by the Liberals.

The Finance Minister has put great effort and consideration and might have accommodated the suggestions given by various government organs, business leaders and others before formulating this budget. It is a budget that has the voice of the people from coast to coast from workers to entrepreneurs, and it is a budget of the people for the people and anyone who opposes this budget is insulting the intelligence of the masses. The direction and true core of the budget leans towards economic stimulation and this has garnered much support from the lower and middle class income earners. The NDP would have supported it if they considered their fundamental goals as more important than political interest. The opposition parties mainly complain whenever a budget of the Conservatives is proposed. They believe that a Conservative budget encourages the entrepreneurs and favors them rather than the common man. But in this budget, this sentiment is far from the truth.

Having a deficit budget right now is inevitable, the global recession has forced almost all industrialized countries to have deficits. There is no magic formula that can keep us away from this and it may have to continue into next year and the following year. How quickly we overcome the recession and reach the recovery stage depends on the consumers, producers, and the global economic situation and government policies. The Finance Minister mentioned that the current situation is somewhat unpredictable and we have to act accordingly. Although interest was reduced to a very low rate the investors and people have to come out and borrow more money; but a good number of them do not have the confidence and are not prepared to face the risk. The common man is very worried about the stability and security of his job and hesitates to spend more money. Unless people spend money and purchase goods and services from service providers, the production will decrease and then the layoffs of workers will continue. It is a chain reaction and a full stop has to be made and it would be better at the consumers end. The stimulation package is not only aimed at the production side but to the consumers as well. The producers and the consumers are both sides of the same coin. Consumer confidence is the backbone of any economy and it cannot be underestimated and after all the main objective of any production is to reach the consumer. Therefore, economic recovery is partially in the hands of every one of us.

The former Conservative government made a very remarkable contribution in paying back the debt of over thirty billion in under three years and today's global economic situation forced them to borrow money. I am very confident that when the economy gets back into shape they will repay the loan and leave the future generations free to a certain extent, from paying back our loans

According to the chief officer of the Central Bank, the nature of this recession is different from the ones that we experienced in the1980's and 1990's. The interest rates of today are low compared to those previous recessions and it will stimulate the home buyers and the investors to borrow more money. Our economy is much stronger than it was when we had the other recessions. In the last two recessions most of the Canadian provinces were very badly affected, but currently oil rich Alberta and some of the other provinces have not felt the gravity of the recession as of yet. The provinces of Ontario and Quebec that depend on a sizeable income from certain manufacturing industries are experiencing a greater adverse effect of the recession.

When the economy is in recession, naturally the amount of revenue for the government will be low and social expenses such employment insurance and social assistance will raise. I have been in one of the Toronto Social Services offices very recently with someone and I could see many recently unemployed people who were there to apply for social assistance after exhausting their employment insurance benefits.

Some are bit panicky about the current recession and they predict that it may go into a deeper state and reach a stage of depression like in 1929-1934. They say that this recession is more severe than the pre—depression of the 1930's. This is a pessimistic approach and I do not think that we are in that kind of situation. We must have the confidence that among the G8 nations, the Canadian economy is stronger and the effect of the cyclone will not produce such a disaster.

The Right Honorable Prime Minister had foreseen the difficulties in implementing the policies of the government effectively and efficiently without having a majority government and this was the main reason for calling the last election. But somehow the decision of the voters allowed for another minority government and we all respect the verdict of the voters. A recent poll indicates that 51% of Canadians did not want the budget to be defeated and thus bring down the government and this is the view of the majority of Canadians.

This budget is only one item that we are looking at and in the future the government should not act in terms of implementing election promises that voters have been expecting and strive to resolve the new problems that may occur in these hard times. We have to have an alternative plan if Mr. Obama dismantles or does not respect and implement the policies of the North American Free Trade Agreement. Concerns over the aging baby boomers, implementation of immigration policies, improving the relationship between the federal government and the provinces and elimination of unemployment need to be discussed and resolved if the nation is to have any peace of mind at all.

The main thing that the opposition parties have to do right now is to put their own differences and agendas aside and put Canada first.

They must work as a team and portray Canada as a role model not only to future politicians, but to the rest of the world.

III. Victory with Vision but the Battle is Not Over

"This is the time for us all to put aside political differences and partisan considerations and to work cooperatively for the benefit of Canada" Stephen Harper said on the evening of, 14th October 2008 at the victory celebration in Calgary. Mr. Stephen Harper is a rare political leader who is down to the earth in both his political views and actions, for example, from the very beginning of the campaign, he predicted that next government would also be a minority government. At the peak of the campaign, on the last weekend, he expressed the belief that the next government would be a minority government formed by either by the Liberals or Conservatives. Whereas the leader of another party was very ambitious, unrealistic, and frequently proclaimed that Harper would make his exit from the prime minister's chair and he would occupy the seat. As usual, his party was pushed into fourth place in the election results though his party did gain more votes in some unexpected places. Harper's prediction has come true, that we would elect another minority government with some unexpected gains.

Harper is a man of vision for Canada and is able to tackle the many multidimensional aspects of our country. As I mentioned in a previous article, Harper was concerned about Arctic sovereignty, the rest of the political leaders did not have the depth of knowledge and focus on this issue. The National Anthem has been sung millions of times, but Harper has given true meaning to the phrase "True North strong and free". Likewise, when all of the other parties were engaged in the beginning of the campaign in various other issues, Harper had foreseen worldwide economic instability and slow down even before the collapse of some American financial institutions. In the middle of the campaign, the other parties were able to realize that what Harper was saying was true and adjusted their campaign messages accordingly.

This minority government is quite different from the other 12 minority governments that we have had in the past. Though this is the second consecutive minority government since Lester B. Pearson, there are some crucial differences. This minority government actually has a mandate which is what Mr. Harper wanted to achieve. For those of us who ask why an election was called, it was clear to Mr. Harper that the previous minority government could not function as freely as what it would have liked. In addition, Mr. Harper wanted to have a clear mandate which would allow the government to do its job more effectively.

It was disappointing to see such a low voter turnout, both in the advance polls and on Election Day. Generally speaking, the voter turnout in Canada has never been less than 60%. In this election, the percentage of eligible voters who cast a ballot fell well below this number. There are many possible reasons for this happening and I could discuss this issue for hours on end. If the turnout had been better, the Conservatives might have won a majority in terms of the voting patterns.

This minority government is facing the major issue of keeping the Canadian economy strong and stable. This is a national issue, and therefore all of the political parties must come out in full force to tackle this challenge head on regardless of their partisan views. Since the international economy is weak, this will not be an easy task; therefore the Opposition should not play politics and focus on the task at hand. It is the moral obligation of every patriotic Canadian particularly those who are elected to public office, to put the country's interest first at this critical time. If so, the government can carry out its plans smoothly without any fear of revolt. I am certain that this is what Canadians want. It is interesting to note that the previous Harper minority government has ruled longer than any other minority government. I am convinced that Mr. Harper with his experience will be in power longer.

Whether we like it or not, the economic cyclone continues to hit hard in many parts of the world. This is not the case in Canada, but we would be fooling ourselves to think that what is happening globally does not affect us here. We understand that our banking system is one of the best in the world and we do not have to panic. Our 1.5 trillion dollars in the economy is safe and sound. And thanks to the previous minority government, our national debt was reduced by almost 40 billion dollars. The interest that has been paid can be used for other purposes such as social amenities. This does not guarantee that the effects of the economic slowdown will not be felt but we have to be prepared.

The Provincial governments have to play their role in improving the economy. This involves motivating investors particularly in the manufacturing sector which has taken a big hit especially in Ontario and Quebec. The Provincial governments must also try to balance their budgets without increasing taxes and not reducing their services.

In this election, the topic of immigration was not emphasized. I found this very surprising. During several media interviews and appearances only one person asked me about this issue. Other than the Conservative Party, other parties did not give prominence to this issue. Immigrants form a very large part of our country and contribute vast amounts of dollars to our economy—why was this not given much air time?

The Election results in Quebec were very interesting. The results show that the people of Quebec place a strong emphasis on their cultural identity and this was reflected in the victory speech of Gilles Duceppe. This shift in votes does not reflect any animosity towards the previous government in fact Harper has done a great job in building a strong relationship with Quebec.

The main opposition party, the Liberals are certainly going to have a leadership review performed at some point in time. There are 2 issues at stake, the first being that having a leadership review will dominate their platform and there will be less focus on parliamentary matters. The second issue is that there might be a complete change in the leadership of the party. The new leader might be more concerned about national issues or more interested in bringing down the minority government and call for an election assuming that he could be the next Prime Minister. This is something that we need to pay close attention to.

Sometimes we need a strong policy; sometimes we need a strong leader. This is the time for a strong leader. There is no doubt that Harper is a strong leader,. He has proven this many times. What Harper has done in less than 3 years in a minority government would not have been accomplished by any other leader in a majority government. His determination, skills, and experience coupled with his vision for a better Canada will certainly make a very positive change and place Canada on the top of the world map.

In conclusion, bad times are ahead but the strong leader is here to transform it for the better.

IV From the World to Toronto and Back Again with a Flourish

"I have never been at a summit where leaders seemed to more deeply feel the necessity of common action and common purpose" said the Right Honorable Prime Minister Stephen Harper, at the end of the G8 summit and it remained with the same spirit at the end of the G20 as well. The entire world was focused, particularly the rest of the world's leaders, finance ministers', investors, terrorist leaders, and the leaders of the leaders. The attention of the intellectual crowd was definitely focused on the summits and this crowd was large in number compared to the crowd of the common men who seemed to focus more on the world cup soccer match and other music and sporting events that add flavor to the warm summer soup. There were some business men in the core of the down town Toronto who were least bothered by the summit and were more concerned about their daily business activities being adversely affected by the pouring rain, coupled with the presence of the police officers on every single meter of the sidewalk and restricted transportation routes. One businesswoman told me that she only read about the recent earthquake in Toronto in the newspapers and it did not change any of her routine business activities. In contrast to her, many others around the world were constantly watching the G8-G20 summits keenly and to them this was a major news event, like the main course of a fancy dinner as opposed to a beer and potato chips.

The media coverage at the initial stage was tuned around Queen's Park, the designated area for the demonstrators to exercise their right to express their support and dissatisfaction on whatever issues that they had. There was much concern by them over the fact this summit spent almost a billion dollars for the security, when to these activists nearly a billion dollars was needed to address human rights violations, maternal issues, exploitation of workers by the capitalist system of economics, native rights, anti-terrorism in many forms, and so on. In fact, Canada being successfully ruled by the democratic system of government has always granted permission and has provided adequate facilities for protestors at the expense of the tax payers. Canada is not a country ruled by the dictates of the government to impose its views; no does the government suppress the freedom of expressing the dissatisfaction and grievances felt by the masses towards the government. But this right, guaranteed by our Constitution should not be turned into paving a way for vandalism and damage to public property such as the burning of police cars, breaking of shop windows, and disruption of the comforts of the general public. The arrest of 602 people in the eyes of Torontonians, certainly looked high, but in light of the gravity of the security concerned it is not really an unusual number. Compared with what has been going on in Paris protesting the rise in the age limit to receive pensions for seniors to 62 from 60. Compared with other summit in other countries, the numbers are really not a concern. At this point many of those who have criticized the allocation of almost one billion dollars for security have to realize that there were very valid reasons for this and they should not be overlooked. To those critics I humbly ask—how much is a human life worth—can we really pay too much for safety?

My thanks go to the Chief of Police, Mr. Bill Blair, for his tireless work and the Mayor of Toronto David Miller for fully backing the organizing committee, although he was not happy that he was not adequately included in the planning. I also thank the Premier of Ontario for all of his help, especially in passing a regulation in granting more powers to the police such as the ability to interrogate individuals, search without warrant, and the ability to deny entry to those deemed to be suspicious who came within 5 meters of the security fence. The powers given to the enforcing officers during the G20 summit in Toronto were only temporary given the nature of the Summit. With all of the support and cooperation the G20 has ended with flying colors and earned a name is history for Canada. Of course the right honorable Prime Minister deserves many thanks as well.

Let me come back to the remarks about the summit made by the right honorable Prime Minster. The mood of the summit appeared to be without any tension; even if the Prime Minister might have had several unanswered questions about security, he might have buried them deep into his heart and thus hosted this meeting cheerfully.

Most of the heads of state appeared to be younger than those who participated in the G20 in 2006. But their faces showed they had become quite stressed out in sailing their economic ships in the troublesome ocean and they still continued to sail into the troubled economic waters and were unable to provide for the demands of the passengers. These factors, combined with the tsunami high debts, sailed these ships dramatically off course. The lifeline for these countries would be to follow Canada's example.

The nature, objectives, priorities and agendas of the G8 and G20 were different. The G8 had its own particular concern around the overall economy worldwide. The G20 had financial stability as the core of its programs and addressed issues of the developed and developing countries. It also focused on constructing and maintaining a bridge between the two in this summit. Both have turned their attention to recovering from the recession quickly and strongly through international cooperation, rather than protecting the individual economies of each nation, as Obama's protectionist policy in the United States.

In this journey, the Canadian ship though not the biggest and heaviest, still in the current weather conditions, is moving steadily and faster from the troubled waters and Canada has been accepted and recognized as a role model of the worlds developed nations. Mr. Harper articulated and insisted to the world's nations to reduce the budget deficits and reduce the debts of member nations within a short period of time without prolonging the recession. It has been well appreciated and accepted with overwhelming support. I am sure some of the leaders would have been envious of Canada in this respect. They have been watching the Minister of Finance and have seen that the financial institutions of Canada have been in smooth operation even at the peak of the recession without leaning for support from the government and none of the financial institution was in the verge of collapsing.

The idea of levying taxes to the banks and maintaining a security reserve fund for keeping away from future financial crises was an important lesson learned by the developed nations including America because of the ongoing recession. But such a need has never arisen and the policy of levying a tax left all member nations to act independently and Canada expressed its plan to get an exemption from it and this has singled out Canada and earned a good name for us and has also won the confidence from the investors and Canada will harvest a hearty yield in the future. The short team pain in tightening the belt will bring long term gain.

I have my own doubts about how the concerned nations could implement and use the allocated funds properly. Our good neighbor in the south is taking economic measures to protect its interests and is partially ignoring the value of sharing their economic interest with its good old friend in the north and how could we expect the rest of the world to commit to this.

I am very pleased to witness that many of them have agreed to allocate funds for the maternally troubled women around the world, particularly in the continent of Africa and South America and a portion of Asia. It is upsetting to hear that every day over one thousand mothers were dying on or pre or post natal time. It goes beyond the issue of money. The education levels of women have to be uplifted. We cannot support the customs and traditions and the norms of ethnic groups in those affected countries that allow for male domination and the deprival of the fundamental rights of women. Abortion is a difficult and contentious issue and it is an issue that the individual countries have to take into consideration by themselves not by others. Mr. Harper made a compromise on this issue with the opposition party members in Parliament and some accommodations were made.

The global terrorists who are threatening the entire world, irrespective of where each nation stands and those who are not prepared to dance according the piper of those organizations are also targeted. Forget about who is a terrorist and the definition of terrorism. As long as it affects the fundamental rights of others and the right to live in peace, we must use all available resources and take precautionary measures against it. Everyone has the right to fight against oppressors but not at the expense of others. In the G20 for example there was much concern and focus given to the issue of nuclear development in Iran and North Korea.

The coolest discussion was on the issue global warming. I think that probably they did not want to add more heat to it by having a serious discussion on it and there was no need to spend more time because of it was thoroughly discussed at the UN meeting in Denmark, not long ago. The second reason was that the decisions' that were made in the summit were not yet implemented as had been expected and there is no point in having another elaborate discussion.

Helping the developing nations is another issue that has been taken into consideration. Many of the smaller nations could not balance their budgets and already their government debts have gone beyond their repaying capacity and their needs have become high and the slow rate of economic growth, corruption in the public sectors, sky rocketing unemployment, fast growing population increase and unstable governments and their poverty have made it hard for those nations to overcome from these difficult situations. In spite of all those needs they have been traditionally dependant on the developed nations. Their problems have been addressed well and the voice of the African Union has not been heard loudly in the developed world.

It has been a great success for Canada in hosting both the summits respectively in Huntsville and Toronto and most of the heads of states were very pleased with the arrangements and warm reception. They have enjoyed it. What is next? The drama is over but we do have a lot of homework to do in terms of capitalizing on the positive image that has been painted on the global mural. I am very certain that the steady progress of the overall economy along with the political maturity of Canadians and the abundant blessings of rich minerals and strong Canadian currency will pave a way in making our economy stronger and steady.

Let me conclude by quoting from US President Obama, "The Success of these summits, the G8 in Muskoka and the G20 here in Toronto—is a tribute to Canadian leadership"

V. Defeat at the Security Council Election, a Blessing in Disguise for Canada.

The rising sun of Canada has been covered by the negativity of the voting results of the non permanent members of the Security Council of the United Nations Organization on 12th October 2010. Though Canada lost in the second round of the vote these are only passing clouds on Canada's raising sun. These clouds will not remain for long and we do not have to do much soul searching; rather we need to bear this in mind, the nations that wanted to vote for any nation that opposed Canada amounted to only a handful. We therefore must take a look at the global perspective surrounding this turn of events.

First of all, the recent journey of Canadian foreign policy has not radically shifted to a new direction from its traditional path. Canada has continued to keep itself from being within the orbit of the American super power, though this was complained about by the opposition parties at the beginning of the first term of the right Honorable Stephen Harper. Mr. Harper has taken a very independent and unbiased stand in maintaining the neutrality of Canada in its foreign policy. But we also should not forget that Canada has long established economic, cultural, industrial, and technological ties that have never before existed except with France and Britain in the early period of Canadian history. It is unavoidable that we must have some sort of inclination towards the United States of America.

The Harper government extended an apology for the head tax that was levied on the Chinese who arrived in Canada as labourers in the late part of the 19th and early 20th centuries. But as a matter of principle, Mr. Harper decided not to visit China to attend the Olympics in Beijing. I believe some might think that it would have been better to compromise the principle with the intention of preserving economic interests, but Mr. Harper decided that it was better to abide by one's principles. Another example is that Mr. Harper decided to call back the Canadian soldiers after he made a state visit to the USA and met with President Obama. There is the possibly that he might have thought that Obama was exclusively concerned with implementing the economic protectionism policy that did not give any consideration for their long time partner and good neighbor in the north. Alongside that concern, Canada did not allow the United States to use our air space for anti missile purposes. Maintaining an arm's length distance from the USA is not a new philosophy for Canada. Mr. Jean Chretien once said about the relationship between Canada and the United States in this way "Canada is your best friend, largest trading partner, and closest ally, but we are also an independent nation. Keeping some distance will be good for us . . . ." This is what the current government is doing but in its own unique way.

Canadian foreign policy with Israel, Arab and other Islamic nations are cordial, even though the reading from the political barometer might be giving off some variations. That being said Canada is not interested in surrendering to one side while totally ignoring the other. For example, when the Palestinians were attacked by the Israelis, the refugees of Palestine were welcomed with as much care as any other refugees. Canada has numerous refugees, skilled workers and their families from many of these countries and the government is very vigilant in terms of protecting their rights. Of course, the public reactions at the time might have deviated from the policy of the government.

When it comes to national security and protection Canada has to take appropriate measures and this is unavoidable. It has been said that once Osama bin Laden mentioned that Canada has been the largest supplier of oil sand to the USA and therefore Canada is in a way allied with it. But we understand that this is business and furthermore, Canada has had some disputes with the USA over the Canadian waters in the north. Mr. Harper is firm in protecting Canada from Russia, the USA and other nations who have disputes with Canada. In spite of the Canadian position in the Middle East crisis and the wars in Iraq and Afghanistan Canada has never participated or formed an alliance with the offensive forces. But just a few days before the election, the endorsement of Israel might have painted the picture with different colors. Out of 192 member nations in the United Nations, 57 of them are Arab and predominantly Islamic nations and they form quite a powerful block. The speculation of some might be that these nations wanted to "punish" Canada for its stance on the attack on the Turkish ship off the coast of Israel by the army; however this is not something that can be easily proved.

Let us move on to Africa where 51 votes were cast and let us read their heart beat. The Canadian government was not very much in favor of funding or donating money for the purpose of providing abortion services to victims of rape and sexual assault and it has been said that those victims number in the millions and their issues have to be addressed immediately rather than though religious edicts. Some of the richer nations including China have been shedding crocodile tears about the progress of African nations, but they do have a hidden agenda in exploiting valuable mineral resources, making investments with a high level of profit, and having potential markets established.

There has been a wrong notion about the Canadian stand on donations, aid, grants and loans to Africa by the members of the G20 nations. When the discussions on the aid for poor nations, particularly to Africa had taken place at the G20 summit, Canada was very sympathetic and generous in encouraging other rich nations to contribute more to those countries. But Canada was particular in saying that those assets should be beneficial to those people in the long run, not for the short term at the expense of the long term. So far this has been supported by the local opposition parties and a couple of the international countries. Quite a good number of leaders might have got the impression that Canada was somehow blocking certain loans and grants that would have been channeled by the rich nations and turned around to vote against Canada's position on the U.N Security Council.

But Canadians also have to consider the Somali Canadian's under aged children who were brain washed or taught and recruited for the purpose of the civil war even without the knowledge of their parents. Most of the parents of these children came and claimed refugee status and chose this country as their new home. They have been treated like any other Canadians and the government is protecting them in accordance with the Canadian charter of rights and freedoms. Whether they like it or not it is the obligation of the government. I strongly feel that there is a miscommunication, a misunderstanding or lack of communication in this regard. Whatever has been said and done Africans should go back and look into the genuine contributions that have been made to them by various countries in the world and then they will be able to gauge the position of Canada in the future.

The decision to withdraw of our soldiers from Afghanistan unilaterally did not please the United States, Afghanistan and the NATO nations. I strongly believe that Canada has realized and carefully reviewed the situation of the war in Afghanistan and the commitments made by both NATO and the USA and decided to the time period for the withdrawal of its soldiers. President Obama himself planned to withdraw the men in uniform from Iraq and Afghanistan without considering the long term benefits and security of his nation and the sacrifices that were made by the soldiers from NATO, the USA and other nations. He should have realized that by unilaterally withdrawing from the war, this would certainly give additional strength and a morale boost and that would have a very positive impact to Al Qaida. In such a situation Canada has no other alternative other than to safe guard its own interests. This decision might have turned some of the nations to vote against Canada.

Some may say that Canada has failed to act seriously on the issues of global warming and climate change. What happened at the UN summit in Copenhagen? Most of the world's nations spoke about plans and remedies loudly enough to reach the ozone layer. What happened later on? In terms of action, nothing was taken seriously; even the USA did not play a serious role in the summit. Rather it was said that the major contribution to climate change was mostly due to nature and that it had been going on for millions of years. The contribution by human beings, they stated, was limited. In my humble opinion, this was a polite way of saying that we do have other urgent and important issues to deal with and that global warming and climate change should not take up the entire agenda.

The European Union has grown multi dimensionally and has expanded its activities from economic cooperation to having common markets to common currency and has now entered into having a common immigration policy. Now it has come to play their cards with the understanding and support of their members without looking and comparing themselves with other competing nations. I should not over emphasis the current weaker economic conditions of Portugal with Canada, the role model economy among the rich nations however it is something to bear in mind in the context of the Security Council vote.

Canada mostly avoids getting involved in any kind of controversial global issues and extends its help without having any strings attached. Canada also has no ulterior motives unlike its former colonial rulers with their former colonies in their umbrella organizations. Canada has no intention of maneuvering or manipulating international issues for its own benefit. Canadian foreign policy from the beginning headed by Sir John A MacDonald to Mr. Harper, regardless, of the policies of the ruling parties is well balanced and has a wider and broader outlook

Let us now compare the capability and the strength of these three nations and objectively arrive at a good conclusion. During the pre industrial era, Spain and Portugal were in a weak economic position. Agriculture provided the main source of income and explorers financed by the ruling elites went around the world to explore new venues in order to expand business and ended up colonizing various countries almost five centuries ago and flourished as a result. The current economic situations of those nations along with Greece are struggling to maintain their economies and were recently on the verge of collapsing. The European Union and some other nations had given their hands and lifted them from the ditch. Furthermore Portugal is not a member of the G8 or G2O, two of the most powerful organizations. With due respect, it would be much better if they were to put their resources including their time into bringing back the local economy rather than deviating into international affairs.

With the recent accomplishment of successfully hosting the International Winter Olympics 2010 in Vancouver, the G8 in Huntsville and the G20 in Toronto, the strength of this country has expanded. The caliber of operating these international events should have given Canada a rightful place at the Security Council. Canada's not being elected to the security council is not a great loss for Canada per se, rather the rest of the world is losing a valuable contribution from a dynamic nation.

Internally, the opposition parties should have forgotten their internal differences and rivalries and joined hands with the government to advocate and support Canada in a potential victory in this election. Let's be united and portray the Canadian image around the globe, rather than considering the affairs that are exclusively the responsibly of the ruling party. If they would have played their role adequately enough, at least our image would have been more impressive. In closing, this defeat at the Security Council shall pass, but the effects of leaving Canada out will be felt, not just by the international community but within Canada as well. That being said, this is Canada, we will survive!

V. Go and Win Canada

It was a very lovely and pleasant evening at the Valentine's Day dinner party. It was organized by my friends in honor of my media services and held at a beautiful restaurant called Chucky Tomatoes around the corner of Woodbine and Steeles Avenue just north of the city of Toronto. Around twenty of us were in one of the party rooms that was located beside the colorfully displayed variety of foods, the sight of which would not allow you to stop the flowing of saliva from your mouth and your eyes from growing larger from the spectacle. We were inside the waiting area for a while until at least half of our guests arrived so we could be seated at our reserved area. I noticed that the restaurant was fully packed with not only youngsters, but guests from all ages and social backgrounds filled all the available seats. While waiting, most of the guests were keenly watching the Winter Olympic Games on a 42 inch wide television. I noticed that there was a remark passed by a gentleman about the negative comments made by some of the British and American media on the winter Olympics 2010 held on our soil. In fact, I had already condemned the negative attitudes held by the foreign media on my television show and in news commentaries on Tamil One Television. I could not contain myself and joined these gentlemen with whom I never had any contact before in their happiness and our patriotic feelings of Canada brought us together as though we were members of the same family. We shared our opinions very objectively. A few days later on the 18th February 2010, I had gone through an article entitled "Shut Up and Enjoy the Games" along with the accompanying editorial in the Toronto Star. I was very pleased and happy about it. It is our moral obligation at a time when the unique country and legacy that our forefathers left behind for us to be patriotic and supportive even when the emphasis in the international media stage is negative. We should not allow foreign media to spoil this beautiful country with their words.

However, I do not disagree with some of the comments. Indeed there are areas where we could have done a little better than what it was. But due to the circumstances we were in, the nature of the winter Olympics and some other factors might have contributed to the arrangements. Some of the comments made by the foreign media were that Canada could have done much better in terms of organization compared to the previous 2 Olympic Games in Montreal in 1986 and Calgary in 1988. But I do not see any justifiable reason to compare apart from expressing personal opinions.

Let us take a closer look at some of the opinions presented by those media outlets:

1. The Games were not well organized and the opening ceremony was not done very well.
2. The accidental death of the Luger from Georgia could have been avoided and that wrong steps were taken in the aftermath.
3. The inadequate arrangements made for training the foreign athletes

4. Our home work was not done on the publicity front, and as a result we had only a few thousand instead of one hundred thousand views.

5. Overall, it was the worst Olympics that we have ever had.

6. The complaint was made by some Quebecers that the French language was not given due place in the opening ceremony.

7. Some First Nations leaders took this as another opportunity to express their long standing grievances by saying that the Winter Olympics was going to take place on stolen land.

I do not want to go into each and every complaint, but I wish to call your attention to what the International Olympic Committee who is in charge of the planning, operating and overseeing the entire program said about the Games. In their humble opinion, the 2010 Olympics were well organized and that there was nothing much to worry about. However, we must all take into consideration that the cooperation we got from nature was not very helpful and we expected more snow, not rain. That being said, however, the weather is still one thing that is beyond our control.

I would like to go behind the presentation of these comments and flesh out some of the hidden motives behind them. The Canadian security and border officials denied entry visas for two critical reporters from United States of America. These incidents might have contributed to the negative comments as well as promoting the idea that criticizing the Games was not allowed. This idea is false because in some Canadian newspapers, there were many pieces critical of the games that were published.

As far as the Canadian public is concerned, the winter Olympic games are primarily a sporting event, not an event that has a hidden agenda in terms of exploiting a given issue.

Let us now examine the other factors that may have prompted some of the world's critics to arrive at such unattractive comments about Canada. The recent report that the image of Canada in the international world scene has diminished compared to the past. The primary reason given is that Canada has not committed sufficient resources for protective measures pertaining to global warming and the human right violations by the Afghanistan government to the detainees who were handed over to them by the Canadian Armed Forces, and the recent independent moves on international issues where the USA has played a vital role is not very pleasing to other western nations, particularly the United States. For example, the Canadian Prime minister announced the decision unilaterally on the withdrawal of the Canadian Forces in Afghanistan in mid 2011. This decision would not have pleased some on the world stage and in some cases it would have antagonized them.

The victories of the Olympics for Canada are many; the first of which I point out is that Canada won more gold medals (8 to be exact) than any other host country in the history of the winter Olympic games. Also, whenever there were some negative and inappropriate criticisms in some of the international media, strong patriotic feelings and sentiments aroused many Canadians and this is another victory for us. On the international level, the image of Canada has been well represented and painted with the right colors and Canada has been placed as a role model to most of the developed and potentially developing nations. Though it has not been part of the games, efforts that have been achieved by government and the strength of the Canadian economy have paved the way for a respectful and heavy presence in the upcoming G20 and G8 summit in Ontario Canada scheduled to take place in the summer. The security and other preparations have been going very well. This is a very beautiful time for Canada because the two summits will be hosted within the same year, so this is our time to shine.

Canada has been in a recession but is now showing early signs of recovery. Our financial policies, the guidance of the government, the Bank of Canada and its institutions are and were in a very sound position, even at the initial stage of the recession when almost all of the developed nations were in a very shaky position, including our neighbor in the south. Compared to Europe and the United States, we have fared well.

The test of security passed with fine marks and could have achieved excellence, if not for some remote incidents that occurred during the Olympics in Vancouver. Though there are no guarantees at any Olympic Games that terrorists might not try to cause problems, still the efforts made are remarkable. In this case the Olympic organizers spent almost a billion dollars. Maybe such a huge amount of money is not required come this summer. Venue wise Toronto is more convenient but security wise it is more complex, due to the reason that it is populated with new immigrants who have migrated from over 170 nations, around the world. The penetration of negative forces in Canada has been watched and monitored by the mighty nations of the globe even before the terrorist attacks on September 11, 2001 in the United States of America. It is not only a question of immigration and security of the lives of local Canadians; rather it is a global concern.

Canadian foreign policy is liberal and impartial, not 90 degrees inclined towards any super power. Even today we have not earned the enmity from any nation, race, religious group or ethnicity. However it is unavoidable to be allied with other nations and that may cause some discomfort and challenges for national security. For example, there was a time when supplying crude oil sand to the States made us a potential terrorist target.

At this critical time, other than a political party that has been backed by trade unions, the political forces in this country is more or less inclined in one direction. I do appreciate the politicians who, despite their differences in many local policies and their bitter fights in parliament and outside, give top most priority to national security and back up necessary actions to prevent any negativity that can arise. There is some criticism on the handing over of the detainees by the Canadian forces to the Afghanistan government that tortured them unduly and inhumanly and Canada should have conducted operations in a different manner. We should also acknowledge that Canada had not joined as a member nation in the American joint force in the war against terrorism in Iraq and Afghanistan from the beginning of Mr. Chretien's, Mr. Paul Martin's or Mr. Harper's leadership. As a nation, we have always acted out of our accord. Canada has always condemned human rights violations in any part of the world, even at the cost of creating a situation where it may earn us some economic losses.

There are some global issues that may crop up at this time in the form of demonstrations or media coverage. Take for example global warming. At the Copenhagen summit all these nations proclaimed their commitments very seriously but in terms of actions they have done nothing tangible. Another issue is human rights. Many aspects regarding human rights violations such as our participation or not are bound to come up. Our support of poor developing countries, the side effects of the war in Afghanistan, these are bound to come up as well. There might also be some local issues mentioned but nothing serious that can be expected.

It is a golden opportunity for Canada to capitalize on these summits in multi dimensional ways. Canada has earned a very high reputation over the years of many sacrifices and its unique qualities and we have not over reacted or have been partially inclined with certain international states. This needs to be made clear to the current leaders around the world and we will reinforce their political and economic plans due to our solid reputation.

Canada has abundance in valuable minerals including the second largest crude oil deposit, uranium, gold, and diamonds and so on. It is the best time to engage in marketing. The Canadian government is also making some smart moves in investing with countries such as India, China, the potential world powers in the east and South American countries. But to some extent, the changes are somewhat limited in Europe due to the 27 member European Union which is a superb economic grouping with investments and trade to non member states.

Canada in terms of immigration is quite literally the world in one country. The Canadian natural increase in population is declining and the rate of increase in seniors has gone up pretty high and the gap between the two has to be bridged by the immigrants. It appears that Canada is very much interested in hiring more skilled workers, so that they can easily fill up the vacancies, if not instantly, in the near future.

We can make use of this opportunity even though it may not be a part of the agenda but this point can be made in many other ways. In this matter, Toronto is the most appropriate venue than any other part of the country.

However the cooperation from the opposition parties is highly required at this junction. The Liberal party leader recently indicated very clearly that he would not vote against the budget, because he is not interested in bringing down the Harper government and because Canadians are not favor of an election. He had learned a bitter lesson when he brought in the no confidence motion last year and after the defeat, the reaction from Canadians. I would prefer even if the time were ripe for an election that in the best interest of the nation let them help this government continue for a while and earn some goodies for Canada where they are the active partners.

I would not want to over emphasis these summits and other international conferences that are going to be held in Canada, like some other developing nations who take such opportunities as a wonderful time to paint a colorful picture of their nation to world leaders. But Canada needs better and stronger foreign markets for exports and investment venues. Although America is a strong trade partner, after I predicted even before the U.S Presidential election, that Obama's economic protectionist policy is harmful to us. It has been exhibited by the recent moves that Obama's administration and he himself has taken on global and Canadian trade matters. The recent moves coupled with George W. Bush on their interest in the economy, global politics and the way they reacted certainly alarmed Canada that they acted in a way that comforts them. Why we should rethink our relationship with them and act accordingly does not mean that we are taking a different road completely, but we are slightly deviated from the traditional path in accordance with the current global changes and the best interests of our nation.

In conclusion, we have gained a smart and unique status around globe. Let's keep it up and work not only hard but wisely so that we can still maintain it and climb up to the top. Oh Canada, win Canada!

VI. Canada—Champion of the World

Recently, Canada is looked upon as a superstar. It is the nation that is the most preferred to migrate to compared to other developed countries. Although many factors contribute to this, the way in which Canada overwhelmingly accepts new immigrants while other receiving countries only tolerate them prompted me to write this article.

It makes us feel proud of who we are in the sense of identity and occasionally when we visit other countries around the world that the reflection of Canadian values wake us up and stirs in us a feeling of pride in our beloved nation of Canada and this has happened to me personally on a few occasions and I have heard similar anecdotes from my friends which had subsequently been buried in their subconscious mind through layers of memories. We who know not and are aware that we know not, will certainly open our eyes and minds to understand and merge with the growing global position of Canada on the international stage.

I appreciate the forefathers of this nation, the builders who made a tremendous sacrifice in constructing the castle of the nation with Canadian values as the bricks and a foundation so solid that even an earthquake would not be able to shake it. I would like to illustrate my point with this example. When some of the disappointed, dissatisfied British alongside the more adventurous and with the French descendants migrated and made their settlements in the northern part of the new world, at that time the Americans were involved in an aggressive and demanding revolution against the British Empire. The American Revolution was between the colonial rulers and the colonized inhabitants and the aim was to sever the connection to the Empire right down to the roots. But the Canadians, the British Loyalists took a different route and won their freedom while maintaining its cordial relationship with the Crown and to this day, we still have the British monarchy as the head of state in Canada, though it is only a symbolic position. Today, particularly since the beginning of the war against terrorism in Iraq and Afghanistan by the United States of America, the U.S and Britain have renewed their relationship, though not in the same vein as the colonial past. Although Canada made a shift in having a close and effective economic relationship with Britain and later on shifting to the States a few decades ago, former Prime Minister Jean Chretien did not want Canada to join the American coalition forces in those wars, without the blessing of the United Nations. There were many occasions in which Canada did not dance to the piper of Great Britain and another example of this was the war in the Suez Canal against Egypt in 1957, Canada did not accept the request to join the British forces and kept itself away. Although Canada has very close ties with America from the cultural industry to our economic relationship, Canada maintains its distance and continues to do so.

Politicians of Canada comparatively have a high level of maturity in exercising their power. Of course, they have their concerns over personality, promotion, party biases and actions but there are times when national interest and challenges overtake the party, regional and other interests and they extend a hand in cooperation and work together. I can cite many occasions where they have exhibited their concerns on the best interests of the nation. When the power of the Quebec nationalists was getting stronger and was on the verge of separating from Canada, the Progressive Conservative Party and the Liberals worked hand in hand and Jean Charest, the national leader of the Conservative Party was viewed as a capable leader who could stand against the Party Quebecois and keep Canada intact. The Conservatives had foregone their party interests and volunteered to lend him to the provincial party leader of the Liberals in Quebec and he is still in power today safeguarding the unity of Canada from the sovereignty movement.

Recently, I have seen the Liberals and other opposition party members bitterly criticize the prorogation of the parliament from December 2009 to March 2010 and were on the verge of dissolving Parliament. But it never happened and though the primary purpose was not because it was in the best interest of Harper or the nation. It was due to the fact that the voters were not ready to go to the ballot box. Furthermore, whoever was the cause for the election would not be able to retain their support and on one occasion Mr. Michael Ignatief openly acknowledged that he did not want to bring down Harper's government because Canadians were not ready for yet another election. Recently there was a heated argument in and outside the parliament buildings on the proposal to spend nearly a million dollars for the security for the G8 and G20 summits and not including the issues of funding abortion and unwanted pregnancies in developing countries on the agenda

The right honourable Prime Minister Steven Harper is very smart and he knows how to move all of the powerful players on the chess board. Once the members of Parliament resumed with the Opposition members plan to bring down Harper's government on the issue of not being presented with the documents of Canadian soldiers who had handed over detainees to the Afghanistan government; Mr. Harper broke his silence on this issue which might have been going on even before he got into power and he might have been given the last stroke at the camel's back. I presume that Harper might have considered that this was a sensitive issue and in the best interest of national security and for the Canadian men and women in uniform and Canadian foreign missions. Whatever the reason, it could be said the members of the opposition were concerned more about integrity than the actual issue itself.

I also wonder why some of the leaders insist or reemphasize the need to include world climate change on the agenda. It is no one nation's issue and most of the nations who attended the summit last year in Copenhagen, talked loudly and added more to the temperature and have since done nothing tangible to implement anything. When Mr. Paul Martin called for the summit in the city of Quebec, America showed a blind eye and now some of the Americans say that climate change is a long term natural phenomenon and we cannot do much about it. I was surprised and disappointed about such comments. Fast growing world super powers such as India, China, and Brazil have not taken the matter very seriously and have not taken adequate measures and the non industrialized nations suffer for others careless or unconcerned acts. It has been taken into consideration in these summits but how it will force any changes is anyone's guess.

I fully agree with Harper taking necessary precautionary measures on security and spending much more money on it compared with such summits held in other countries. We have to look into the current global developments on terrorism and counter terrorist activities and the timing. Usually terrorists think that Canada is a safe haven for their operations, because Canada has never earned any enemies. Canadian foreign policy is such that people who belong to opposing camps of rival ethnic groups who migrate to Canada, under the refugee category or skilled workers sponsorship, after living in this country for some time, inherit some of our Canadian values. Upon seeing the miniature world structure and the coexistence of many cultures, religions and political views, these new Canadians come to respect the rights of others. But Canada has been cautioned by our neighbor in the south that some of the terrorists have taken the widely opened immigration door as a sign of its weakness, rather than a generosity of spirit and lack of human resources.

We have to see the other side of the coin also that Toronto in particular, and Canada in general, is also in the targeted area of the terrorist attack list. The results of the enquiry and the verdict of the judiciary system revealed that Toronto—18 terrorists had already planned and prepared to carry out an attack of the Canadian financial capital city, Toronto in many vital points. Once it has been said that Bin Laden warned Canada not to supply oil sand to America considered the prime enemy of the Islamic revolution. Most of the Arab nations are not very pleased and feel that Canada should have acted more fairly for the people of Gaza in terms of the boarding of the four Turkish ships in international waters by the Israelis. Although it is a recent development, this did not influence the planning for the security of the summits. I know that terrorists are the least concerned about attacking Canada but the leaders representing the other nations may not be considered in a similar ranking. Those countries have almost two thirds of the world's population and a very high percentage of the GDP and wealth. At the initial stages, such summits were done in remote areas around the world, but recently it has been determined that these summits would be better held in advanced cities.

Certainly the success of the summit in the long run places the positive image of Canada on the globe so high that many of us might have not even thought of this. Canada has carried itself well in handling the recession. Our financial policies and management have proven to the world that Canada is a role model. In the economic ocean, international ships have faced tough waters and cyclones. They could not sail their ships and struggled very hard. The ship of Greece like the Titanic was on the verge of sinking and those of Portugal, Italy, Spain, United Kingdom and the United States of America found the economic ocean rough. But the Canadian ship was navigated safely without any major mishaps but with the light shake of the mild ocean waves. Bravo to the Prime Minster and the Finance Minister.

Recently, Canadian currency has been elevated by some of the developed countries and Canadian currency has gotten closer to the almighty American dollar in terms of value. The Canadian economy is going to boom and many developed nations and developing nations are going to come closer to us when it comes to trade and will prefer to have investments in Canada. I can see these as positive signs. The Prime Minister of China arrived a few days before the beginning of the summits and it appears that he would like have more trade relationships with us. Although our Prime Minster did not attend the summer Olympics of 2008 in China and was almost the last leader of the G8 to visit China, China did not mind this and is coming closer to us. I am certain Canada will gain many more economic benefits from the world.

Canada's high rising image will certainly pave the way to have more skilled workers emigrate here and resolve the shortage of quality man power. According to recent statistics, within two decades Canada will have more seniors than children. The natural rate of population increase has gone down. Canada requires an increase of at least one percent of the existing population, but Canada has been accepting fewer immigrants. The current population of Canada is almost 34 million and the current acceptance of new immigrants is just above two hundred and fifty thousand.

Overall, Canada has been making use of the wonderful opportunities that it has received and the image of Canada is going to be on the top of the ladder. There are other countries that have made similar developments but only in certain aspects. Canada is the only country that has balanced development with spirit. Once again, travel outside Canada with a Canadian passport; you will see what I mean.

CHAPTER FOURTEEN

Jack Layton, the Legend from the Left

'My friends, love is better than anger, hope is better than fear, optimism is better than despair. So let us be loving, hopeful and optimistic and we'll change the world'"

These are the fruits of long years of commitment and honest and tireless contributions that Jack Layton harvested from the seeds that were planted in the Canadian political landscape. It proves beyond doubt that he was not merely a politician; rather he was a statesman and he exhibited his vision for not only the NDP but also to the entire nation of Canada as a whole. I am personally very impressed that the government of Canada under the leadership of Harper decided to honor him by declaring his funeral as a state funeral. This kind of funeral is a privilege that is only given to the Prime Minister, Governor General and other government ministers.

"To other Canadians who are on journeys to defeat cancer and to live their lives, I say this: please don't be discouraged that my journey hasn't gone as I had hoped. You must not lose your own hope.' When

I read those words I wonder about the message Jack Layton wanted to convey to all Canadians when he was fighting for his survival. I am thinking particularly about his loyal team who are to carry his touch without him and pass it on to the next generation. In fact I wonder if some instinct and his strong will to survive might have prompted him in the last election to accommodate the record breaking number of younger aged candidates in the political history of Canada.

The untimely death of Mr. Layton reminded me of some prominent politicians, artists, musicians and movie stars who died just after their sudden rise, like a lamp the gives off a bright flame just before it burns out. In the sixty year history of the New Democratic Party the glory that was achieved in the parliamentary election of May 4, 2011 was due to three reasons. The dynamic leadership of Jack Layton with his personal skills, experience and political diplomacy brought him a very high rating in the leadership polls next to Prime Minister Harper. Also the decline of the popular vote for the Liberals who did not have a strong and people oriented leader for the party in the last two consecutive terms was another factor. The third factor that contributed to this victory was the rising awareness of the youth in Quebec and their desire to support a federalist party in this case the NDP rather than the Bloc Quebecois and the Liberals.

I had been keenly watching the slight changes in the wording of policies and the presentation to the masses regarding the labels "leftist" and "socialists". These are two terms that many Canadians are sensitive to and may balk at any perceived threats to their abundant freedom. I agree up to certain point regarding these worries but it must be pointed out that a socialist government or any sort of dictatorship be it a so called system of proletariat government or the dictatorship of monarchies and self proclaimed leaders such as Moammar Ghadhafi are very different from the system of governance of the Canadian political left. I do not think that the nature of the agenda that the current NDP in particular under the leadership of Jack Layton was inclined towards the socialist system; rather it leans towards the model of welfare capitalism in a democratic government. Mr. Layton during the last election campaign put the emphasis more on social reforms and the expansion of social services such as low income housing, extended health services, qualitative education, and keeping the corporate tax level as it was and sharing a portion of it to cover the cost of fundamental services for low income earners. This was a brilliant move in securing support from undecided voters.

During the campaign of the 2011 election, it was crystal clear that the Conservatives would form the next government, but the question was the margin and whether or not the majority government would be formed by Harper. It was the time when the Liberals wanted to keep their identity for the long term benefits by forgoing short term gains and thus kept away from the idea of a coalition during the pre election period. But the Liberals did not close the door tightly. It was during the middle of the campaign that the glimmerings of a glorious victory for the NDP pushing the Liberals into third place sprouted mutterings of a coalition. But Jack Layton played his cards very well by abstaining without making any substantial comment.

Some of his political moves during the short period of governing by Paul Martin are hard to understand but there was a vision behind them. He never extended unconditional support to Martin and never expected any form of coalition. He was a man of determination, courage and concerned with achieving his mission at any cost; the belief that the "ends justify the means" was in the background even though Mr. Layton never resorted to selling himself short and did not compromise his integrity.

Although his uncle, grandfather and father were more inclined towards conservative philosophies, Jack Layton defied his traditional family background and worked for the people on the grass roots level from day one of his public life to his last breath. I met with him and had a couple of meetings with him when he was a City Councilor in Toronto in the early 1990's. He was a very kind hearted person and identified himself as an associate of a blue collar worker. He was dressed in blue jeans, like Castro in his army uniform and Mao Tze Tung in his collarless shirt and this truly reflected his state of mind. The people of Toronto claim that he was more of a Torontonian and that his love of this city superseded others. However, members and supporters of the NDP also claim ownership and the Quebecers determined him to be the better politician among the federal leaders. People like me who are Conservatives respect him as a smart Canadian.

He was highly concerned about the fair distribution of national wealth. Both Liberal and Conservative governments have done enough to assist blue collar workers in particular and the Canadian masses in general. As an example during the last election campaign the Conservatives want to give tax relief to entrepreneurs so that they would be able to reduce the cost of production and sell their products at a cheaper rate. This in turn would control inflation and give ample opportunity to provide more employment and encourage foreign countries to buy our products in a competitive market when our Canadian dollar has high exchange value. Even the Liberals were somewhat supportive of this idea for a while though at a later stage changed their views. But Layton was deathly against this and wanted the corporate tax rate to remain as it was and that a certain percentage be put towards social programming.

However, this is not the time for recounting political differences. Canada lost a vibrant man who led a remarkable life with dignity and grace. Torontonians will miss him as he is one of our own who cared deeply about this city. The NDP will miss him for he leaves behind very large shoes to fill. And finally Canadians will miss him for though he was an extraordinary man, he saw himself as ordinary, as one of us. I hope that we can all live up to his expectations and change the world.

CHAPTER FIFTEEN

The U.S.A and Canada Today

Barrack Obama, an American Who Happened to Be a Black Man

"Our challenges may be new. The instruments with which we meet them may be new. But those values upon, which our success depends—honesty and hard work, courage, and fair play, tolerance and curiosity, loyalty and patriotism—these things are old." This comes from, the inauguration speech made by Mr. Barrack Obama the 44th president of America made on 20th January 2008. Mr. Barrack Obama is an American who happens to be a black man, not a black man who happens to be an American. It is the main waves of his speech in the inauguration ceremony and his earlier election campaign speeches. He emphasized everyone in America, regardless, of political ideology, ethnic background or economic status, everyone is a proud American and they all should put America first. Therefore, it is crystal clear that Mr. Obama is an American and he continues to look after the American interests first and the rest behind, but not forgotten.

How do I look at him? Do I look at him as a follow human being or as a fellow colored man, or an American or all of the above? Mr. Obama made history in many ways in the sense that he is the first African American to be elected to the White House and received an 80% approval rating. The unsuccessful foreign policy of the previous political regime influenced the American voters to find an alternative president who did follow in the same vein. This contributed to a high proportion of his votes. If he would have contested under any other circumstances, he might not have had such a high rate of success.

Mr. Obama is at the initial stage in his career in the Oval Office. He was a hard-line left wing person and while sailing his political ship in the turf ocean. Later, he cooled down and shifted his direction and accommodated others as well.

His political role model is Abraham Lincoln who came from the grass roots level to the top position as the American President. Obama's loyalty was exhibited at the inauguration ceremony when he took the oath by swearing on the red covered Bible that Lincoln used in his inauguration ceremony.

Unfortunately, he has taken office at a very critical situation in which American government is in debt over a trillion dollars. America is in the middle of a recession and already financial institutions are shaking and the unemployment rate is high. The engagements in Iraq and Afghanistan swallow a big portion of the national cake and the yield is very negative; the progress made is not encouraging the Americans to extend the war. But Americans should not underestimate the danger from terrorists and the volcanic lava can erupt at any time.

As Obama mentioned in his inauguration speech, all of these problems cannot be resolved in a short time. It indeed takes time but nobody can predict the future and it depends on the capability of the President, the plans and strength of the terrorists and the rate of economic recovery.

I am surprised to see that at this early stage in office he included the Middle East crisis as one of the topics in his agenda. This is a very complex and time consuming issue and it will occupy a reasonable amount of time and energy. Mr. Obama needs to concentrate on the other main concerns that occupied the minds of the voters in the presidential election campaign such as the improvement of the economy, Pulling out the troops in Iraq without finding an alternative solution is not a wise idea. Otherwise the parents, relatives and fellow citizens will ask "Why were these sacrifices made, was it all for nothing?" Can we allow the Iraqis to become influenced by the fundamentalists? I would prefer if the complex Middle East agenda would have been taken up once Mr. Obama got settled in. Anyhow let us wait and see how far it will go.

I am a Canadian who wants to know where my country is placed on his list. I am very pleased that he proposed even before he officially took oath as president, that his first state visit will be Canada and this is an honor for us. But what are at stake are at least three main issues. When he was canvassing in the presidential election he made it very clear that he is not going to accept the current North American Free Trade Agreement and in his view it was not working well for the states. Canada is very dependent on its exports to the United States; it accounts for 85% of the export income. What worries me is the possible application of protectionist policies. These policies would protect American jobs, but not Canadian jobs. The second important issue is that he should take adequate interest in resolving the dispute over the rights of Canadians in the Arctic Ocean. It is ours and America, Denmark or any other nations have the right to go into our waters. This is a violation of our sovereignty and it may be a minor issue to them but it is a serious issue for us. The intensified border checking and other restrictions contribute adversely to our economy; there must be an alternative system that can prevent the smuggling of terrorists but not delay the exports. Americans who want to visit Canada in the summer and Canadian snowbirds are also having an awful time. According to the Bush administration, pretty soon both Canadians and Americans have to have a passport to visit both Canada and the United States as they do when they travel to other countries. Mr. Obama has also stated that the oil sands are a major cause of pollution. This concern and his actions around it will have a direct impact on our oil exports.

I hope his first visit that is proposed to occur sometime in February 2009 will accommodate these issues and some tangible, bilateral agreements will be made. We can only indicate our priorities but he does have his own as well. Let us wait and see.

Mr. Obama, we Canadians wish you the very best in your undertakings and we hope we will have a better and peaceful world for all of us to live. We are always with you as long as you consider us as a good friend of yours.

America—From the Space Age to Stone Age
The First Mini World War

I was at Pearson international airport, Toronto at about 9.00 pm. on 10th September 2010 to board an Air Transat flight to Heathrow, London, United Kingdom and the scheduled departure time was 11:55 am, five minutes ahead of the sorrowful 9th remembrance day of the victims of the September 11, 2001 attack in New York and Washington. It appeared quite normal and I did not notice any alerting signs or extra uniformed security officers. I was heading to the security check, after obtaining my boarding pass. We the passengers were heading to the security check counter. There were a few Canadians of South Asian heritage behind me and I appeared very casual and was dressed in fashionable skin tight name brand New York jeans and a t-shirt and my head was completely shaved. I noticed Canadians of Asian descent went in and out of the security check easily and when my turn came, I handed in my luggage and placed all the belongings I had on myself in a small plastic box and everything passed through without any trouble. I reached the officer who was performing the personal security check he searched every part of my body and asked me to be seated on a nearby chair and re-searched me from top to bottom and asked me to remove my pair of shoes and he scanned them and finally asked me to proceed. I appreciate his dedication to his service but did not care for his search because I know pretty well my records are clear and that I have nothing to do with terrorist activities. Probably my appearance would have made him to do such a search. The only thing that bothered me was that at least the officer could have show a sign in his body language that I was the wrong person for the search and expressed some concern of my being in such an embarrassing situation. It was exactly this event that prompted me to write this article while it was on the plane and by the time the airplane landed at Heathrow airport, I had completed and saved it.

The first mini world war that began on 11th September 2001 in Washington and New York, respectively the capital city and the financial capital of the U.S.A, the only superpower in the world. Although initially no one claimed responsibility, in short while al-Qaida claimed responsibility for it and it was said that Osama bin **Laden** mentioned that it was only a small attempt to make America realize how they had been suffering from the adverse effects of the political maneuvers planted by the U.S.A in the Middle East. Whether it was true or not, he further said that it was only the beginning and not the end of their retaliation.

It was not just planned and executed overnight; rather it had been revolving underneath the surface as volcanic lava and erupted with minor force many times as at the US foreign missions and the countries of the Arabs and those with a predominantly Muslim population such as Malaysia, Bosnia and Indonesia. Though America is the main target of their attacking process, it also linked with the nations that have backed, politically motivated or associated or considered to be assisting America for undermining or destroying their activities. In fact there have been two things going on at the same time. The first is that all the non Muslim countries whose activities go against their interest are open to attack. The second thing is that Islamic nations are being pushed by the extremist groups directly or indirectly to purify their life, system of government and reform the judiciary system in accordance with Islamic Sharia law. These nations have been considered brothers and they are reminded that it is their moral obligation and duty to act as Muslims, not as people corrupted by the western systems. I remember that when I was working in Nigeria, the President Sahu Sahari once said he preferred to have his people ignorant, rather than ill-educated under a western system.

The modern war began on a small scale and shifted its location from the Middle East after the creation of Israel, a Jewish nation 1948 and was considered to be the last straw. The Arab nations felt the pinch of the expansion of the territory of Israel into the surrounding nations and during the Six Day War in the year 1967; Israel went into the Sinai Peninsula of Egypt and alerted the Arab nations. It was a wonderful opportunity for the Soviet Union to have a great influence in the Middle East and slowly penetrate into the African nations and spread anti capitalism and anti American propaganda against the rival world power. In fact it woke up the Arabs and they slowly got away from the American domination in economic activities, political control over the royals and other leaders who had been manipulated behind the scene. Although the backbone of their economy is the crude oil in abundant quantities, in the absence of technology, they had to solely depend on the west, particularly on the Americans who were able to make the required investments as well.

But somehow they got away from the economic domination, undue political interference, investments, over dependency on technology, lack of modern education and inter rival conflicts and wanted to develop a strong Islamic brotherhood. The focus on achieving these goals began with the oil embargo and manipulation of the price mechanism in increasing the price by reducing the supply. They were aware that the industrialized nations heavily depended on the oil and the Middle East is the main producer and supplier. The second reason for it was that most of the western nations support and protect the survival of the

Jews in Israel and the arms and ammunition that helps to fight against their enemy. Their oil made a significant contribution in producing them and some of the radicals mentioned that their oil became weapon for their distraction by selling to the western world that supports their enemy. How far it goes as a valid point is another matter.

The war got into many dimensions as such the psychological war, economical war, political war, intellectual war, diplomatic war, and all they are in operation simultaneously.

CHAPTER SIXTEEN

The Dragon and the Elephant under the Rising Sun

My friends invited me for dinner in honor of the launching of my recent book entitled **"Canada the Meat of the World Sandwich"** at a local Chinese restaurant along with the massive crowd of multi ethnic supporters at Victoria park Avenue and Sheppard Avenue East, Scarborough. I honored the invitation and while I was enjoying my meal at this particular place, I noticed to my surprise that the spicy meal from the soup to the main course had a mixture of flavors from both the Indian and Chinese cultures. I ended up wondering about the combination of the two cultures in the meal in contrast to their political rivalries. Later on I discovered that the owner of the restaurant and the staff were born and raised in the state of Bengal India, descendants of the Chinese who had been residing in India over many generations. The delicious meal that I ate in that establishment prompted me to write this article.

The proliferation of Chinese goods and Indian services are rampant even in remote villages around the world and the invisible and invisible exports of these two potential world powers are rising at lightning fast speed. Last year, the President of Mexico once warned the American President and the Prime Minister of Canada that the time had come to enforce some trade restrictions regarding the importing of Chinese products. There was a concern that domestic industries would face serious challenges. The recent "Buy America" Policy of US president barrack Obama indiscriminately made some changes in the American trade policies to allow the recover from the rescission. However, Chinese products till dominate the shelves.

It is inevitable that these two nations are booming rapidly and there is a gowning shift in the world economic power from the west to the east with the exception of Brazil in South America. While the sun sets in the west, it rises in the east and the powerful rays of the sun fall on China and India. With that additional energy they are flourishing and have reach the stage of prominent world powers and the focus has shifted from painting these 2 countries with the proverbial brushes of poverty in India and human rights violations in China. Of course, the domination of economic power does not in any way erase the issues of poverty and human rights violations and as these 2 countries grown in their economic strength these issues will have to be addressed.

The progress rate and the patterns of these two countries have many similarities and the contrasts. Both of them have very rich and old civilizations and that is being analyzed and studies with the help of archaeologists and the anthropologists. In India, the recently discovered Mohenjo-Daro and Harappa settlements at the Indian border with Pakistan, and the Lemurian civilization that sank into the Indian Ocean at the southern tip of India have yet to be fully recognized by historians in India. Chinese settlements that are around 5000 years old still inspire awe and the beauty of them is that the core elements of that civilization never died out even during the suppressing colonial rules of the west for almost 500 years. Although they were paralyzed during the colonial era, after gaining independence from the British on 15th August 1946 in a non violent resistance led by Mahatma Gandhi in India and establishment of a socialist system of government based on Marxist philosophy in China on October 1st, 1949, their people began to revive and became proud of who and what they are and made the world recognize their identity and respect their values and merits.

Both the nations are the richest in terms of human resources which encompasses almost one third of the entire global population. Today, it has not been considered as an economic burden as it used to be in the recent past. The age distribution in China demonstrates that the country now has more of a middle aged population and the working age population is going to reach one billion and the rest of the population will be seniors and children. Furthermore, based on the current trend it will reach its peak in 2015 and then it will shrink steadily. If China does not adapt the policy of one child per family (the maximum established in 1979) today china would have had 400 million additions to the current population. That is more than the combined population of Canada and the USA.

The population growth rate and the age distribution of the Indian population have evolved somewhat differently. Though family planning has been a pressing issue since the 1960's, and the objectives could not be achieved as planned. One of the reasons for this is that many in

India are illiterate and unlike China the life of the common people is very much influenced by religious beliefs. None of the religious groups were in favor of artificial or natural ways of family planning particularly the Muslim community and orthodox Hindus when it came to the issue of abortion to control the population increase. The government also does not have the power to force anyone to control the population increase. The government also does not have the power to force anyone to use condoms and in turn, this has contributed to an increase in the number of people infected with HIV/AIDS. In China, it is very hard to obtain independent statistics regarding HIV/AIDS other than those provided by the government. Whereas in India, one can easily obtain the numbers as there are many local and national health agencies keeping up to date statistics.

The type of government also matters in their development. India is the most populous democratic government in the world and exercises its duties along with employing a wide range of fundamental freedoms to the masses such as freedom of expression, freedom of the press and private ownership of property. In India after achieving independence, the India Congress (one of the major political parties) was in power for a long time and there appeared to be a one party system of government. Later on the JBP joined and the government turned into a two party system.

The practice the multi-party system of government has its own pros and cons but it most widely accepted by the common person. To get the full level of benefits in a democracy, the masses have to be somewhat educated to be able to decide and cast their vote in an election. But in many parts of India election malpractice and the tendency towards hero worship amongst the undereducated of the electorate, has allowed corrupt politicians to abuse the system. The essence of democracy has been diluted and mixed with unwanted elements.

In contrast to the western democratic system of government, in China the system of government is a centralized proletariat dictatorship ruled by the communist party and there is no room for existence of another party. No one has the right to question the ideology or advocate for an alternative system. The economic system is almost a monopoly system. According to Karl Marx even the optimum level of capitalism leads to private monopoly, and it is better to have the state own the monopoly rather than the private sector. The wealth of the nation belongs to the state and private enterprises are not welcomed or encouraged. It would be easy for the government to push the plans without wasting time in the debate and taking time for implementation. People have to undergo a lot of sacrifices for the nation.

A striking example of this is that on June 4th, 1989 a million post-secondary students and supporters gathered on Tiananmen Square and on that Saturday night it has been said that thousands of them were mercilessly killed. On the following day, the local and state media were prohibited from reporting about this event. Even to this very day, the Chinese government keeps a tight leash on what is said or not said about the events of Tiananmen Square.

Both these nations have deviated from their original paths. China was for a long time isolated by the western world. The entire world criticized its suppression of human rights and poverty. The closed door system was as impenetrable as The Great Wall for it did not allow the outside world to gain any authentic information other than what was given by the government officials. Then Dr. Henry Kissinger in the 1970s knocked at the gate and it opened. He employed triangular political maneuvers in which he wanted to weaken the enemy by becoming friendly with the enemy of his enemy. In order to attack the Soviet Union, America became close to the enemy of the Soviet Union even though both of them practiced the some ideology. As a result, many countries began to recognize the Chinese government and established diplomatic relationships.

India was inclined towards the former Soviet Union against America while Pakistan was backed by the USA against India. The United States meanwhile kept a superficial friendly relationship with India. Drastic changes in the global system occurred after the disintegration of the Soviet Union and dismantling of Socialist governments in Eastern Europe. America became the only superpower in the world. India had no other choice but to turn to the USA and had come to the stage of reaching an agreement regarding atomic energy. China does not criticize the capitalistic system as the former Soviet Union did. China allowed foreign investment and established bilateral economic actives. These days the water tight compartments of west and east and the right wing and left wing have come down to a mixed economic system and intricate levels of diplomacy and global communication.

It is inevitable that every country, whether big or small, developed or developing, free-market, or socialist, to a certain degree has to embrace the concept of globalization. It is evident to witness that economic co operation such as European Union, the G20, the United Nations, NATO, NAFTA, and other organizations are some of the grounds for it. These two nations have an excessive number of skilled professionals and their man power is in high demand by developed countries such as the USA, UK, Canada, Germany, France, and Australia. The countries that receive these skilled workers do not make any investment in them whereas the governments of India and China have invested much time and money in developing these skilled workers. In the next 20 years exports from India and China will remain stable. Later on, the high growth of their economies at a rapid rate and the high percentage of the aging population will absorb these highly skilled workers. However, as the local economy improves, the migration of these skilled workers will decrease even though the developed nations will still have a demand for them.

The pulling force of the migration of manpower is the higher wages and better standard of living in western countries and Australia and the main pushing force is mass unemployment. The rapid economic and infrastructure development eventually case a decline in the exporting of skilled man power. Even today some of these skilled workers migrate to Canada work for a short period of time, obtain Canadian citizenship and go back to their home with their new sophisticated experience and remain. For example, quit a few Chinese migrated from Hong Kong to Canada in the late 1990s just before the British handing over of the island to China. They were afraid that the Chinese government would interfere and place restrictions on their business actives. After a few years, many of these business people, some of whom obtained Canadian citizenship, regained their confidence and moved back to Hong Kong.

Having a bulk of the local population and high rate of economic growth broadens the local market for their products and it is another added advantage. The global market for their products will have some changes. The quality of their goods will have marked improvement by years of experience and with the use of high technology will fetch better market. The prices of their exports might not remain cheap as it is today due to the face that the standard of living and cost of living are raising and the production higher and the export prices also will go up. China has a very high market for low cost consumer goods around the world and the prices might not remain the same, some countries have place restrictions on these imports to protect local producers and due to the poor quality of these good according to their standards.

These two countries have not only contributed positively but also adversely to the glove in some ways such as in climate change, and global warming. These two countries consume a high percentage of cheap sources of energy and it adds a high percentage to air pollution and global warming. China burns fuel five times less effectively than the west and it also added to the death toll in millions. Low levels of literacy in the rural areas, neglect of compulsory universal education for children between the age of 5-14, child labor, inaccessibility of medical faculties and poor health services also attribute to this.

The rivalry of the regional level is not a healthy sign; the Border States such as Bhutan, Nepal, Tibet and Sri Lanka are caught in between. And when the dragons and elephants fight, those caught on the field will suffer although in some cases they get undue advantages, for example, China wants to get Sri Lanka on its side by using the Buddhist sentiment of the majority population in Sri Lanka to help them win more political influence over the Tamil population. China is doing to Sri Lanka what the Soviet Union did to the U.S.A by influencing Cuba. Already there is an undeclared war in infiltrating these small nations. Tibet was invaded by China, the Maoist influence is very high in Nepal and there is an uneasy situation at the Indian border with China and according to the Indian government, the huge number of soldiers brought to the border is an indication that tensions are mounting. The friendly and close relationship with Pakistan by China is viewed with suspicion by India. This current situation is reminiscent of how during the colonial era, France and the United Kingdom fought each other and of the Soviet Union and USA during the Cold War. Though these super powers are working together, the playing cards are not always on full display.

The gates of the Great Wall of China are no longer closed and locked and they are slowly opening and the Taj Mahal, the monument of love has turned to a love of growth and power. The effects of these changes have brought not only changes within the elephant and the dragon but have shifted the focus of the world towards the East.

CHAPTER SEVENTEEN

The Arab spring

Tuned in Tunisia; Burning in the Arab World

In Egypt a camel has given birth to a sheep by caesarean delivery after having labour pains for eighteen days. The end of the dictatorial rule of Hosni Mubarak is not the beginning of a new era; rather it is the beginning of another form of dictatorship by men in uniform. It has been promised that they will suspend the constitution and dissolve parliament and they have also claimed that they will act as transitional rulers until another duly elected government is sworn in. This is nice and sweet to hear and is a big relief for the Egyptians and all those who have been suffering under various forms of dictatorship around the world.

This spirit has already spread out like a wild fire in the Middle East and in North African Arab nations. It was centered in Tunisia and then the cyclonic winds moved to Egypt and then to Jordan, Yemen, Morocco, Algeria, Bahrain, Libya and Iran and I do not know which direction this wind is going to move. Already the dictators are in a panicked mood and are probably going through sleepless nights. Under a constitutional monarchy, the elected members of the government are symbolic figures with no independent voice and have to dance according to the tune of the dictators. I have experienced this when I was working in Ethiopia under the constitutional monarchy rule of the emperor Haile Selassie. It is true that absolute power corrupts absolutely and the rule of Hosni Mubarak would not be an exception. It was very unfortunate that he had no other choice other than follow the footsteps of Sadat who was assassinated in the Independence Day celebrations by one of the men in uniform during the parade of honour. Sadat could not follow the footsteps of President Nasser being of radical thinking, counterattacking Israel and pouring out anti western views. He was able to fight against Britain, their former colonial ruler and who constructed the Suez Canal of 190 km in length with the help of a French company in 1869. Britain then withheld Egypt's independence and President Nasser won the subsequent battle. He never recognized the existence of Israel as a sovereign state. He once said that the wiping out Israel is not difficult task and if all Arabs line up and urinate, it will be easily done.

Later on during the Six Day War Israel capture the Sinai Peninsula and reached the Suez Canal. It was at that time Sadat realized the strength of Israel and the strong backing of the western world. The question of peaceful existence of not Israel, but Egypt became a very big challenge. Sadat came down to the earth in his plans and took a drastic stand by making secret deals with Israel through America. Dr. Henry Kissinger was the main player in making these deals. I can still remember that when Kissinger arrived at the airport in Egypt President Sadat welcomed him by calling him by his first name instead of his family name and expose to the world in general and the Arab world in particularly that their relationship was a deep one and not superficial. Although working closely with the western world and somehow accepting Israel as a nation antagonized the radial Arabs leaders when Hosni Mubarak replaced Sadat even if he wanted to change the political climate it was very costly and very bold step and he did not want to make such a move.

We should not forget that the relationship between Israel and Egypt is historically significant and dates back many years. According to the Old Testament of the Bible, the holiday of Passover for the Jews and the action taken by Moses clearly indicates their close relationship and thus the birth of the modern state of Israel does not limit the relationship between the two nations.

The political views of the Arabs are in four camps. The first are the radical Islamic activists branded recently as terrorist are determined and committed to translating their agenda into action at any cost. They follow the Holy Quran ran their scripture from word to word and anything that is to the contrary is to be fought and destroyed at any cost. It is not just a war, rather a holy war and as Zaeef of the Mujahedeen said **"May God be praised. We weren't concerned with the world or with our lives; our intentions were pure and every one of us was ready to die as a martyr. "**They are clear in what they have been doing and do not hesitate in carrying out what are convinced is right and have no regard for what others say. It may appear to others that they are trying to go back to an old fashioned way of life but they see themselves as liberated from the so called modern life of materialistic slavery. When former US President George W. Bush said the civilized world is challenged by Islamic extremists this might have given the implication that they are not civilized.

The second Arab political camp is demonstrated by the dictator of Libya, Muammar Gaddafi. He made several attempts to stop this kind of behaviour and spoke out against Islamic extremism but he did not have continuity and action plans. Arafat, the leader of the P.L.O (Palestinian Liberation Organization) was more inclined towards this path as well but later on could not withstand the constant attacks of the Israelis. He then cooled down and then Hamas took over the radical path. They have two main agendas such as their fight against America and the western world and their supportive nations. It started with the attacks on the American embassies in Nairobi and Darussalam along with the hostage taking incidents during the foreign mission in Iran and finally leading to the attacks of September 11th, 2001. The second phase is purification of the Islamic world and the destruction of western cultural, political and other influences. The recent Tunisian and Egyptian revolutions have not yet backed by them but I have my doubts they will try to infiltrate it.

The third group more or less accepts western influences in most aspects of life from dress to defence. The Shah of Iran and some other Arab leaders followed this path. The fourth does not fall into any of these extreme camps and swings between the two like the pendulum of a clock. Where do we position the now deposed leader of Egypt? He expressed his stand that he is the man of two worlds, the Arab world and the western and he expected the rest of the Arab world would follow his example until the crushing mass of protesters surrounded him.

The current political turmoil has brought in a new and forceful group that is deviating from the all others in that they emphasize the importance of having a western multi party democratic system of government. It does not mean however that they accept the culture, way of life or civilization of the west; it is confined to the political arena. When it comes to the way of life it is what they have been practising based on the teachings of Islam. They do not want to have any form of dictatorship be it a monarchy with blue blood like in Saudi Arabia or a de facto leader like Gaddafi in Libya. Even a form of Islamic dictatorship is not accepted as a form of democracy for "Power to the people" is their slogan. Even the Communists claim that their system of government is the people's government and all rules are elected by the people for a defined period of time. But the basic difference between the western system of democracy and the communist system is the multi party system versus single party system of government. Furthermore in the Communist system of government it is a dictatorship of so called proletariats. The democratic way of ruling does not require particular cultural or religious background and it can be practised in any part of the world.

Now, here we come to the question of the link between religion and state. There was a time in history when various religions exerted a high degree of influence and directed the government in their own way. In certain countries, they become part of the government and play dual roles under the same roof. In certain cases, the religious aspects superseded the political agenda. In the lands of the Arabs Islam is much more concerned about the five times of worship and other religious activities. Although all religions advocate for religious activities, they are not confined within the halls of the places of worship, rather they extend into every part of private and community life. But in the case of the radical Muslims everything should be parallel and religion and state are inseparable.

I am pretty sure that on the soil of the Arab world their religious influence will be strong and would not have any contradictions. The second important aspect is economic principles and they would not be inclined towards Marxist ideologies. The only system that would work is free enterprise what we call the capitalist economic system. Therefore, there would not be any basic differences in their multi party system of government. The effective operation of the democratic government should have the masses; the voters which make the government should have sound education and political awareness. The recent demonstrations have evidently exhibited that political awareness has awakened. But knowing the rights and the responsibilities of a citizen is highly demanded. In the absence of it, the democratic system of government can be manipulated by a handful of people. This is what we have been witnessing in some of the South American countries. It turns back into a dictatorship by a group of people instead of individuals, under the cover of people's democracy.

The wave of the current political movement brings down power to the people and allows them to think of their rights and then their duties and responsibilities. This awakening in turn will lead them to become leaders instead of followers. They will begin to analyze things in a critical manner and make their own decisions. The younger generation is certainly questioning the many things that they are asked to accept and this will not be comfortable for the older generation. This will widen the generation gap and pave a way for conflicts and deviate their way of life. At this stage, they will realize that so called western education and lifestyle is the product of modernization and it is not confined or owned by the western world as such; rather it is global and whether we like it or not it is penetrating around the world as a by product of technological development.

We should also look into the prevailing economic factors in the Arab world. Most of those countries mainly or solely depend on oil as a single commodity. Alternative sources of energy though do not play an active role in the energy market. However the rest of the world is looking at other sources of energy and is slowly moving away from foreign sources of petroleum. The Arab world will have to look into other ways of keeping their respective economies working and that means working with other nations to foster interdependence. When their life gets closer to the global village the concept of brotherhood will be extended to include a wider circle and bring about a better understanding and earn respect from other ethnic groups.

Although U.S President Obama and others shifted their support from the rulers to the people, this new development is dangerous but unavoidable. The awakened common masses will no longer accept foreign interference, infiltration and any form of domination and this can encourage anti American feelings. This will also be another challenge for Israel and the degree of support from the west will determine its course. The awakened sleeping camel will not go back to sleep, rather it will actively carry on the different political loads. Apart from the positive changes in the political sphere there is a draw back in terms of atomic power development in Iran. These days the government of Iran is able to carry on its atomic development, either in a constructive way or destructive manner and can do this very quickly. Once the opposition parties get liberated, there is no telling what the political establishment can do.

In conclusion, this is just a beginning, not the end.

An Adamant Radical Challenged by Empowered Radicals

I remember once that Muammar Abu Minyar al-Gaddafi sarcastically said that Tunisia was a nation without a leader and he was a leader without a country and the intention behind those words was to conquer Tunisia and merge the two nations of Tunisia and Libya and become the leader of this expanded nation with glory. The revolving ambition of Gaddafi is to be super Arab leader who would spontaneously challenge the Western World whenever he made a plan to attack them.

This is the first time that Gaddafi has accused al-Qaeda, not the Western powers by saying that Al-Qaeda was behind the problems facing Libya and that the youth were on drugs and misbehaving. 'It is obvious now that this issue is run by Al-Qaeda". He further said. "Those armed youngsters, our children, are incited by people who are wanted by America and the Western world. They have been brainwashing the kids in this area and telling them to misbehave. These are the ones who are under Bin Laden's influence and authority, under the influence of drugs".

I remember how he used to accuse the western powers for challenges that he faced. In those days in his emotional roaring speeches he blamed the west by saying "Get ready to fight for Libya, get ready to fight for dignity, get ready to fight for petroleum. We can crush any enemy. We can crush it with the people's will" He cuts two of his enemies by a double edged sword.

I have been closely observing most of his major moves and in fact I began to work as an instructor at a teachers college in Jimma,

Ethiopia where the head quarters of the organization of the African Unity (O.A.U.) the one that has since been replaced by the Union of Africa (U.A). On September1, 1969 Colonel Gaddafi led a small group of junior military officers in a bloodless coup d'état and overthrew King Idris while he was in Turkey receiving medical treatment. Although Libya is a part of Africa and a member of the OAU and UA its ethnic and political sentiments are more confined and limited to the Berber states of Northern Sudan. It is different world of Africa from the sub Saharan countries and their peoples who are ethnically and linguistically different. Although Gaddafi was once elected and functioned as the chairman of the O.A.U and has contributed to some extent, his heart is more inclined towards to the Arab world.

His early days of the regime was full of radical changes and it reflected his mission that was proclaimed as the "Great Revolution of the Socialist people's Libyan Arab Jamahiriya" It is important to ask; what were the targets and aims of this revolution? Was it a revolution against dictatorship and colonial rule? Was it a revolution to establish power to the people? To move from private enterprises to the state owned socialist system of economics? Was this a revolution against western cultural, political and economic domination? Or was this revolution a means to purify Arab world? I believe that Gaddafi's goals were a mixture of all these things. He also had multi dimensional schools of thought and expressed them variously as "Islamic Socialism" "Arab nationalism", "popular democracy" and "Pan Arabism". He had a vision of achieving something extraordinary for the Arab world while having oil rich Libya as its base. Let's examine the nature of each of these points. Islamic socialism aims to overhaul the present governmental and economic systems of the Arab world along with daily life. It is a complex and difficult task to achieve with other sovereign Arab states having their own interpretations of economics, governance and daily living. In contrast, according to Karl Marx, there is only one kind of socialism that can be practiced and that is scientific socialism, not African socialism or Arab socialism. A popular democracy is what the people of Libya along with the other nations where the people have been revolting against the dictatorship governments want. I would have preferred that Gaddafi talked about the Arab culture and the promotion of Islamic nations rather than delving into international political philosophies which are much beyond his intellectual capacities.

The political life of Gaddafi was in his youth, highly influenced by the president of Egypt the radical of that time. Gamal Abdel Nasser advocated for Arab Nationalism by condemning western domination. He was very aggressive in provoking the sleeping masses in the Arab world against the western world in the late 1940's and early fifties and Gaddafi was one of the young ones who worshipped him as a hero. When he was an elementary school child Palestine was defeated by the Israelis in 1948 and the establishment of Israel was considered by the radical Arabs as a thorn in the flesh, a foreign painful material and it has to be removed sooner rather than later. Most of those countries, including Egypt at the initial stage did not recognize Israel as a sovereign state and it did not exist on their world map. Gaddafi being a high school graduate with militarily training was inclined towards the military solution rather than political maneuvers or the manipulation of international affairs in terms of reaching his goal. The Americans were clearly watching his political moves and reacted not spontaneously but slowly and quietly eventually cornering him.

Gaddafi realized the powerful backing of the western world and the strength of Israel and the ineffective unity among the Arab nations only after the defeat of the six day war in 1967. This prompted him in overthrowing king Idris on 1st September 1969. Though Gaddafi is pro communist, his political activities in spreading the ideas of the promotion of Arab nationalism and fight against anti-imperialism and fight against the western world almost similar to the fight against anti-imperialism by Ernesto Che Guevara in South America. He formed the Revolutionary Command Council with himself as head, though originally he gave the title of his position as the prime minister and then colonel. That being said, he was the only person who was behind entire operation. Unlike the former Egyptian president Hosni Mubarak who was almost a figurehead and most of the planning and policy making was done by the senior military officers. Although he has frequently said that "Libya's society is ruled by the people" it is a one-man show. He hardly ever listens to his advisers, intellectuals' and members of his cabinet; rather he wants them to listen and accept his decisions as though they are a divine vision. Though the blood that circulates in his body is not royal blue blood, he acts like a divine ruler and a representative of god. This behavior has clouded his vision and judgment not to mention his perception of reality. If it would have been as he claims that his government is a government by the masses, the people would not be revolting against him and that he should not have launched attacks against them resulting on the deaths of over 100 people.

He has pretty much ignored the concerns and fundamental needs of Libyans. The system of education was not reformed to include new techniques and educational expansion has not been done sufficiently. The removal of foreign language instruction particularly English and French in the school system kept them isolated from the outside world. The medical services provided in Libya compared with some of the other Arab nations are not adequate enough for their growing needs. Overall the infrastructure of Libya has been well established and Gaddafi deviate most of his time, resources and energy in building Arab nationalism and this sped up after the death of Nasser of Egypt on 28th November 1970. It was witnessed when he proclaimed the "Federation of the Arab Republic" and proposed to merge Egypt, Syria and Libya. He signed a merger agreement with Tunisia but this proposal was not accepted by those countries and resulted in an utter failure. He then made very aggressive moves which had multi-dimensional purposes. His forces entered the country Chad, a sub-Saharan nation with a substantial Muslim population and sizeable Christian population, not for the purpose of capturing a portion of the desert with very little resources, but because the ruler of Chad was a Christian and a black African. Libya occupied a portion of Chad between the period of 1973 and June 1994. He never spared Egypt and sent his troops to its borders for a brief period of time in 1977.

Since the slogans of Arab nationalism did not achieve his burning desire, he began to focus on Islamic aspects and created the Islamic Legion in 1972 and its existence and growth moved towards fighting against the so called oppression to their own development. he had gone far in establishing nuclear and chemical weapons and the western world and the peace loving nations were very much alarmed and drew a line in their dealings and relationship with him. I do not know how he could have liked and supported the terror of Idi Admin of Uganda for Gaddafi's daughter married him though their marriage was short lived. Gaddafi sent his troops to Uganda against Tanzania, a nation that got independence under Julius Nyerere, a peace loving leader with courage, honesty, and dignity. When he sent his troops to Chad, France the former colonial ruler having close business ties to the country was deathly against it and Gaddafi responded by threatening France. When the Japanese Red Army massacred innocent civilians at the Lod (now Ben Gurion) Airport in Tel Aviv Israel in 1972, Gaddafi encouraged the Palestinians to initiate similar moves against western nations. There was also a very upsetting situation at the Summer Olympics in Munich Germany when anti Israel in 1972; Gaddafi encouraged the Palestinians to initiate similar moves against western nations. There was also a very upsetting situation at the Summer Olympics in Munich Germany when anti Israelis massacred innocent participants. Gaddafi financed this operation and the pain of the victims remains a bleeding wound to this day. His involvement in the Philippines in supporting the Muslims terrorists who have been fighting for the creation of a separate state involved financing, military advise and other assistance through various means. As such in the 1980's he continued and his aborted plan to assassinate US President Ronald Reagan was a shock to Americans. Reagan once called Gaddafi the "Mad Dog of the Middle East".

In other words Gaddafi has made use of every possible means in taking revenge against the western world. Not only that, he is not afraid to use his vast arsenal against his own people. It is clear that the so called "Mad Dog of the Middle East" is not going to leave quietly, but the noose is tightening. If Colonel Gaddafi does end up losing power then for the people of Libya, like those in Tunisia and Egypt, this will not be the end, only another beginning.

CHAPTER EIGHTEEN

Ontario—Where Are We Heading?

It was a pleasant morning, with the bright sun and the color of the skirt of the sky was flowing from royal blue to snow white. I entered into the Scarborough Town Centre and made an inaugural speech at the Guinness World Record Breaking event of bicycling for five days by Mr. Suresh Jokin who is the second highest number world record breaker. After completing my speech, I mingled with the audience and the topic turned from the weather to politics. The most interesting and timely discussion that we had was on the current state of Ontario politics ranging from the broken promises made by Dalton McGuinty's government to the ineffective and inefficient managing of government tasks at the expense of the taxpayers' money. Premier Dalton McGuinty started off his first term by blaming the previous Conservative government for keeping the treasury virtually empty leaving nothing for him to carry out his assignments. It was an exaggeration from the reality and provided an inappropriate and lame excuse for his execution of his policies. All of his consecutive budgets have had high levels of deficit and the last budget's (the 2010/2011 budget) deficit has climbed up to $24.7 billion. If we include the 2011/2012 provincial budget even though the deficit will be less than $5 billion dollars this still does not bode well for Ontario tax payers. Former Deputy Prime Minister and Finance Minister John Manley expressed concern over Ontario's debt and alerted Mr. McGuinty of the potential for trouble. He is reported to have said something along the lines of not wanting the debt of Ontarians being passed onto the next generation. Mr. Manley of course had every right to be concerned. Along with that, Dalton McGuinty broke many promises, such as the one stating that no new taxes would be introduced, but then the Health Premium was put into effect, and collected billions of dollars from Ontarians as a result. The workers who had contributed to the Health Premium realized with a shock that not all of the money from this premium had gone entirely to the support of health care services. Almost two billion out of the three billion dollars collected had gone into the general treasury. The accountability, the trustworthiness, and the reliability have not been well kept. Many have lost confidence in these kinds of broken promises and the inappropriate execution of power. In the absence of maintaining the same level of social services that had been previously provided, the increasing of taxes cannot be justified, and the lack of efficient management has made many Ontarians disappointed. Mr. Dalton McGuinty should take the blame for the inappropriate spending of the taxpayers' money, in some cases billions of dollars. Ontarians had a very high hope in the investing of billions of dollars on the E-Health project, but the government auditor's report indicates that it has not been properly carried over. At the time of the recession, this hurt many Ontarians. Furthermore, over a million Ontarians still do not have a family doctor. The Canadian Doctors' Association met recently and drew up a list of recommendations to contribute to the betterment of a more extended health care system. But, the existing health care system has itself become sick. How can we expect patients to have access to fair treatment in a sickly system? As was mentioned during the election campaign of 2004, the waiting periods have never improved. The long-term waiting period for surgeries has not improved either. Due to these problems, some of the doctors in Ontario have pulled up stakes and have migrated elsewhere. During these two terms, the health care system has not improved; rather it is getting more deteriorated.

I would like to pinpoint certain areas where the provincial government could have taken an alternative step. For example, at the initial stage itself, presently, the Eco tax was quietly levied under the cover of charging the companies that over pollute the air by using inefficient or lower quality sources of energy. It wasn't somehow passed to the customers from the concerned producers, and the prices of certain household items skyrocketed. The Toronto Star, though it is more inclined in elevating the Liberal government, brought the cat out of the bag. The consumers had to carry the tax burden and pocket out more money. I don't know why this was so poorly planned and secretly implemented. The concern over the danger of air pollution (which is certainly legitimate) had given the green light to the government by the Ontarians under the notion that it would bring a greener and brighter future. But the way it was planned and executed appears to be aimed at generating more revenue at any cost to be lavishly spent as it was spent on the E-Health record project. When a little opposition cropped up, the concerned minister immediately took a step back and then brought forward a modification; implementation would remain suspended for ninety days and then the Eco tax would come back in a different form. It appears that the confused government was creating more confusion among the people. In fact, more than the private sector, some of the government sectors are polluting the air very badly by using poor sources of power such as coal. Why isn't the government levying a tax against itself? The McGuinty government had made a promise in their first term to replace plants that had been powered by coal to a more efficient source of power, but this has yet to be seen. Until then, how many more "eco-fees" are we going to see?

Another issue that the McGuinty government tried to capitalize on was the use of wind energy. Mr. McGuinty tried to have us all convinced that wind farms were the way to go in this province. However, not all Ontarians shared his enthusiasm. Many Ontarians who lived in regions where wind farms were established reported various health concerns and finally Mr. McGuinty had to pull the plug on future wind energy projects. I do not want to come across as too negative however, Mr. McGuinty is still committed to finding alternative sources of energy and is putting time and research into other projects such as the use of solar panels. This research is necessary because coal is a limited resource and is a major polluter and we cannot depend on it forever.

Just before levying the HST on the first of July, 2010, the government decided to pay almost a thousand dollars in three installments in June 2010, December 2010, and June 2011 to middle and low income Ontarians. The first installment cheque was to soften the blow just before the hit of the tax. With the second installment, we are given a break from the HST during the holiday season, and the third installment paid just before the election, aiming to get more votes of support from Ontarians. I think McGuinty`s government has underestimated the intelligence of Ontarians and their patriotic commitments to their province. His political cousin the respectful Paul Martin did the same thing by providing hundred dollar cheques to lower income Canadians just before the federal elections. People did not hesitate in receiving the cheques for they had come from their own taxpayers` treasury and cast their votes to the efficient and appropriate politicians thus disappointing Paul Martin by not giving enough support for him to form a government.

Let us move onto the future of the younger generation and what types of concerns this government has for them. Much more than planning ahead for their future, and allocating more investments, it is highly required that we should not mortgage their lives and pass our tax burdens onto them and make our lives much more comfortable than what we deserve. The provincial government debt is climbing up and the deficit has been growing upwards ever since Bob Rae of the Liberals, who had been the Premier of Ontario under the NDP, left the government treasury almost empty and passed it on to the Progressive Conservative party under the leadership of Mike Harris. The Progressive Conservative government balanced the budget and had a surplus in the treasury and paid quite a sum of money to cancel the debt. Today Harper's Conservative government, when the economy was in good shape, paid almost 40 billion dollars, and brought down the national debt. We, the taxpayers, pay millions as interest for the government debt and that again takes proportionately a certain amount of money from other services. The McGuinty government should have considered the exemplary measures taken by the Federal government. A sincere government with a long-term commitment with creating a better future for our children should have taken the short-term pain for the long-term gain.

The province of Ontario, the former Upper Canada, the backbone of the Canadian economy, is losing its economic influence and is on the verge of becoming a have-not province. Our forefathers shed their blood, put in their hard work and made this province the heart of the Canadian economy. Their marvelous contributions along with a diversified economy brought a substantial achievement that should be maintained by the provincial government. It is mandatory for them to do so. The oil sands in Alberta and the recent discovery of oil in Newfoundland along with the discovery of valuable minerals in the so-called Northern desert serve to shift the focus from Ontario to the North, the West and the East. We have to come to a more balanced state and create better economic plans, implement more efficient management, and develop strong interprovincial initiatives which in turn will build better relationships between all of the provinces. Better relationships build a stronger economy.

At the recent Premier's Summit in Winnipeg, Manitoba, some of the Western premiers did not want more dependency on the federal government and started taking initiatives in their economies by having international development in their trade agreements. Whereas Ontario's government has not been adequate enough in focusing and progressing on these types of projects. The premier made a visit to Israel and made some progress in promoting Ontario's trade, but he has a long way to go and has to explore better markets from the European Union to China.

It is very unfortunate that the weakened American economy somewhat affected the Canadians, particularly the state of Canadian exports. Furthermore, the protectionist policy implemented in President Obama's economy reduced, shifted and permanently closed some industries, mainly the automobile production facilities in Canada. The Ontario government should have made some alternative arrangements and brought forth some more initiatives in terms of building up better relationships in maintaining the economy. It is very unfortunate that the unemployment rate of Ontario is higher than the national average. Right now, the national unemployment rate is 7.9% and Ontario`s has not come down from 9%.

Ontario is blessed with many natural resources but is finding it difficult to have educated human resources. The natural increase of population is slowing down and the numbers of seniors are both very high and Ontario needs more skilled workers. Though it is the responsibility of the federal government, the provincial governments have some access in choosing immigrants in accordance with a specific need of the province. There are some provinces, like Manitoba, working extensively hard in choosing apples from oranges. The Ontario government has not gone far enough in having a better selection process of new immigrants who can be directly absorbed into the current labor market or current economy. Ontario received over 50% of the new immigrants to Canada, mainly processed under the federal skilled workers category, and once they came here, most of them could not find jobs in their field of expertise due to various preventing factors such as acceptance of credentials, lack of Canadian experience and lack of sufficient guidance in exploring the right jobs. I have seen doctors, engineers, accountants, and lawyers who have been working as limousine and taxi drivers and delivering pizza.

Let us look into the educational fabric of Ontario. There are a number of people making complaints about the closing of certain schools. My concern is that we need to channel more money into the classroom. The money that we spend for our education is more of an investment than expenditure. I have not seen much structural change and the current provincial government have not made any attempt to resolve long overdue problems. When Janet Ecker was the Minister of Education, a couple of drastic measures were taken and some of them were controversial, but the ones that have been accepted and implemented are very fruitful. The example of common examinations for grade 3, grade 6, grade 9, and the grade 10 literacy test, has been slightly deviated and moving on in a different direction. It was clearly proclaimed that such common examinations were a good evaluation tool, but right now, it has been said by some, that the examinations are made easier and marks are inflated. If so, it defeated the purpose and misled the educators and children. The dropout rate is another problem in Ontario. Almost 30% of high school students and 40% of first-year students in certain universities cannot cope with their studies and end up dropping out. There has been talk about the creation of special schools to help certain groups of children who are at risk of dropping out. However, this is a controversial idea as the opening of a school with an afro-centric curriculum in Toronto has pointed out. Many Ontarians object to these kinds of schools out of the fear that this will lead to segregation. The reasons why students drop out of school are diverse but it is mainly because of the lack of proper learning and teaching processes and there is no point in blaming the parents or the kids and allowing the government to wash their collective hands. We expect a qualitative education in line with today`s fast-changing world so our young people are equipped to face this brave new world.

It is high time for Ontarians to have a change of government. It is not for the sake of change, but rather for the betterment of the province by having a leader who can face all the challenges, solve all the accumulated problems, wipe out deficiencies with qualitative leadership, and build a better Ontario for us and the future generations. Change is one of the few guarantees in life and I have faith in change.

Red Shouldn't Always be Red.

I do not usually watch any thriller movies or dramas. But I enjoy the movies from the comedy of nature and the occasional hit like "Avatar" produced by Cameron. These days, I am fortunate enough to watch a thrilling drama with a gourmet pinch and dash of comedy and seriousness on the stage known as the Ontario Legislative Assembly or Queen's Park. Premier Dalton McGuinty stars as the valiant hero, the rest of his colleagues in supporting roles, the villains and back benchers star as the silent backdrop who always dances to whatever tune is playing on the political sound system.

The title of the drama is **"Ontario on Top"**. Now before I get into the current act, let me take you back to some of the interesting scenes that have taken place recently and have ceased to be the centre of attention. Just a couple of weeks before the by—election in the riding of Toronto Center, voters did not pay much attention assuming that it was nothing more than a by—election and that there would not be any drastic change in the government except for the possibility that it would be an indicator of the heart beat of the voters and the other ridings would take heed and gauge their support. Furthermore, Toronto Center is a traditionally Liberal riding. Even in the last federal election, Mr. Bob Rae former NDP Premier of Ontario and a former leadership candidate of the Liberal Party and the political critic of that party won in the federal election with an over whelming majority.

A few weeks prior to the provincial by-election a political bombshell was dropped on the voting public by saying that Toronto Grace Hospital located in the same riding, was going to be closed due to the lack of funds. This woke up the entire population residing in that riding and surrounding areas that have been making use of those facilities. It was the talk and concern of the entire city. The government might have become engaged in finding the resources or reallocating them. However, my concern is that the timing of conveying the decision of the government not to close Toronto Grace as additional funding (by some miracle) would be made available was deliberately made to get the masses on their side and garner more votes. Personally I really enjoyed watching this scene and came to appreciate the gravity of political maneuvering.

After a short intermission, the annual show began as the Provincial Budget for the financial year 2010 opened. The center attraction was the Finance Minister the Hon. Dwight Duncan, the hero who was seated beside the Premier Dalton McGuinty and accompanied by cabinet ministers and other colleagues. The Minster for Finance appeared very relaxed and stood firmly, probably due to the new shoes that he was wearing. These shoes by the way would have been produced while we were in the peak of the recession when manufacturers did not have many sales and had ample time to produce them. While he was comfortable delivering the budget, his colleagues constantly aroused their emotional support by giving rounds of applause, but not to the level of a standing ovation.

The opening ballad that was played was the proposal of the creation of employment for thousands and thousands. At first glance this appeared to be rather encouraging, a sweet and tasty appetizer for the spring patio. But as I watched for a couple more minutes, my appetite quickly spoiled when I realized the proposed plans, structure and the strategy that were presented was nothing but the same old wine in a colored glass served alongside stale crackers. There was nothing much to get excited about.

There was nothing new and by now sounded all too familiar with the broken promises made by this government. It was not very realistic and I began to grind my popcorn between my teeth. We heard a similar melody but with different lyrics in Ottawa a couple weeks before when the Federal Budget was presented in the House of Commons. Did Queen's Park borrow the Federal Government's script but leave out the sense of vision that the Federal Government espoused?

Then Act Two began and the freezing of salaries for the legislature's, and non unionized public service employees was presented. This adds up to just over a million dollars for this year and the forthcoming couple of years. This appeared to be a good example to others and was at least symbolic of the idea that charity begins at home. At that time, my mind went back to the archives and I remembered the generous increase in salary for the members of provincial parliament (M.P.P's) within the last few years. This was done when the economy was in a terrible state. The timing of these salary freezes is wonderful for the government because 70% of the contracts will not be renewed before 2012 after the October 2011 election. This will not cause any adverse effects by the contract and unionized workers by causing strikes and other unpleasant actions against the government.

I am so happy that the McGuinty government had the courage to listen to Mr. Jim Flaherty, the Federal Finance Minister by giving tax breaks to the corporate sector. This had been advised earlier but fell on deaf ears. At this time however, it was taken into serious consideration and a tax break on the harmonized sales tax would add up to over two billion dollars. This will certainly help in motivating entrepreneurs by reducing the cost of production and in turn will encourage sales and a boom in sales will keep current employees working and provide more employment opportunities. In particular, mass unemployed workers, those who had been laid off and retrained and new immigrants in the skilled workers category will benefit the most. The current unemployment rate of Ontario (9. %) is higher than the national unemployment rate of 8.3 % and most of the unemployed are directly or indirectly attached to the manufacturing industries. We cannot wipe out the reality that a sizable number of jobs have permanently disappeared although the reason for this is very controversial; some of these industries could have been retained if proper care had been taken and if we had listened to the Feds earlier.

Dalton McGuinty somewhat deviates from the standard and traditional Liberal path on tax reduction and relief for the corporate sector. A few days after this budget was presented at the Legislative Assembly, the Federal Liberals disagreed with Mr. Stephen Harper's tax reductions in the corporate sectors and were determined to eliminate or take an alternative stand on it, if they were to form a government sooner or later. The Liberals are always in favor of keeping taxes intact and as far as possible avoiding tax reductions with the intention of reducing personal income tax. Mr. Paul Martin, as the finance minister, under the Chrétien government took a firm stand on reducing personal income tax during the recovery stage of the recession of the early 1990's. Though the provincial party has its own agenda and freedom to plan and execute their policies, underneath there might be some pressure that may slow them down, if not, at least prompt a 'U' turn.

There are two issues that are of top concern to Ontarians; the regaining of lost employment and opening avenues for new employment. Reasonable security of employment is also important in order to plan and execute their plans with confidence. Many more are concerned and centered on the manufacturing sectors and service industry. They cannot be satisfied with fabulous promises with all sorts of magnified supporting figures. Of course at this critical time of recovery at the tail end of a recession, the global economy is one of the main factors that determine economic growth and increase in employment opportunities. This should be coupled with as the right honorable Prime Minster Steven Harper said when U.S President Barrack Obama was in Ottawa on his first state visit to Canada that the stimulation of our economy along with the American economy is required. This means that the USA is our single major trade partner with 85 percent of our visible and invisible exports going to that country. Their strength in purchasing power will determine our level of exports and it does not guarantee that when there is an economic boom in the U.S that it will buy proportionally more from us. The recent trend and the complexity of the political and economic interaction with Canada and other nations with the States is, in reality, not giving due recognition to Canada. Although Canada and the States are partners in the North American Free Trade Agreement, the USA expects Canada to always dance to her tune. It is always possible that the reaction when Canada deviates from the path would be an adverse affect in the economic relationship. We experienced the restrictions made on soft wood lumber and meat exports for example. The protectionist policy of President Obama and having a free trade agreement with China are very much a concern for our economy. We have to play our cards well and open new venues in our exports and investments. This is a very timely but necessary challenge.

There was nothing much in the provincial budget in terms of health care expenditure and capital investment this year. The rising health care costs accounts for 46% of government expenditures today and will be up to 70% in 12 years time. This is not only alarming but we never get any answers to our questions regarding health care spending nor does the government propose any projects or plans. It is possibly because of the fear of questions surrounding the improper spending of over a billion dollars of tax payer's money on e-health. Furthermore, the public has not forgotten that McGuinty in the past promised in the election campaign that he would not introduce any new taxes but then brought in a new tax as the health care premium, thus breaking his promise.

Though our cosmopolitan city of Toronto is the capital of the province of Ontario, it is regarded as the most important city in Canada, having the head offices of the most powerful financial institutions on Bay Street just like Wall Street in the U.S. It is a miniature globe having the constant inflow of new immigrants from over 170 countries. It is the most populous city in Canada and the 5th in North America. It has been chosen for the G 20 Summit on 26-27 June 2010 and the Pan Am Games in 2015. The infrastructure of Toronto, including public transportation has been deteriorating day by day. The maintenance of the subway is very poor and there are broken ceilings, insufficient lights and many other repairs are required. I being a Torontonian, expected like many others, that there might be some kind of inclusion of capital projects on the extension of the subway lines but no word was substantially mentioned. Many such pressing issues were ignored and more concentration was given to the North. I do not under value the problems that those Ontarians have been facing and I do believe that they have to be addressed sooner or later, but not at the expense of one to the other. I do not know whether it is an oversight or having the motivation of gaining more political support by trying to turn the political tide in the Liberals favor.

Let me compare this budget to that of the recent Federal Budget and see if the Provincial Budget has any substantial vision that will lead to the future of Ontario becoming stronger, brighter and competitive in the fast moving global economy. The Feds are smarter than the rest of the developed nations these days. They have very solid policies and supervision of the monetary and other economic sectors. It has been shown that during the current recession where most of the financial institutions were shaking and were unable to survive without support from their respective governments before their operations were finally secured, in Canada such a situation never arose. In fact Canada was late to join and first to get out of the recession. The Feds planned to have checks and balances on the interest rates, inflation, and investment and began to plan and act well in advance. The Feds are smart in capitalizing international events by hosting the G8 and G20 Summits and the 2015 Pan Am Games in Toronto. The only vision that I have seen in the Provincial Budget is to foresee the future of Northern Ontario and other than that there is no vision on infrastructure, health care, replacing the job vacancies created by the baby boomers, welcoming and integrating new immigrants into the work force, investors and post secondary education. If this budget was a drama—I would not even step into the theatre.

It is high time for the Government of Ontario to stop this province from running off a cliff and falling into the dust.

CHAPTER NINETEEN

Canada's Mission and Vision

There are many factors that have contributed to the weaving of the fabric of Canada. It began geologically in the pre – Cambrian era and during the structural changes over many eras, it blessed this country with over sixty valuable resources such as the oil sands which ranks second in the world when it comes to size, uranium, zinc, gold, copper, diamonds, and nickel. But only a small portion has been mined in two hundred locations and has generated $34.7 billion in 2010 and accounts for 2.8 % of the national GDP. We are also privileged with having abundant fresh water that accounts for 7% of the world's total renewable fresh water supply and is the third highest in the world. We also have a very large amount of arable land for agriculture. But even with all of these valuable resources Canada still has a long way to go in terms of using them for finished products, increasing their export, and reducing the export of raw materials.

Global warming is another issue that is going to be a challenge in the lives of Canadians and for the economy. However, it is more than a matter of climactic change that causes droughts which affect the sector of agriculture. Most of the birds that cross the border without any entry visa during the fall season in order to avoid the shivering cold winter in the north would have been happy to remain there if it were not for the resources and their habitats that bring them back north each spring. The question of protecting our sovereignty has also become a challenge and keeping the undue claims on our bodies of water by the main countries in the Arctic region and others such as the United States of America, Russia, and Denmark at bay requires much vigilance. Prime Minister Harper has frequently mentioned that we have to protect our north and keep it strong and free and it is highly appreciated that a portion of our men in uniform having returned from Afghanistan, are stationed in the north.

Our good old traditional friends south of broader abandoned their British traditions, and discontinued their relationship with the British Commonwealth as a sign of their true independence. They proclaimed that they established a brand new nation with its own constitution, cultural mosaic and foreign policies and proved to the world that with freedom of expression, freedom of the press and with rights that are enshrined in law, they would be able to reach the top of the ladder as a world power. In contrast, the British, the Germans, the Scandinavians and the Japanese have been building up their nations in their own unique ways. Once upon a time, the ancient Egyptians, Babylonians, the Romans and Greeks threw light into the world but the Egyptians eventually lost their identity the rest are no more the leaders of the developed world, they have been reduced to followers. We do have another exceptional country rising up in the case of Brazil, the southern star of the Amazon River basin and I believe that after the Mayan civilization in Central America, that it is going to the next super power south of the United States of America.

The nature of the Canadian structure is very complex in many sections of its fabric. As such, the main issues that Canada is facing are as follows:

1. The dispute with the first inhabitants who arrived in Canada
2. The entry and flourishing of the Europeans
3. The evolution of the political process and its independence
4. The system of government
5. The foreign policy
6. The technological challenges
7. The future and current economy and Dutch disease
8. The intact or disintegration of regions.
9. Could Canada be a potential super power?

The time will come sooner rather than later in terms of addressing and resolving the grievance from the First Nations and an everlasting amalgamated solution for the both parties and is only a wish rather than the will. I do not think it will die by itself because it has revived and received international attention and some of the international bodies have pinpointed and accused Canada of violating the human rights of the first nations. Though it is a partial exaggeration, still it cannot be ignored.

There is also the question of reforming the parliamentary system in Canada by the introduction of Senate reform through amending the constitution and there is also the question of whether or not to keep the office of the Governor General in place since this office represents the British monarchy. It is fair to ask if Canada's democracy would be better reflected if we actually voted for our Senators and for the Governor General rather than having them appointed by the Prime Minister.

It is unavoidable but an accepted fact that whether or not Canada likes it, the door for the constant inflow of immigrants is to be widely opened. There is not much in change in the number and type of immigrants that are being welcomed, recruited and accepted but the source countries will be shifting from its traditional favoured regions. It is not the prediction or the desire of the politicians or those who want to maintain the current identity of the Canadian mosaic at the expense of maintaining the healthy economic progress in a very competitive global economy. The human resources department is gradually shedding its regional and ethnic sentiments and is focusing more on productivity, the foreign supply in the labour market. The elasticity of the supply of human capital is more flexible than ever before and the trend will continue at least for another three decades due to the number of baby boomers that will be retiring from the workforce.

One of the top most secrets for the overall success of Canada and the unique image that has been portrayed internationally is the stable consecutive governments that Canada has been experiencing and there is no doubt that this will continue in the immediate future. The Canadian population compared to its resources both natural and manmade are abundant and the country is able to provide a decent life for everybody one way or other and also the density of population within the easily inhabitable land is pretty low. This prevents the creation of slum areas where the life of the people is below the poverty line and becomes a center of crime growing with the business of illegal drugs, the flourishing of the underground economy, increased prostitution, high concentrations of illegal immigrants and criminals which, when taken together, create an unhealthy environment for everyone, but especially children.

There are hardly any conflicts in Canadian politics. Though some political parties make use of the political freedom of information in order to assert their own agenda and there some parties that have Marxist leanings, their influence is very low. I have been keenly watching the growth and the adjustments in political ideology of a popular national party, the New Democratic Party (NDP). Their inclination towards the socialist ideology is not based on the scientific socialism based on Marxism; rather they accept private enterprise as the means of the economic structure and are not moving towards a state monopoly. The policies of the Liberals and the Conservatives are basically similar with the Republican and Democratic parties in the U.S.A and the Conservative and Labour parties in England.

The celebration of the victory of the bicentennial year of the War of 1812 between the United States of America and the British Empire, reminds us of how the Quebecers attached themselves to Canada. When there is a foreign attack, interference and aggressive moves made, it is the wish and will of the majority of Quebecers that economic interests and national sovereignty trump ethnicity.

Former Liberal leader Michael Ignatief recently commented that Quebec eventually will become an independent country and that a victory for Scottish separatists in an expected 2014 referendum will launch a new effort by Quebec nationalists to fulfil their sovereignty dreams. He also mentioned that Quebec and the rest of Canada have little to say to each other and that the two already are "almost" separate countries. He said in British Broadcasting Corporation (BBC) interview with Glen Campbell that the devolution of central powers, whether from London to Edinburgh or from Ottawa to Quebec City, likely will be only temporary.

The Result of the Quebec Election 2012

In spite of the differences and changes in opinion the worst did not come to pass. The decision that was made and expressed by the Quebecers in the provincial election has not given the indication that the sentiment around Quebec sovereignty is dead nor is it aggressively moving on. Although the Party Quebecois won the majority of the votes to reign the province, it only gained 32% of the cast votes with 32 seats while the Liberals were able to reach 31% of the votes with 50 provincial members of parliament.

The main reason for the victory of the Party Quebecois in this election was the weaker situation of the Liberals in the last three teams and the people wanted a change hoping that the political mechanization would work for better than allowing the same government to continue and make the situation worse. It is evident that the incumbent Quebec Premier Jean Charest was defeated in his own riding of Sherbrooke and being the Premier since 2003 was bold enough to accept the responsibility of defeat. He should have taken more serious measures in adjusting the economic plans and appropriate measures well in advance. Since he was a national leader for the Progressive Conservative Party and from the time he was Premier in 2003 till the election in 2012 he had a better chance and opportunity than anyone else to be in the same position. The high level of deficit in the pre election budget and the loan by the province of $183.7 billion also was not a good sign of maintaining a healthy economy. The spending of tax payer's money in some contracts became an intense issue just before the election campaign. The prolonged strike on the issue of the increase in tuition fees by the student unions was not resolved and it earned the provincial government a bad reputation and brought down the image a bit. I would not under estimate the other side of the coin of the victory for Ms. Pauline Marois and her party for it also has significant supporters for Quebec sovereignty. Now the ball is in the court of the right honourable Prime Minister in handling the case by satisfying the demand of the provincial minority government. Already Ms. Marois has proposed a list of items including new powers for Quebec over employment insurance, culture and communications, immigration and foreign policy. I hope the grievances will be healed and be together and that time will provide the right solutions.

Another unique feature of our political system is that due to our stability, we do not allow ourselves to be overly influenced by the opinions of others within and without. I would cite a simple example of how various leaders reacted when the American government requested Canada to allow them to have special access in using our space for their protection from any air attacks made by Russia. All of our recent Prime Ministers such as Jean Chretien, Paul Martin and Steven Harper did not agree to spare even an inch and rejected their request. I also happy to notice the trend of the NDP in the past few years in attempting to have a more concerned and broad outlook on national issues rather than concerns of their own party.

In spite of the successful operation of parliament, still the questions of structural changes are pending and an overhaul is in the air and it has to be addressed before the issue mushrooms. The reformation of the Senate is an issue has been lingering for years and the NDP once said it would be better for us to eliminate it and the conservatives wants to have an elected House of Senators.

It appears that Canada has only one place in the government where the people's voice can be placed directly and that is in only the House of Commons. As far as the head of state is concerned, let the Queen of Canada remain as long as she is. There is a question of what would be next in terms of whether or not to accept her heir and there are many who hold the attitude of waiting and seeing. But there are opinions that Canada should become a republic. There was another opinion expressed during the provincial election of Quebec 2012 by a politician that it is a waste of money and resources in having a Governor General as a representative of the Queen but it appears that this comment targeted the institution, not the individual.

The modern world is highly influenced by the infiltration of technology from the bed room to space craft and Canada is not an exception to this. It has become a high yielding business and is dominated by a handful of nations and marketing around the globe and Canada is one of the fast growing markets but is not efficient enough in capitalizing the world market. It is another area where we have to have more development in production and marketing research.

The national economic growth and international challenges in the current world even before the recession of 2008 have a very high impact on the Canadian economy internally and internationally. The mining and manufacturing industrial sectors contribute a substantial portion of the GDP. The oil sand exports have saved Canada from a weaker economic position like the United States of America, European Union and other major world economic powers. The high level of export of oil sand has also have a negative impact on the exports of the manufacturing sectors, mainly because of the high value of the Canadian dollar in the foreign exchange market. Our manufactured products find difficulty in competing with other producers in the international market. Alberta primarily depends on oil sand as a single commodity for its revenue whereas the back bone of the income of the provinces of Ontario and Quebec come from the manufacturing sector. These industries are both necessary and some sort of compromise will have to be reached.

The regions from the west and the north are quite dormant but sometimes feel like their voices are not heard but they do have somewhat of a fair share in the national cake, though there are certain areas where their demands have not been fully met. However, when watching the trends in the meetings of the provincial governments and the discussions by the Premiers I could easily predict that for another decade or more it would not be a pressing concern for national unity.

Canada is a nation that has its own identity, goals and vision and wants to always be sound. It is a well reputed and respectful player and is not self aggrandizing nor overly ambitious for its own good. We do things in a way that is unique to us as a nation and world player.

I am forever proud to be a citizen of this wonderful nation and may God bless my Canada.

REFERENCE

Authors	Titles of the Book
Valerie Knowles	Strangers at Our Gates
(Edited by)Jon H. Pammett	The Canadian Federal Election of 2006
(Edited by) Andre Pratte	Quebec Federalists Speak up for Change
(edited by) Elspeth Cameron	Multiculturalism & Immigration in Canada
(edited by) James Bickerton & Alain-G. Gagnon	Canadian Politics
(edited by) Peter S. Li	Race and Ethnic Relations in Canada
(edited by) Stephen white, Judy Batt & Paul G. Lewis	Naming Canada
Alan Rayburn	Naming Canada
Alexander Himelfarb / C.James Richardson	Sociology For Canadians
Barbara A. Crow / Lise Gotell	Open Boundaries
Benjamin Drew	The Refugee
Bennett Jaenen Brune Skeoch	Canada a north American Nation

Bill Clinton	My Life
Bruce Hutchison	The Incredible Canadian
D. F. Putnam / R. G. Putnam	Canada: a regional analysis
Daiva Stasiulis, Rejean Lachapelle & Ilze Peterson Taylor	Cultural Boundaries and The Cohesion Of Canada
David Matas with Ilana	Closing The Doors
Evelyn Kallen	Ethnicity and Human Rights in Canada
George W. Bush	Decision Points
Jean Chretien	My years as Prime Minister
Joe Clark	A Nation Too Good To Lose
John English	Citizen of the World: The Life of Pierre Elliott
John R. Barber	Modern European History
John Sawatsky	Mulroney The Politics of Ambition
Leo Diredger (Editor)	The Canadian Ethnic Mosaic
Marc Lynch	The Arab Uprising
Mario Pei	The Story of Language
Marvin Harris	Culture, People, Nature
Merton / Nisbet	Contemporary Social Problems
Micheal Bliss	Right Honourable Men
Myrna Kostash	The Next Canada

Norine Dresser	Multicultural Manners
Peter C. Newman	The Canadian Establishment
Peter Stalker	The Work of Strangers: A survey of international labour migration
Preston Manning	The New Canada
Roger Riendeau	A Brief History of Canada
Stewart Bell	Cold Terror
Stuart A. Queen / Robert W. Habenstein	The Famly in Various Cultures
W. E. Mann	Canada: A Sociological Profile
W. Gunther Plaut	Refugee Determination in Canada
William Johnson	Stephen Harper and the future of Canada

APPENDIX

Tables

Permanent residents

Facts and Figures 2009—Immigration overview:
Permanent and Temporary Residents

Canada—Permanent residents by gender and category, 1985 to 2009

Category	1985	1986	1987	1988	1989	1990		1991	1992	1993	1194	1995	1996
Family class	59,933	50,868	55,260	60,610	66,786	62,287	65,116	62,263	63,364	70,513	66,241	65,577	65,200
Economic immigrants	128,350	97,912	109,246	136,285	155,720	137,863	121,045	133,747	156,312	138,251	131,244	149,070	153,498
Refugees	24,307	22,842	24,397	30,091	27,915	25,115	25,984	32,686	35,775	32,499	27,955	21,860	22,846
Other immigrants	3,400	2,547	1,031	460	206	3,780	9,200	7,124	6,787	10,375	11,312	10,737	10,634
Category not stated	0	0	0	0	1	0	1	0	2	2	1	2	1
Gender not stated	48	29	18	9	12	4	2	5	1	2	1	1	0
Total	**216,038**	**174,198**	**189,952**	**227,455**	**250,640**	**229,049**	**221,348**	**235,825**	**262,241**	**251,642**	**236,754**	**247,247**	**252,179**

Category	1985	1986	1987	1988	1989	1990	1991	1992	1993	1994	1995	1996
Family class	41.4	37.1	29.9	26.7	27.8	30.8	33.1	34.4	39.5	37.9	31.7	25.5
Economic immigrants	31.1	37.9	51.9	51.4	47.7	45.7	36.8	37.9	42.6	47.9	52.7	58.4
Refugees	25.0	23.2	16.6	20.0	22.7	22.0	28.4	25.5	14.7	10.7	15.1	14.0
Other immigrants	2.4	1.7	1.7	1.9	1.7	1.6	1.7	2.2	3.2	3.5	0.5	2.1
Category not stated	0.0	0.0	0.0	0.0	0.0	0.0	0.0	0.0	0.0	0.0	0.0	0.0
Males	**100.0**	**100.0**	**100.0**	**100.0**	**100.0**	**100.0**	**100.0**	**100.0**	**100.0**	**100.0**	**100.0**	**100.0**
Family class	51.4	48.2	41.0	36.7	35.8	38.3	42.6	44.8	47.7	45.6	40.7	34.8
Economic immigrants	30.9	34.3	45.5	48.0	46.4	44.8	37.5	37.3	39.9	43.5	47.7	52.6
Refugees	15.2	15.5	11.6	13.3	15.8	15.1	18.0	15.7	9.5	7.7	11.4	11.3
Other immigrants	2.6	2.0	1.8	2.0	2.0	1.7	1.9	2.2	2.8	3.2	0.3	1.3

Category not stated	0.0	0.0	0.0	0.0	0.0	0.0	0.0	0.0	0.0	0.0	0.0	0.0
Females	**100.0**	**100.0**	**100.0**	**100.0**	**100.0**	**100.0**	**100.0**	**100.0**	**100.0**	**100.0**	**100.0**	**100.0**
Family class	46.5	42.7	35.4	31.8	31.8	34.5	37.8	39.7	43.9	42.0	36.4	30.2
Economic immigrants	30.9	36.0	48.7	49.6	47.1	45.2	37.2	37.6	41.2	45.6	50.1	55.5
Refugees	19.8	19.3	14.1	16.6	19.2	18.6	23.2	20.5	11.9	9.1	13.2	12.6
Other immigrants	2.5	1.8	1.8	2.0	1.9	1.7	1.8	2.2	3.0	3.3	0.4	1.7
Category not stated	0.0	0.0	0.0	0.0	0.0	0.0	0.0	0.0	0.0	0.0	0.0	0.0
Gender not stated	0.3	0.2	0.1	0.0	0.0	0.0	0.0	0.0	0.0	0.0	0.0	0.0
Total	**100.0**	**100.0**	**100.0**	**100.0**	**100.0**	**100.0**	**100.0**	**100.0**	**100.0**	**100.0**	**100.0**	**100.0**

Category	1997	1998	1999	2000	2001	2002	2003	2004	2005	2006	2007	2008	2009
Family class	22.7	23.4	23.1	20.7	21.1	21.5	23.4	20.8	19.6	23.3	23.2	22.5	22.1
Economic immigrants	62.9	60.5	62.2	64.7	66.8	65.3	60.0	61.4	63.3	58.9	59.5	63.9	64.1
Refugees	12.7	14.5	14.2	14.4	12.1	11.7	13.0	14.9	14.5	13.7	12.5	9.3	9.5
Other immigrants	1.8	1.6	0.6	0.2	0.1	1.4	3.6	3.0	2.6	4.1	4.7	4.3	4.3
Category not stated	0.0	0.0	0.0	0.0	0.0	0.0	0.0	0.0	0.0	0.0	0.0	0.0	0.0
Males	**100.0**	**100.0**	**100.0**	**100.0**	**100.0**	**100.0**	**100.0**	**100.0**	**100.0**	**100.0**	**100.0**	**100.0**	**100.0**
Family class	32.7	34.7	34.9	32.4	32.1	32.7	35.0	31.7	28.5	32.4	32.4	30.2	29.4
Economic immigrants	56.1	52.2	53.1	55.3	57.6	55.2	49.7	52.3	56.1	51.2	51.6	57.0	57.8
Refugees	9.9	11.8	11.6	12.1	10.2	10.2	10.6	12.9	12.8	12.2	11.1	8.4	8.6
Other immigrants	1.4	1.3	0.5	0.2	0.1	1.9	4.6	3.1	2.6	4.1	4.8	4.3	4.2

Category not stated	0.0	0.0	0.0	0.0	0.0	0.0	0.0	0.0	0.0	0.0	0.0	0.0	0.0
Females	**100.0**	**100.0**	**100.0**	**100.0**	**100.0**	**100.0**	**100.0**	**100.0**	**100.0**	**100.0**	**100.0**	**100.0**	**100.0**
Family class	27.7	29.2	29.1	26.6	26.6	27.2	29.4	26.4	24.2	28.0	28.0	26.5	25.9
Economic immigrants	59.4	56.2	57.5	59.9	62.1	60.2	54.7	56.7	59.6	54.9	55.4	60.3	60.9
Refugees	11.3	13.1	12.8	13.2	11.1	11.0	11.7	13.9	13.6	12.9	11.8	8.8	9.1
Other immigrants	1.6	1.5	0.5	0.2	0.1	1.7	4.2	3.0	2.6	4.1	4.8	4.3	4.2
Category not stated	0.0	0.0	0.0	0.0	0.0	0.0	0.0	0.0	0.0	0.0	0.0	0.0	0.0
Gender not stated	0.0	0.0	0.0	0.0	0.0	0.0	0.0	0.0	0.0	0.0	0.0	0.0	0.0

Facts and figures 2009 – Immigration overview:
Permanent and temporary residents
Permanent residents

Category	2000	2001	2002	2003	2004	2005	2006	2007	2008	2009
Spouses and partners	36,814	39,402	34,197	39,676	44,218	45,448	45,303	44,912	44,204	43,894
Sons and daughters	3,951	3,932	3,645	3,618	3,037	3,232	3,191	3,338	3,255	3,027
Parents and grandparents	17,771	21,341	22,244	19,385	12,733	12,475	20,005	15,813	16,599	17,179
Others	2,080	2,119	2,205	2,438	2,278	2,209	2,016	2,179	1,519	1,100
Family class	**60,616**	**66,794**	**62,291**	**65,117**	**62,266**	**63,364**	**70,515**	**66,242**	**65,577**	**65,200**
Skilled workers—p.a.*	52,120	58,911	52,974	45,377	47,894	52,269	44,161	41,251	43,360	40,735
Skilled workers—s.d.**	66,468	78,323	69,756	59,847	65,557	77,969	61,783	56,601	60,374	55,227
Canadian experience class—p.a.*										1,775
Canadian experience class—s.d.**										770

Entrepreneurs—p.a.*	1,658	1,608	1,176	781	668	750	820	581	446	372
Entrepreneurs—s.d.**	4,529	4,479	3,302	2,197	1,800	2,098	2,273	1,579	1,255	943
Self-employed—p.a.*	795	705	636	446	366	302	320	203	164	179
Self-employed—s.d.**	1,732	1,451	1,271	981	824	714	632	373	341	358
Investors—p.a.*	1,390	1,768	1,234	972	1,671	2,591	2,201	2,025	2,832	2,872
Investors—s.d.**	3,561	4,574	3,402	2,723	4,428	7,020	5,830	5,420	7,370	7,435
Provincial/territorial nominees—p.a.*	368	410	680	1,417	2,086	2,643	4,672	6,329	8,343	11,801
Provincial/territorial nominees—s.d.**	884	864	1,447	3,001	4,162	5,404	8,664	10,765	14,075	18,577
Live-in caregivers—p.a.*	1,759	1,874	1,521	2,230	2,496	3,063	3,547	3,433	6,157	6,273
Live-in caregivers—s.d.**	1,023	753	464	1,074	1,796	1,489	3,348	2,684	4,354	6,181
Economic immigrants	**136,287**	**155,720**	**137,863**	**121,046**	**133,748**	**156,312**	**138,251**	**131,244**	**149,071**	**153,498**
Government-assisted refugees	10,669	8,697	7,505	7,508	7,411	7,424	7,326	7,573	7,295	7,425

Privately sponsored refugees	5,036	3,512	3,588	3,337	2,976	3,116	3,252	3,043	3,576	2,933
Refugees landed in Canada	7,204	6,994	11,696	15,884	19,935	15,901	11,264	10,546	11,897	12,993
Refugee dependants	3,181	4,059	5,098	5,952	5,441	6,259	3,960	4,021	3,749	3,497
Refugees	**22,846**	**21,860**	**27,955**	**32,499**	**35,776**	**32,687**	**25,984**	**25,115**	**27,919**	**30,092**
Retirees, DROC and PDRCC* *	6	2	15	23	20	53	79	—	206	460
Temporary resident permit holders	106	113	107	136	123	148	97	—	0	0
H and C* * * cases	3,142	3,452	4,346	4,312	3,110	2,984	2,375	619	0	0
Other H and C cases outside the family class / Public Policy	7,380	7,170	6,844	5,904	3,534	3,939	6,649	3,026	0	0
Other immigrants	**10,634**	**10,737**	**11,312**	**10,375**	**6,787**	**7,124**	**9,200**	**3,780**	**206**	**460**
Category not stated	1	2	1	2	2	0	1	0	1	0
Total	**252,179**	**247,247**	**236,754**	**251,642**	**262,241**	**235,825**	**221,348**	**229,049**	**250,640**	**227,455**

Canada—Permanent residents by gender and age, 2009

Facts and figures 2009—Immigration overview:

Permanent and temporary residents

Permanent residents

Source area	2000	2001	2002	2003	2004	2005	2006	2007	2008	2009
Africa and the Middle East	40,908	48,238	46,340	43,676	49,531	49,279	51,860	48,564	51,312	56,154
Asia and Pacific	120,736	132,938	119,055	113,727	114,568	138,050	126,472	112,657	117,480	117,178
South and Central America	17,004	20,212	19,470	20,349	22,254	24,640	24,303	25,890	26,495	26,778
United States	5,828	5,909	5,294	6,013	7,507	9,263	10,942	10,449	11,216	9,723
Europe and the United Kingdom	42,958	43,293	38,866	37,570	41,902	40,906	37,944	39,070	40,650	42,313
Source area not stated	12	38	20	11	58	102	119	123	93	33
Gender not stated	9	12	4	2	5	1	2	1	1	0
Total	227,455	250,640	229,049	221,348	235,825	262,241	251,642	236,754	247,247	252,179

Source area	2000	2001	2002	2003	2004	2005	2006	2007	2008	2009
Africa and the Middle East	18.0	19.2	20.2	19.7	21.0	18.8	20.6	20.5	20.8	22.3
Asia and Pacific	53.1	53.0	52.0	51.4	48.6	52.6	50.3	47.6	47.5	46.5
South and Central America	7.5	8.1	8.5	9.2	9.4	9.4	9.7	10.9	10.7	10.6
United States	2.6	2.4	2.3	2.7	3.2	3.5	4.3	4.4	4.5	3.9
Europe and the United Kingdom	18.9	17.3	17.0	17.0	17.8	15.6	15.1	16.5	16.4	16.8
Source area not stated	0.0	0.0	0.0	0.0	0.0	0.0	0.0	0.1	0.0	0.0
Gender not stated	0.0	0.0	0.0	0.0	0.0	0.0	0.0	0.0	0.0	0.0
Total	**100.0**	**100.0**	**100.0**	**100.0**	**100.0**	**100.0**	**100.0**	**100.0**	**100.0**	**100.0**

Facts and figures 2009—Immigration overview:
Permanent and temporary residents—Permanent residents
Canada—Permanent residents by category and source area

Source area	2000	2001	2002	2003	2004	2005	2006	2007	2008	2009
Africa and the Middle East	7,060	7,810	6,389	7,463	7,903	7,625	8,353	8,966	9,313	9,686
Asia and Pacific	32,531	35,262	36,650	38,685	34,072	36,537	43,011	37,565	34,619	34,425
South and Central America	8,745	10,039	7,832	7,387	7,447	7,170	7,042	7,372	7,711	7,736
United States	3,180	3,614	2,783	2,987	3,706	4,146	4,468	3,952	4,685	4,453
Europe and the United Kingdom	9,095	10,054	8,629	8,588	9,115	7,864	7,625	8,362	9,226	8,892
Source area not stated	5	15	8	7	23	22	16	25	23	8
Family class	**60,616**	**66,794**	**62,291**	**65,117**	**62,266**	**63,364**	**70,515**	**66,242**	**65,577**	**65,200**
Africa and the Middle East	23,410	30,706	30,604	25,385	27,591	28,650	31,346	28,175	31,225	33,873
Asia and Pacific	78,659	87,727	71,212	62,241	66,480	87,740	69,423	62,298	73,303	73,156

South and Central America	5,955	7,475	8,040	7,313	8,454	8,205	7,191	9,466	11,392	12,392
United States	2,575	2,240	1,938	1,703	2,977	3,804	4,498	4,785	4,926	3,695
Europe and the United Kingdom	25,685	27,553	26,059	24,403	28,242	27,912	25,791	26,520	28,225	30,382
Source area not stated	3	19	10	1	4	1	2	0	0	0
Economic immigrants	**136,287**	**155,720**	**137,863**	**121,046**	**133,748**	**156,312**	**138,251**	**131,244**	**149,071**	**153,498**
Africa and the Middle East	10,340	9,662	8,820	9,535	12,592	11,443	10,222	9,252	9,015	10,832
Asia and Pacific	9,326	9,858	10,198	10,166	12,159	11,849	10,573	9,569	6,399	6,648
South and Central America	2,220	2,657	2,842	3,712	4,596	7,634	7,601	6,077	4,699	3,678
United States	69	55	33	45	132	772	1,246	831	482	537
Europe and the United Kingdom	8,133	5,683	3,220	2,523	3,177	4,007	2,764	2,153	1,223	1,132
Source area not stated	4	4	2	3	31	71	93	73	42	19

299

Refugees	30,092	27,919	25,115	25,984	32,687	35,776	32,499	27,955	21,860	22,846
Africa and the Middle East	101	61	527	1,293	1,445	1,562	1,937	2,171	1,760	1,763
Asia and Pacific	224	99	998	2,637	1,862	1,922	3,466	3,224	3,159	2,949
South and Central America	85	41	756	1,937	1,757	1,631	2,469	2,975	2,691	2,972
United States	4	0	540	1,278	692	541	731	881	1,123	1,038
Europe and the United Kingdom	46	5	959	2,055	1,368	1,123	1,764	2,036	1,976	1,906
Source area not stated	0	0	0	0	0	8	8	25	28	6
Other immigrants	460	206	3,780	9,200	7,124	6,787	10,375	11,312	10,737	10,634
Africa and the Middle East	40,911	48,239	46,340	43,676	49,531	49,280	51,858	48,564	51,313	56,154
Asia and Pacific	120,740	132,946	119,058	113,729	114,573	138,048	126,473	112,656	117,480	117,178
South and Central America	17,005	20,212	19,470	20,349	22,254	24,640	24,303	25,890	26,493	26,778

United States	5,828	5,909	5,294	6,013	7,507	9,263	10,943	10,449	11,216	9,723
Europe and the United Kingdom	42,959	43,295	38,867	37,569	41,902	40,906	37,944	39,071	40,650	42,312
Source area not stated	12	38	20	11	58	102	119	123	93	33
Category not stated	0	1	0	1	0	2	2	1	2	1
Total	**227,455**	**250,640**	**229,049**	**221,348**	**235,825**	**262,241**	**251,642**	**236,754**	**247,247**	**252,179**

Canada—Permanent residents, 1860 to 2009

Year		Year		Year		Year		Year		Year		Year		Year	
1860	6276	1880	38,505	1900	41,681	1920	138,824	1940	11,324	1960	104,111	1980	143,117	2000	227,465
1861	13,599	1881	47,991	1901	55,747	1921	91,728	1941	9,329	1961	71,698	1981	128,618	2001	250,638
1862	18,294	1882	112,458	1902	89,102	1922	84,224	1942	7,576	1962	74,586	1982	121,147	2002	229,040
1863	21,000	1883	133,624	1903	138,660	1923	133,729	1943	8,504	1963	93,151	1983	89,157	2003	221,355
1864	24,779	1884	103,824	1904	131,252	1924	124,164	1944	12,801	1964	112,606	1984	88,239	2004	235,824
1865	18,958	1885	79,169	1905	141,465	1925	84,907	1945	22,722	1965	146,758	1985	84,302	2005	262,239
1866	11,427	1886	69,152	1906	211,653	1926	135,982	1946	71,719	1966	194,743	1986	99,219	2006	251,649

Year	Value	Year	Value	Year	Value	Year	Value	Year	Value	Year	Value	Year	Value
1867	10,666	1887	84,526	1907	272,409	1927	135,962	1947	64,127	1967	222,876	1987	152,098
1868	12,765	1888	88,766	1908	143,326	1928	158,886	1948	125,414	1968	183,974	1988	161,929
1869	18,830	1889	91,600	1909	173,694	1929	166,783	1949	95,217	1969	164,531	1989	192,001
1870	24,708	1890	75,067	1910	286,839	1930	104,806	1950	73,912	1970	147,713	1990	241,230
1871	27,773	1891	82,165	1911	331,288	1931	27,530	1951	194,391	1971	121,900	1991	230,781
1872	36,578	1892	30,996	1912	375,756	1932	20,591	1952	164,498	1972	122,006	1992	252,842
1873	50,050	1893	29,633	1913	400,870	1933	14382	1953	168,868	1973	184,200	1993	254,321

Year	Value	Year	Value	Year	Value	Year	Value	Year	Value	Year	Value	Year	Value
1874	39,373	1894	20,829	1914	150,484	1934	12,476	1954	154,227	1974	218,465	1994	217,950
1875	27,382	1895	18,790	1915	36,665	1935	11,277	1955	109,946	1975	187,881	1995	212869
1876	25,633	1896	16,835	1916	55,914	1936	11,643	1956	164,857	1976	149,429	1996	225,313
1877	27,082	1897	21,716	1917	72,910	1937	15,101	1957	282,164	1977	114,914	1997	216,038
1878	29,807	1898	31,900	1918	41,845	1938	17,244	1958	124,851	1978	86,313	1998	174,200
1879	40,492	1899	44,543	1919	107,698	1939	16,994	1959	106,928	1979	112,093	1999	189,966
TOTAL	485472		1,222,089		3,259,258		11,342		1,973,375		2,813,948		3,475,337

1,678,210

Canada—Permanent residents, 1860 to 2009

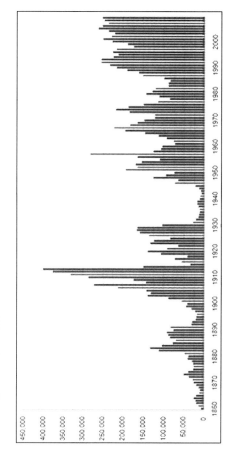

Canada—Permanent residents by category and source area, 2009

Source area	2000	2001	2002	2003	2004	2005	2006	2007	2008	2009
Africa and the Middle East	11.6	11.7	10.3	11.5	12.7	12.0	11.8	13.5	14.2	14.9
Asia and Pacific	53.7	52.8	58.8	59.4	54.7	57.7	61.0	56.7	52.8	52.8
South and Central America	14.4	15.0	12.6	11.3	12.0	11.3	10.0	11.1	11.8	11.9
United States	5.2	5.4	4.5	4.6	6.0	6.5	6.3	6.0	7.1	6.8
Europe and the United Kingdom	15.0	15.1	13.9	13.2	14.6	12.4	10.8	12.6	14.1	13.6
Source area not stated	0.0	0.0	0.0	0.0	0.0	0.0	0.0	0.0	0.0	0.0
Family class	**100.0**	**100.0**	**100.0**	**100.0**	**100.0**	**100.0**	**100.0**	**100.0**	**100.0**	**100.0**
Africa and the Middle East	17.2	19.7	22.2	21.0	20.6	18.3	22.7	21.5	20.9	22.1
Asia and Pacific	57.7	56.3	51.7	51.4	49.7	56.1	50.2	47.5	49.2	47.7

South and Central America	4.4	4.8	5.8	6.0	6.3	5.2	5.2	7.2	7.6	8.1
United States	1.9	1.4	1.4	1.4	2.2	2.4	3.3	3.6	3.3	2.4
Europe and the United Kingdom	18.8	17.7	18.9	20.2	21.1	17.9	18.7	20.2	18.9	19.8
Source area not stated	0.0	0.0	0.0	0.0	0.0	0.0	0.0	0.0	0.0	0.0
Economic immigrants	**100.0**	**100.0**	**100.0**	**100.0**	**100.0**	**100.0**	**100.0**	**100.0**	**100.0**	**100.0**
Africa and the Middle East	34.4	34.6	35.1	36.7	38.5	32.0	31.5	33.1	41.2	47.4
Asia and Pacific	31.0	35.3	40.6	39.1	37.2	33.1	32.5	34.2	29.3	29.1
South and Central America	7.4	9.5	11.3	14.3	14.1	21.3	23.4	21.7	21.5	16.1
United States	0.2	0.2	0.1	0.2	0.4	2.2	3.8	3.0	2.2	2.4
Europe and the United Kingdom	27.0	20.4	12.8	9.7	9.7	11.2	8.5	7.7	5.6	5.0

Source area not stated	0.0	0.0	0.0	0.0	0.1	0.2	0.3	0.3	0.2	0.1
Refugees	**100.0**	**100.0**	**100.0**	**100.0**	**100.0**	**100.0**	**100.0**	**100.0**	**100.0**	**100.0**
Africa and the Middle East	22.0	29.6	13.9	14.1	20.3	23.0	18.7	19.2	16.4	16.6
Asia and Pacific	48.7	48.1	26.4	28.7	26.1	28.3	33.4	28.5	29.4	27.7
South and Central America	18.5	19.9	20.0	21.1	24.7	24.0	23.8	26.3	25.1	27.9
United States	0.9	0.0	14.3	13.9	9.7	8.0	7.0	7.8	10.5	9.8
Europe and the United Kingdom	10.0	2.4	25.4	22.3	19.2	16.5	17.0	18.0	18.4	17.9
Source area not stated	0.0	0.0	0.0	0.0	0.0	0.1	0.1	0.2	0.3	0.1
Other immigrants	**100.0**	**100.0**	**100.0**	**100.0**	**100.0**	**100.0**	**100.0**	**100.0**	**100.0**	**100.0**
Africa and the Middle East	18.0	19.2	20.2	19.7	21.0	18.8	20.6	20.5	20.8	22.3

Asia and Pacific	53.1	53.0	52.0	51.4	48.6	52.6	50.3	47.6	47.5	46.5
South and Central America	7.5	8.1	8.5	9.2	9.4	9.4	9.7	10.9	10.7	10.6
United States	2.6	2.4	2.3	2.7	3.2	3.5	4.3	4.4	4.5	3.9
Europe and the United Kingdom	18.9	17.3	17.0	17.0	17.8	15.6	15.1	16.5	16.4	16.8
Source area not stated	0.0	0.0	0.0	0.0	0.0	0.0	0.0	0.1	0.0	0.0
Category not stated	0.0	0.0	0.0	0.0	0.0	0.0	0.0	0.0	0.0	0.0
Total	**100.0**	**100.0**	**100.0**	**100.0**	**100.0**	**100.0**	**100.0**	**100.0**	**100.0**	**100.0**

Canada—Permanent residents by age and source area

Source area	2000	2001	2002	2003	2004	2005	2006	2007	2008	2009
Africa and the Middle East	10,485	12,517	11,686	10,379	11,920	12,036	12,254	11,003	12,500	13,774
Asia and Pacific	25,332	29,544	25,622	23,074	23,762	28,758	23,294	21,453	21,544	20,939
South and Central America	3,834	4,425	4,280	4,408	4,750	5,137	4,898	5,144	5,363	5,100
United States	1,979	1,819	1,549	1,613	2,275	3,279	3,462	3,140	3,002	2,501
Europe and the United Kingdom	9,552	8,978	7,821	7,160	8,182	8,344	7,343	7,475	7,848	7,960
Source area not stated	0	7	4	1	24	41	67	59	46	18
0 to 14 years of age	**51,182**	**57,290**	**50,962**	**46,635**	**50,913**	**57,595**	**51,318**	**48,274**	**50,303**	**50,292**
Africa and the Middle East	6,711	7,426	6,728	6,911	8,299	8,270	8,441	7,802	7,835	8,075
Asia and Pacific	16,622	17,322	16,401	17,260	17,852	22,002	22,095	19,937	19,413	19,328
South and Central America	3,074	3,574	3,266	3,489	3,693	4,174	4,333	4,367	4,305	4,063

United States	607	597	587	633	756	963	1,158	1,057	1,223	1,090
Europe and the United Kingdom	5,677	5,432	4,619	4,724	5,256	5,146	4,630	4,697	4,634	4,781
Source area not stated	4	9	5	2	15	21	18	22	15	3
15 to 24 years of age	**32,695**	**34,360**	**31,606**	**33,019**	**35,871**	**40,576**	**40,675**	**37,882**	**37,425**	**37,340**
Africa and the Middle East	19,051	22,846	22,878	21,313	24,315	23,397	25,031	23,485	24,264	26,783
Asia and Pacific	63,085	67,972	57,776	56,505	58,096	68,571	57,887	52,064	56,285	55,750
South and Central America	8,211	9,682	9,413	9,704	11,128	12,563	11,997	13,190	13,476	14,142
United States	2,266	2,371	2,109	2,544	2,913	3,421	4,114	4,056	4,629	4,060
Europe and the United Kingdom	22,382	23,245	21,272	20,483	23,284	23,243	21,407	21,875	22,111	23,310
Source area not stated	7	19	10	6	15	30	26	32	27	7
25 to 44 years of age	**115,002**	**126,135**	**113,458**	**110,555**	**119,751**	**131,225**	**120,462**	**114,702**	**120,792**	**124,052**

Africa and the Middle East	3,800	4,494	4,204	4,108	4,294	4,903	5,250	5,292	5,594	6,124
Asia and Pacific	12,837	14,816	15,333	13,243	11,839	16,393	18,547	15,531	16,773	17,292
South and Central America	1,587	2,161	2,138	2,296	2,301	2,489	2,722	2,796	2,870	2,957
United States	742	899	822	945	1,265	1,370	1,944	1,918	1,985	1,718
Europe and the United Kingdom	4,046	4,243	3,820	3,856	4,066	3,612	3,808	3,997	4,546	4,858
Source area not stated	1	1	1	2	4	7	6	9	4	4
45 to 64 years of age	**23,013**	**26,614**	**26,318**	**24,450**	**23,769**	**28,774**	**32,277**	**29,543**	**31,772**	**32,953**
Africa and the Middle East	864	956	844	965	703	674	884	982	1,120	1,398
Asia and Pacific	2,864	3,292	3,926	3,647	3,024	2,326	4,650	3,672	3,465	3,869
South and Central America	299	370	373	452	382	277	353	393	481	516
United States	233	223	227	278	298	230	265	278	377	354

Europe and the United Kingdom	1,302	1,398	1,335	1,347	1,114	561	756	1,027	1,511	1,404
Source area not stated	0	2	0	0	0	3	2	1	1	1
65 years of age or more	**5,562**	**6,241**	**6,705**	**6,689**	**5,521**	**4,071**	**6,910**	**6,353**	**6,955**	**7,542**
Africa and the Middle East	40,911	48,239	46,340	43,676	49,531	49,280	51,860	48,564	51,313	56,154
Asia and Pacific	120,740	132,946	119,058	113,729	114,573	138,050	126,473	112,657	117,480	117,178
South and Central America	17,005	20,212	19,470	20,349	22,254	24,640	24,303	25,890	26,495	26,778
United States	5,827	5,909	5,294	6,013	7,507	9,263	10,943	10,449	11,216	9,723
Europe and the United Kingdom	42,959	43,296	38,867	37,570	41,902	40,906	37,944	39,071	40,650	42,313
Source area not stated	12	38	20	11	58	102	119	123	93	33
Age not stated	1	0	0	0	0	0	0	0	0	0
Total	**227,455**	**250,640**	**229,049**	**221,348**	**235,825**	**262,241**	**251,642**	**236,754**	**247,247**	**252,179**

313

Source area									
Africa and the Middle East	27.5	24.8	22.8	24.0	20.9	23.4	22.1	23.0	21.8	20.5
Asia and Pacific	41.6	42.8	44.4	45.4	49.9	46.7	49.5	50.3	51.6	49.5
South and Central America	10.1	10.7	10.7	9.5	8.9	9.3	9.5	8.4	7.7	7.5
United States	5.0	6.0	6.5	6.7	5.7	4.5	3.5	3.0	3.2	3.9
Europe and the United Kingdom	15.8	15.6	15.5	14.3	14.5	16.1	15.4	15.3	15.7	18.7
Source area not stated	0.0	0.1	0.1	0.1	0.1	0.0	0.0	0.0	0.0	0.0
0 to 14 years of age	**100.0**	**100.0**	**100.0**	**100.0**	**100.0**	**100.0**	**100.0**	**100.0**	**100.0**	**100.0**
Africa and the Middle East	21.6	20.9	20.6	20.8	20.4	23.1	20.9	21.3	21.6	20.5
Asia and Pacific	51.8	51.9	52.6	54.3	54.2	49.8	52.3	51.9	50.4	50.8
South and Central America	10.9	11.5	11.5	10.7	10.3	10.3	10.6	10.3	10.4	9.4
United States	2.9	3.3	2.8	2.8	2.4	2.1	1.9	1.9	1.7	1.9

Europe and the United Kingdom	17.4	15.8	14.6	14.3	14.7	12.7	11.4	12.4	12.4	12.8
Source area not stated	0.0	0.0	0.0	0.0	0.0	0.1	0.0	0.1	0.0	0.0
15 to 24 years of age	**100.0**	**100.0**	**100.0**	**100.0**	**100.0**	**100.0**	**100.0**	**100.0**	**100.0**	**100.0**
Africa and the Middle East	16.6	18.1	20.2	19.3	20.3	17.8	20.8	20.5	20.1	21.6
Asia and Pacific	54.9	53.9	50.9	51.1	48.5	52.3	48.1	45.4	46.6	44.9
South and Central America	7.1	7.7	8.3	8.8	9.3	9.6	10.0	11.5	11.2	11.4
United States	2.0	1.9	1.9	2.3	2.4	2.6	3.4	3.5	3.8	3.3
Europe and the United Kingdom	19.5	18.4	18.7	18.5	19.4	17.7	17.8	19.1	18.3	18.8
Source area not stated	0.0	0.0	0.0	0.0	0.0	0.0	0.0	0.0	0.0	0.0
25 to 44 years of age	**100.0**	**100.0**	**100.0**	**100.0**	**100.0**	**100.0**	**100.0**	**100.0**	**100.0**	**100.0**
Africa and the Middle East	16.5	16.9	16.0	16.8	18.1	17.0	16.3	17.9	17.6	18.6

Asia and Pacific	55.8	55.7	58.3	54.2	49.8	57.0	57.5	52.6	52.8	52.5
South and Central America	6.9	8.1	8.1	9.4	9.7	8.7	8.4	9.5	9.0	9.0
United States	3.2	3.4	3.1	3.9	5.3	4.8	6.0	6.5	6.2	5.2
Europe and the United Kingdom	17.6	15.9	14.5	15.8	17.1	12.6	11.8	13.5	14.3	14.7
Source area not stated	0.0	0.0	0.0	0.0	0.0	0.0	0.0	0.0	0.0	0.0
45 to 64 years of age	**100.0**	**100.0**	**100.0**	**100.0**	**100.0**	**100.0**	**100.0**	**100.0**	**100.0**	**100.0**
Africa and the Middle East	3.8	3.6	3.2	3.9	3.0	2.3	2.7	3.3	3.5	4.2
Asia and Pacific	12.4	12.4	14.9	14.9	12.7	8.1	14.4	12.4	10.9	11.7
South and Central America	1.3	1.4	1.4	1.8	1.6	1.0	1.1	1.3	1.5	1.6
United States	1.0	0.8	0.9	1.1	1.3	0.8	0.8	0.9	1.2	1.1
Europe and the United Kingdom	5.7	5.3	5.1	5.5	4.7	1.9	2.3	3.5	4.8	4.3

Source area not stated	0.0	0.0	0.0	0.0	0.0	0.0	0.0	0.0	0.0	0.0
65 years of age or more	**100.0**	**100.0**	**100.0**	**100.0**	**100.0**	**100.0**	**100.0**	**100.0**	**100.0**	**100.0**
Africa and the Middle East	18.0	19.2	20.2	19.7	21.0	18.8	20.6	20.5	20.8	22.3
Asia and Pacific	53.1	53.0	52.0	51.4	48.6	52.6	50.3	47.6	47.5	46.5
South and Central America	7.5	8.1	8.5	9.2	9.4	9.4	9.7	10.9	10.7	10.6
United States	2.6	2.4	2.3	2.7	3.2	3.5	4.3	4.4	4.5	3.9
Europe and the United Kingdom	18.9	17.3	17.0	17.0	17.8	15.6	15.1	16.5	16.4	16.8
Source area not stated	0.0	0.0	0.0	0.0	0.0	0.0	0.0	0.1	0.0	0.0
Age not stated	0.0	0.0	0.0	0.0	0.0	0.0	0.0	0.0	0.0	0.0
Total	**100.0**	**100.0**	**100.0**	**100.0**	**100.0**	**100.0**	**100.0**	**100.0**	**100.0**	**100.0**

Canada—Permanent residents by age and source area, 2009

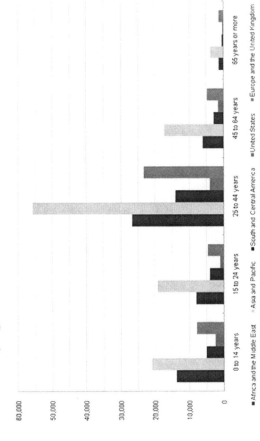

Facts and figures 2009—Immigration overview:
Permanent and temporary residents—Permanent residents
Canada—Permanent residents by source country

Source country	2000	2001	2002	2003	2004	2005	2006	2007	2008	2009
China, People's Republic of	36,749	40,365	33,305	36,251	36,429	42,292	33,079	27,013	29,337	29,049
Philippines	10,119	12,928	11,011	11,988	13,303	17,525	17,718	19,066	23,726	27,277
India	26,122	27,902	28,838	24,594	25,573	33,142	30,750	26,049	24,548	26,122
United States	5,828	5,909	5,294	6,013	7,507	9,263	10,943	10,449	11,216	9,723
United Kingdom	4,649	5,360	4,724	5,199	6,062	5,864	6,541	8,129	9,243	9,566
France	4,345	4,428	3,962	4,127	5,028	5,430	4,915	5,526	6,384	7,300
Pakistan	14,201	15,353	14,173	12,351	12,793	13,575	12,329	9,545	8,052	6,214
Iran	5,616	5,746	7,889	5,651	6,063	5,502	7,073	6,663	6,010	6,065
Korea, Republic of	7,639	9,608	7,334	7,089	5,337	5,819	6,178	5,866	7,246	5,864

Morocco	2,560	3,951	4,057	3,243	3,471	2,692	3,109	3,789	3,906	5,222
Algeria	2,529	3,009	3,030	2,786	3,209	3,131	4,513	3,172	3,228	4,785
United Arab Emirates	3,084	4,523	4,444	3,321	4,358	4,053	4,100	3,368	4,695	4,640
Iraq	1,384	1,597	1,365	969	1,140	1,316	977	1,601	2,570	4,567
Sri Lanka	5,849	5,520	4,968	4,448	4,135	4,690	4,490	3,934	4,509	4,269
Colombia	2,228	2,967	3,225	4,273	4,438	6,031	5,813	4,833	4,995	4,240
Germany	2,369	1,846	1,624	2,098	2,387	2,635	3,030	2,555	4,057	4,080
Mexico	1,658	1,939	1,919	1,738	2,245	2,851	2,830	3,224	2,831	3,104
Russia	3,523	4,073	3,677	3,520	3,685	3,607	2,850	2,854	2,547	2,799
Nigeria	1,088	1,325	1,281	931	1,369	2,034	2,481	2,255	1,837	2,662
Taiwan	3,535	3,114	2,910	2,126	1,992	3,092	2,823	2,779	2,972	2,543

Lebanon	1,682	2,071	1,723	2,600	2,673	3,122	3,290	3,018	2,827	2,531
Egypt	1,737	1,915	1,634	1,929	2,051	2,062	1,651	1,969	2,314	2,486
Brazil	842	857	759	865	934	976	1,209	1,759	2,127	2,480
Jamaica	2,463	2,775	2,457	1,983	2,130	1,880	1,686	2,113	2,312	2,427
Israel	2,601	2,479	2,605	2,366	2,857	2,549	2,692	2,446	2,633	2,364
Ukraine	3,323	3,590	3,576	2,781	2,401	2,317	1,880	2,170	1,874	2,300
Vietnam, Socialist Republic of	1,800	2,097	2,282	1,686	1,803	1,820	3,121	2,549	1,740	2,141
Haiti	1,653	2,484	2,217	1,945	1,657	1,719	1,650	1,614	2,509	2,085
Saudi Arabia	2,029	3,564	2,538	2,042	2,111	2,364	2,227	1,649	2,357	2,025
Romania	4,430	5,589	5,689	5,466	5,658	4,964	4,393	3,770	2,754	1,994
Peru	605	852	859	1,021	1,455	1,658	1,479	1,475	1,078	1,872

Country										
Bangladesh	2,715	3,393	2,615	1,896	2,374	3,940	3,838	2,735	2,716	1,854
Moldova	294	518	628	606	632	634	790	1,080	1,119	1,535
Afghanistan	2,845	3,182	2,971	3,010	2,527	2,908	2,552	2,262	1,810	1,507
Turkey	1,097	1,223	1,356	1,444	1,796	2,060	1,698	1,481	1,190	1,455
Cuba	854	971	866	876	857	979	1,044	1,338	1,296	1,421
Venezuela	475	572	554	710	1,259	1,235	1,221	1,373	1,259	1,385
Japan	1,305	1,645	1,080	1,008	1,264	1,346	1,367	1,388	1,442	1,323
South Africa, Republic of	1,953	2,090	1,631	1,452	1,332	1,102	1,267	1,297	1,227	1,316
Congo, Democratique Republic of	1,145	1,164	1,022	1,127	1,400	1,381	1,414	1,314	1,133	1,274
Ethiopia	1,039	1,009	802	1,326	1,439	1,370	1,647	1,424	1,473	1,212
Australia	718	959	957	1,040	1,021	1,042	949	1,097	1,097	1,199

Country										
Tunisia	440	789	653	654	759	726	1,010	850	900	1,164
Guyana	1,274	1,665	1,432	1,394	1,321	1,176	1,263	1,248	1,089	1,152
Trinidad and Tobago	896	917	937	693	724	844	804	990	1,019	1,147
Somalia, Republic of	1,361	988	598	799	1,172	980	896	982	750	988
Poland	1,334	1,168	1,117	1,079	1,329	1,206	1,191	1,158	1,183	981
Myanmar (Burma)	104	76	130	228	140	183	185	446	647	961
Hong Kong	2,865	1,965	1,541	1,472	1,547	1,783	1,489	1,131	1,324	924
Kuwait	1,222	1,713	947	1,074	917	1,140	946	697	1,046	896
Cameroon	198	169	184	255	301	519	606	834	959	872
Mauritius	182	376	343	558	690	684	504	493	691	840
El Salvador	552	446	469	441	437	428	421	923	1,107	825

Jordan	1,283	1,239	981	1,038	1,034	1,324	1,207	969	929	812
Syria	1,049	804	681	958	861	1,199	944	923	800	803
Netherlands	879	815	685	662	826	929	892	630	841	795
Bulgaria	1,097	1,188	1,474	1,424	1,945	1,685	1,401	1,132	976	757
Thailand	289	403	587	489	439	596	1,292	1,931	885	741
Singapore	753	842	939	716	482	629	433	1,228	1,383	740
Malaysia	378	494	468	419	454	629	612	643	701	706
Belgium	496	524	480	442	597	575	430	596	570	702
Ghana	1,004	789	716	567	836	1,082	809	735	770	675
Albania	1,773	1,613	985	819	1,378	1,207	810	660	506	669
Eritrea	97	154	115	194	303	378	492	389	470	662

Côte-d'Ivoire, Republic of	160	171	236	204	294	331	436	669	681	649
Nepal	247	273	418	440	594	714	640	564	639	627
Portugal	397	481	319	283	323	291	405	399	653	610
Italy	481	527	446	401	432	344	421	425	547	583
New Zealand	202	381	367	401	395	457	376	374	506	583
Switzerland	619	568	409	477	513	447	445	506	629	581
Kenya	804	1,004	855	987	887	896	824	544	567	558
Ecuador	355	366	446	380	506	561	620	591	642	529
Zimbabwe	97	114	200	687	1,456	639	449	650	597	527
Ireland, Republic of	180	215	205	260	284	244	314	352	493	503
Indonesia	1,155	930	712	498	509	598	585	624	685	499

Saint Vincent and the Grenadines	267	283	240	193	291	340	374	566	428	497
Argentina	455	625	844	1,783	1,648	1,169	894	624	542	492
Qatar	322	394	327	464	327	362	311	382	515	485
Senegal	117	95	182	152	205	208	365	386	454	465
Burundi	281	297	326	352	512	565	405	476	390	464
Sudan, Republic of	761	1,179	1,368	1,533	1,508	1,039	832	703	723	455
Belarus	550	476	453	468	598	643	441	581	511	454
Kazakhstan	527	569	481	590	576	548	484	480	384	429
Chile	374	377	437	343	375	392	452	546	359	388
Libya	406	499	562	246	254	418	468	340	402	380
Dominican Republic	237	266	204	245	272	288	245	288	414	380

Oman	242	413	372	483	409	366	542	391	540	346
Rwanda	344	263	195	251	253	302	315	337	288	337
Grenada	369	345	248	219	288	288	357	357	287	318
Hungary	439	639	562	492	685	542	531	429	387	315
Fiji	460	669	616	566	492	304	273	302	316	306
Bahrain	269	241	268	307	258	251	347	278	341	293
Benin, Republic of	32	48	62	67	82	76	105	182	172	280
Guatemala	341	255	248	178	217	192	215	259	255	273
Uzbekistan	109	139	158	171	203	340	307	261	196	269
Sweden	215	239	198	178	160	234	165	224	225	268
Armenia	100	85	133	154	159	233	210	190	210	268

Country									
Saint Lucia	103	116	83	94	113	188	189	269	289	260
Spain	104	110	140	96	157	167	152	165	223	253
Guinea, Republic of	200	238	265	244	504	395	341	369	292	246
Costa Rica	109	136	115	120	173	206	320	305	282	240
Uganda	96	133	163	155	181	263	199	205	221	225
Bolivia	31	79	59	63	98	137	149	111	164	222
Greece	362	346	211	179	210	145	138	189	248	205
Yemen, Republic of	102	213	209	102	141	195	109	158	225	201
Macedonia	239	296	349	635	450	292	249	210	180	196
Cambodia	239	252	229	274	354	385	562	455	349	196
Togo	36	64	79	86	138	125	103	145	154	174

Country										
Bosnia-Herzegovina	987	871	466	265	180	215	253	251	246	168
Palestinian Authority (Gaza/West Bank)	161	171	246	212	223	319	409	328	270	166
Honduras	204	179	147	113	132	160	160	160	177	166
Kyrgyzstan	73	94	162	104	225	177	165	134	163	163
Czech Republic	487	315	237	198	230	205	159	140	104	161
Azerbaijan	78	115	179	176	266	354	258	217	127	153
Madagascar	29	41	53	45	66	76	89	95	83	147
Burkina Faso	22	38	36	38	74	96	143	128	125	140
Tanzania, United Republic of	210	322	294	391	308	270	299	182	230	134
Barbados	128	157	132	79	89	124	100	140	144	133
Mali	55	54	67	67	77	86	137	142	136	128

Austria	128	158	111	155	155	132	115	106	121	121
Georgia	78	114	119	117	106	118	116	132	107	121
Mongolia, People's Republic of	17	18	19	25	34	67	69	87	58	118
Norway	144	139	135	111	98	83	92	107	88	117
Slovak Republic	460	579	614	501	588	356	236	206	117	115
Denmark	104	112	87	96	100	101	105	109	128	115
Nicaragua	131	102	63	82	62	75	89	67	121	110
Uruguay	79	73	103	108	149	294	202	175	161	108
Paraguay	39	53	85	108	83	78	105	124	123	101
Latvia	230	286	250	157	136	94	73	113	66	86
Finland	135	111	116	105	84	58	78	92	109	86

Croatia	959	518	347	172	121	110	84	87	100	82
Chad, Republic of	145	74	59	55	84	115	81	110	93	82
Panama, Republic of	51	57	53	50	46	66	72	72	59	80
Zambia	71	127	130	109	118	114	98	110	69	74
Gabon	24	38	49	82	49	105	87	105	93	70
Djibouti, Republic of	193	127	56	52	71	100	59	46	48	60
Namibia	20	12	19	11	19	47	31	19	37	59
Angola	54	161	169	155	256	291	172	101	70	59
Niger, Republic of	16	20	20	28	35	55	57	60	69	57
Lithuania	112	176	123	193	222	160	110	101	103	55
Sierra Leone	167	280	289	253	251	136	87	63	66	54

Country										
Dominica	71	74	66	58	46	49	73	74	54	54
Tajikistan, Republic of	6	23	25	19	16	171	59	38	17	51
Brunei	22	16	14	19	18	11	8	47	74	50
Congo, Republic of the	117	98	75	70	104	93	110	48	53	45
Mauritania	8	19	16	17	50	55	66	65	41	45
Bahamas, The	17	22	20	22	24	34	42	31	70	45
Bermuda	15	24	22	34	27	36	47	38	47	44
Antigua and Barbuda	13	35	16	27	15	30	37	20	43	44
Laos	35	38	53	24	37	38	74	58	37	43
Belize	26	23	33	15	26	36	29	30	53	41
Malawi	12	10	15	14	36	32	35	52	51	38

Liberia	47	51	43	110	88	196	127	55	16	30
Slovenia	29	24	17	14	17	21	8	23	19	26
Botswana, Republic of	57	24	50	45	74	55	39	56	61	26
Cyprus	44	44	27	59	40	30	34	19	33	26
Macao	74	60	60	36	38	33	56	14	19	26
Malta	92	66	42	39	48	32	38	10	29	24
Estonia	66	43	55	70	28	25	21	36	36	23
Turkmenistan	6	23	25	26	14	138	47	40	22	19
Yugoslavia (former)	4,740	2,802	1,623	940	708	272	126	49	59	16
Luxembourg	13	17	28	9	12	13	10	20	19	14
Martinique	8	12	20	16	12	18	21	10	15	13

Surinam	15	20	19	15	22	12	10	25	10	13
Central African Republic	18	6	10	9	9	37	9	21	10	11
Gambia	73	37	31	91	49	56	46	32	33	11
Saint Kitts and Nevis	14	11	11	13	10	7	7	11	28	11
Seychelles	24	11	10	17	20	32	12	11	21	11
Guadeloupe	18	18	14	5	13	24	10	9	22	5
Country not stated	10	38	20	10	53	96	115	121	91	32
Other countries	**233**	**251**	**242**	**321**	**303**	**728**	**1,028**	**1,142**	**1,006**	**1,835**
Total	**227,455**	**250,640**	**229,049**	**221,348**	**235,825**	**262,241**	**251,642**	**236,754**	**247,247**	**252,179**

Canada—Permanent residents by province or territory and language ability

Language ability	2000	2001	2002	2003	2004	2005	2006	2007	2008	2009
English	814	951	792	802	1,105	1,301	1,763	1,777	1,953	1,821
French	14	9	13	24	21	13	22	19	27	22
Both French and English	50	69	58	111	172	192	162	138	202	132
Neither	730	669	556	537	473	423	639	589	469	449
Nova Scotia	**1,608**	**1,698**	**1,419**	**1,474**	**1,771**	**1,929**	**2,586**	**2,523**	**2,651**	**2,424**
English	341	353	319	350	449	604	1,014	951	1,099	1,066
French	67	67	46	59	38	58	58	64	90	80
Both French and English	56	77	61	66	129	142	110	129	131	198
Neither	294	301	279	191	179	287	464	499	536	569
New Brunswick	**758**	**798**	**705**	**666**	**795**	**1,091**	**1,646**	**1,643**	**1,856**	**1,913**

English	386	284	279	276	506	459	608	725	943	948
French	5	2	9	0	12	10	11	3	7	11
Both French and English	6	25	14	20	47	33	30	32	58	57
Neither	209	216	210	217	324	325	424	778	1,051	1,310
Other Atlantic provinces*	**606**	**527**	**512**	**513**	**889**	**827**	**1,073**	**1,538**	**2,059**	**2,326**
English	6,008	6,013	5,951	6,638	7,842	8,049	8,796	8,283	8,474	7,980
French	8,734	9,555	9,170	8,614	9,732	10,239	10,697	10,759	10,590	11,634
Both French and English	5,968	8,114	9,285	11,488	14,742	14,601	15,098	16,513	16,711	20,079
Neither	11,788	13,916	13,175	12,815	11,929	10,426	10,093	9,646	9,445	9,800
Quebec	**32,498**	**37,598**	**37,581**	**39,555**	**44,245**	**43,315**	**44,684**	**45,201**	**45,220**	**49,493**
English	71,951	77,704	67,592	62,205	72,329	84,372	78,633	71,413	74,360	73,566
French	1,206	1,385	1,156	1,018	1,148	1,274	1,198	1,350	1,402	1,315

	C1	C2	C3	C4	C5	C6	C7	C8	C9	C10
Both French and English	2,889	3,731	3,327	3,399	5,355	5,562	4,748	4,719	4,887	4,668
Neither	57,464	65,821	61,513	53,100	46,262	49,317	41,313	33,833	30,229	27,318
Ontario	**133,510**	**148,641**	**133,588**	**119,722**	**125,094**	**140,525**	**125,892**	**111,315**	**110,878**	**106,867**
English	2,083	2,117	1,851	2,728	3,788	4,078	5,276	5,809	6,354	8,331
French	72	50	42	45	57	144	100	182	98	135
Both French and English	78	96	61	114	180	201	164	152	166	214
Neither	2,402	2,328	2,661	3,616	3,401	3,673	4,507	4,811	4,600	4,840
Manitoba	**4,635**	**4,591**	**4,615**	**6,503**	**7,426**	**8,096**	**10,047**	**10,954**	**11,218**	**13,520**
English	992	837	794	881	1,155	1,198	1,637	1,973	2,855	4,299
French	8	8	11	—	20	24	25	32	29	20
Both French and English	23	25	34	—	139	108	65	73	96	135
Neither	859	834	828	735	629	789	997	1,438	1,855	2,436

Saskatchewan	1,882	1,704	1,667	1,668	1,943	2,119	2,724	3,516	4,835	6,890
English	7,524	8,528	7,311	7,743	9,321	10,878	12,354	13,179	16,832	19,053
French	110	116	85	99	155	176	273	269	285	310
Both French and English	291	360	330	399	688	798	876	904	862	1,041
Neither	6,438	7,401	7,057	7,598	6,311	7,552	7,213	6,509	6,220	6,613
Alberta	**14,363**	**16,405**	**14,783**	**15,839**	**16,475**	**19,404**	**20,716**	**20,861**	**24,199**	**27,017**
English	17,643	17,964	14,527	15,084	18,120	21,995	22,916	22,924	26,920	25,619
French	151	139	100	108	118	125	176	145	159	168
Both French and English	545	543	544	585	1,139	1,367	1,376	1,427	1,488	1,383
Neither	19,089	19,836	18,886	19,452	17,651	21,283	17,615	14,465	15,425	14,268
British Columbia	**37,428**	**38,482**	**34,057**	**35,229**	**37,028**	**44,770**	**42,083**	**38,961**	**43,992**	**41,438**
English	98	125	81	86	94	103	117	139	215	224

French	0	1	1	1	1	2	1	1	5	5
Both French and English	5	3	5	14	17	6	28	12	25	25
Neither	52	44	35	63	47	50	29	38	42	37
Territories**	**155**	**173**	**122**	**164**	**159**	**161**	**175**	**190**	**287**	**291**
English	107,840	114,876	99,497	96,793	114,709	133,037	133,114	127,173	140,005	142,907
French	10,367	11,332	10,633	9,972	11,302	12,065	12,561	12,824	12,692	13,700
Both French and English	9,911	13,043	13,719	16,244	22,608	23,010	22,657	24,099	24,626	27,932
Neither	99,325	111,366	105,200	98,324	87,206	94,125	83,294	72,606	69,872	67,640
Province or territory not stated	12	23	0	15	0	4	16	52	52	0
Total	**227,455**	**250,640**	**229,049**	**221,348**	**235,825**	**262,241**	**251,642**	**236,754**	**247,247**	**252,179**

Language ability	2000	2001	2002	2003	2004	2005	2006	2007	2008	2009
	100.0	100.0	100.0	100.0	100.0	100.0	100.0	100.0	100.0	100.0
English	50.6	56.0	55.8	54.4	62.4	67.4	68.2	70.4	73.7	75.1
French	0.9	0.5	0.9	1.6	1.2	0.7	0.9	0.8	1.0	0.9
Both French and English	3.1	4.1	4.1	7.5	9.7	10.0	6.3	5.5	7.6	5.4
Neither	45.4	39.4	39.2	36.4	26.7	21.9	24.7	23.3	17.7	18.5
Nova Scotia	100.0	100.0	100.0	100.0	100.0	100.0	100.0	100.0	100.0	100.0
English	45.0	44.2	45.2	52.6	56.5	55.4	61.6	57.9	59.2	55.7
French	8.8	8.4	6.5	8.9	4.8	5.3	3.5	3.9	4.8	4.2
Both French and English	7.4	9.6	8.7	9.9	16.2	13.0	6.7	7.9	7.1	10.4
Neither	38.8	37.7	39.6	28.7	22.5	26.3	28.2	30.4	28.9	29.7
New Brunswick	**100.0**	**100.0**	**100.0**	**100.0**	**100.0**	**100.0**	**100.0**	**100.0**	**100.0**	**100.0**
English	63.7	53.9	54.5	53.8	56.9	55.5	56.7	47.1	45.8	40.8

French	0.8	0.4	1.8	0.0	1.3	1.2	1.0	0.2	0.3	0.5
Both French and English	1.0	4.7	2.7	3.9	5.3	4.0	2.8	2.1	2.8	2.5
Neither	34.5	41.0	41.0	42.3	36.4	39.3	39.5	50.6	51.0	56.3
Other Atlantic provinces*	**100.0**	**100.0**	**100.0**	**100.0**	**100.0**	**100.0**	**100.0**	**100.0**	**100.0**	**100.0**
English	18.5	16.0	15.8	16.8	17.7	18.6	19.7	18.3	18.7	16.1
French	26.9	25.4	24.4	21.8	22.0	23.6	23.9	23.8	23.4	23.5
Both French and English	18.4	21.6	24.7	29.0	33.3	33.7	33.8	36.5	37.0	40.6
Neither	36.3	37.0	35.1	32.4	27.0	24.1	22.6	21.3	20.9	19.8
Quebec	**100.0**	**100.0**	**100.0**	**100.0**	**100.0**	**100.0**	**100.0**	**100.0**	**100.0**	**100.0**
English	53.9	52.3	50.6	52.0	57.8	60.0	62.5	64.2	67.1	68.8
French	0.9	0.9	0.9	0.9	0.9	0.9	1.0	1.2	1.3	1.2
Both French and English	2.2	2.5	2.5	2.8	4.3	4.0	3.8	4.2	4.4	4.4

Neither	25.6	27.3	30.4	32.8	35.1	37.0	44.4	46.0	44.3	43.0
Ontario	**100.0**	**100.0**	**100.0**	**100.0**	**100.0**	**100.0**	**100.0**	**100.0**	**100.0**	**100.0**
English	61.6	56.6	53.0	52.5	50.4	51.0	41.9	40.1	46.1	44.9
French	1.0	0.9	1.7	1.0	1.8	0.8	0.7	0.9	1.1	1.6
Both French and English	1.6	1.5	1.4	1.6	2.5	2.4	1.8	1.3	2.1	1.7
Neither	35.8	41.0	43.9	44.9	45.4	45.8	55.6	57.7	50.7	51.8
Manitoba	**100.0**	**100.0**	**100.0**	**100.0**	**100.0**	**100.0**	**100.0**	**100.0**	**100.0**	**100.0**
English	62.4	59.0	56.1	60.1	56.5	59.4	52.8	47.6	49.1	52.7
French	0.3	0.6	0.9	0.9	1.1	1.0	—	0.7	0.5	0.4
Both French and English	2.0	2.0	2.1	2.4	5.1	7.2	—	2.0	1.5	1.2
Neither	35.4	38.4	40.9	36.6	37.2	32.4	44.1	49.7	48.9	45.6
Saskatchewan	**100.0**	**100.0**	**100.0**	**100.0**	**100.0**	**100.0**	**100.0**	**100.0**	**100.0**	**100.0**

English	52.4	52.0	49.5	48.9	56.6	56.1	59.6	63.2	69.6	70.5
French	0.8	0.7	0.6	0.6	0.9	0.9	1.3	1.3	1.2	1.1
Both French and English	2.0	2.2	2.2	2.5	4.2	4.1	4.2	4.3	3.6	3.9
Neither	44.8	45.1	47.7	48.0	38.3	38.9	34.8	31.2	25.7	24.5
Alberta	**100.0**	**100.0**	**100.0**	**100.0**	**100.0**	**100.0**	**100.0**	**100.0**	**100.0**	**100.0**
English	47.1	46.7	42.7	42.8	48.9	49.1	54.5	58.8	61.2	61.8
French	0.4	0.4	0.3	0.3	0.3	0.3	0.4	0.4	0.4	0.4
Both French and English	1.5	1.4	1.6	1.7	3.1	3.1	3.3	3.7	3.4	3.3
Neither	51.0	51.5	55.5	55.2	47.7	47.5	41.9	37.1	35.1	34.4
British Columbia	**100.0**	**100.0**	**100.0**	**100.0**	**100.0**	**100.0**	**100.0**	**100.0**	**100.0**	**100.0**
English	63.2	72.3	66.4	52.4	59.1	64.0	66.9	73.2	74.9	77.0
French	0.0	0.6	0.8	0.6	0.6	1.2	0.6	0.5	1.7	1.7

Both French and English	3.2	1.7	4.1	8.5	10.7	3.7	16.0	6.3	8.7	8.6
Neither	33.5	25.4	28.7	38.4	29.6	31.1	16.6	20.0	14.6	12.7
	100.0	**100.0**	**100.0**	**100.0**	**100.0**	**100.0**	**100.0**	**100.0**	**100.0**	**100.0**
Territories**	**100.0**	**100.0**	**100.0**	**100.0**	**100.0**	**100.0**	**100.0**	**100.0**	**100.0**	**100.0**
English	47.4	45.8	43.4	43.7	48.6	50.7	52.9	53.7	56.6	56.7
French	4.6	4.5	4.6	4.5	4.8	4.6	5.0	5.4	5.1	5.4
Both French and English	4.4	5.2	6.0	7.3	9.6	8.8	9.0	10.2	10.0	11.1
Neither	43.7	44.4	45.9	44.4	37.0	35.9	33.1	30.7	28.3	26.8
Province or territory not stated	0.0	0.0	0.0	0.0	0.0	0.0	0.0	0.0	0.0	0.0
Total	**100.0**	**100.0**	**100.0**	**100.0**	**100.0**	**100.0**	**100.0**	**100.0**	**100.0**	**100.0**

*Newfoundland and Labrador and Prince Edward Island

**Yukon, Northwest Territories and Nunavut

Permanent and temporary residents—Permanent residents
Canada—Permanent residents by province or territory and source area

Source area	2000	2001	2002	2003	2004	2005	2006	2007	2008	2009
Africa and the Middle East	680	721	546	619	749	730	795	775	881	825
Asia and Pacific	362	352	409	365	404	556	925	903	740	593
South and Central America	64	84	98	70	119	84	135	84	144	121
United States	111	126	101	124	176	159	245	206	289	210
Europe and the United Kingdom	391	415	265	296	322	400	485	555	597	675
Source area not stated	0	0	0	0	1	0	1	0	0	0
Nova Scotia	**1,608**	**1,698**	**1,419**	**1,474**	**1,771**	**1,929**	**2,586**	**2,523**	**2,651**	**2,424**
Africa and the Middle East	438	450	385	348	443	390	476	537	531	714
Asia and Pacific	306	332	372	369	649	830	1,419	1,715	2,332	2,545

South and Central America	83	97	112	101	123	164	162	147	207	168
United States	93	114	107	114	169	172	223	188	238	211
Europe and the United Kingdom	444	331	241	247	298	362	438	594	607	601
Source area not stated	0	1	0	0	2	0	1	0	0	0
Other Atlantic provinces*	**1,364**	**1,325**	**1,217**	**1,179**	**1,684**	**1,918**	**2,719**	**3,181**	**3,915**	**4,239**
Africa and the Middle East	9,686	12,328	12,265	12,609	14,097	13,845	16,179	16,306	16,204	19,680
Asia and Pacific	9,324	9,767	8,711	8,798	9,260	8,850	8,671	7,205	7,730	7,507
South and Central America	4,195	5,553	5,476	6,833	7,830	8,312	8,200	9,169	9,243	9,153
United States	493	501	521	701	775	732	1,006	982	1,039	983
Europe and the United Kingdom	8,799	9,448	10,601	10,613	12,271	11,551	10,613	11,510	10,981	12,167
Source area not stated	1	1	7	1	12	25	15	29	23	3

Quebec	32,498	37,598	37,581	39,555	44,245	43,315	44,684	45,201	45,220	49,493
Africa and the Middle East	22,850	26,642	25,461	22,202	25,345	25,665	24,176	21,649	22,965	23,232
Asia and Pacific	73,854	83,393	74,359	66,297	65,680	78,897	68,504	57,414	55,858	52,444
South and Central America	10,207	11,785	11,190	10,214	10,924	12,513	12,118	12,218	12,101	12,330
United States	3,286	3,255	2,845	3,099	3,849	5,147	5,698	5,134	5,335	4,736
Europe and the United Kingdom	23,305	23,542	19,727	17,902	19,262	18,234	15,311	14,845	14,570	14,103
Source area not stated	8	24	6	8	34	69	85	55	49	22
Ontario	133,510	148,641	133,588	119,722	125,094	140,525	125,892	111,315	110,878	106,867
Africa and the Middle East	1,044	1,089	957	1,347	1,671	1,570	1,922	1,764	1,870	1,960
Asia and Pacific	1,731	1,814	2,055	2,696	3,264	3,807	5,090	5,872	5,804	8,209
South and Central America	263	267	415	614	563	555	433	811	737	773

United States	99	135	107	139	155	207	195	210	237	227
Europe and the United Kingdom	1,498	1,286	1,081	1,707	1,771	1,957	2,407	2,294	2,570	2,351
Source area not stated	0	0	0	0	2	0	0	3	0	0
Manitoba	**4,635**	**4,591**	**4,615**	**6,503**	**7,426**	**8,096**	**10,047**	**10,954**	**11,218**	**13,520**
Africa and the Middle East	507	508	509	488	582	558	618	646	904	1,061
Asia and Pacific	719	702	693	639	735	848	1,053	1,710	2,442	4,124
South and Central America	53	51	53	99	87	139	206	186	222	169
United States	82	88	106	104	116	124	142	133	170	189
Europe and the United Kingdom	521	355	306	338	423	449	705	841	1,097	1,347
Source area not stated	0	0	0	0	0	1	0	0	0	0
Saskatchewan	**1,882**	**1,704**	**1,667**	**1,668**	**1,943**	**2,119**	**2,724**	**3,516**	**4,835**	**6,890**

Africa and the Middle East	2,155	2,863	2,755	2,734	2,972	3,025	3,760	3,527	4,176	4,899
Asia and Pacific	7,462	8,624	7,781	8,792	8,644	11,024	11,243	11,212	12,263	13,841
South and Central America	774	1,008	932	1,155	1,164	1,356	1,545	1,782	2,196	2,384
United States	549	581	474	555	759	758	980	938	1,224	1,076
Europe and the United Kingdom	3,423	3,325	2,840	2,603	2,932	3,241	3,179	3,384	4,327	4,812
Source area not stated	0	4	1	0	4	0	9	18	13	5
Alberta	**14,363**	**16,405**	**14,783**	**15,839**	**16,475**	**19,404**	**20,716**	**20,861**	**24,199**	**27,017**
Africa and the Middle East	3,538	3,628	3,441	3,307	3,655	3,475	3,903	3,338	3,743	3,765
Asia and Pacific	26,904	27,845	24,629	25,682	25,861	33,159	29,474	26,502	30,147	27,743
South and Central America	1,357	1,362	1,187	1,252	1,430	1,504	1,499	1,477	1,625	1,663
United States	1,090	1,083	1,020	1,162	1,496	1,954	2,436	2,632	2,657	2,073

Europe and the United Kingdom	4,536	4,556	3,774	3,824	4,583	4,671	4,763	4,994	5,812	6,191
Source area not stated	3	8	6	2	3	7	8	18	8	3
British Columbia	37,428	38,482	34,057	35,229	37,028	44,770	42,083	38,961	43,992	41,438
Africa and the Middle East	9	10	21	18	17	22	31	21	29	18
Asia and Pacific	75	96	49	85	76	75	85	93	140	172
South and Central America	9	4	7	9	14	13	5	16	19	17
United States	25	25	13	15	12	10	11	18	20	18
Europe and the United Kingdom	37	38	32	37	40	41	43	42	79	66
Territories**	155	173	122	164	159	161	175	190	287	291
Africa and the Middle East	40,907	48,239	46,340	43,672	49,531	49,280	51,860	48,563	51,303	56,154
Asia and Pacific	120,737	132,925	119,058	113,723	114,573	138,046	126,464	112,626	117,456	117,178

South and Central America	17,005	20,211	19,470	20,347	22,254	24,640	24,303	25,890	26,494	26,778
United States	5,828	5,908	5,294	6,013	7,507	9,263	10,936	10,441	11,209	9,723
Europe and the United Kingdom	42,954	43,296	38,867	37,567	41,902	40,906	37,944	39,059	40,640	42,313
Source area not stated	12	38	20	11	58	102	119	123	93	33
Province or territory not stated	12	23	0	15	0	4	16	52	52	0
Total	**227,455**	**250,640**	**229,049**	**221,348**	**235,825**	**262,241**	**251,642**	**236,754**	**247,247**	**252,179**

Source area	2000	2001	2002	2003	2004	2005	2006	2007	2008	2009
Africa and the Middle East	42.3	42.5	38.5	42.0	42.3	37.8	30.7	30.7	33.2	34.0
Asia and Pacific	22.5	20.7	28.8	24.8	22.8	28.8	35.8	35.8	27.9	24.5
South and Central America	4.0	4.9	6.9	4.7	6.7	4.4	5.2	3.3	5.4	5.0
United States	6.9	7.4	7.1	8.4	9.9	8.2	9.5	8.2	10.9	8.7
Europe and the United Kingdom	24.3	24.4	18.7	20.1	18.2	20.7	18.8	22.0	22.5	27.8
Source area not stated	0.0	0.0	0.0	0.0	0.1	0.0	0.0	0.0	0.0	0.0

INDEX

354

H

I

U

Ukrainians 52

Ulrich Beck 168

Undesirable 11, 39, 51, 56, 60-1

Unemployed 124, 141, 185, 268

UNICEF 157

The United nations Organization
26, 79, 157, 197

V

Vacation 14

Vegetarian 129

Vietnam 27, 73, 75, 81, 321

Vietnamese 81, 103

Vision xxi-xxii, 4, 151, 187, 190,
219, 221, 251, 253, 267, 271,
273, 281

W

War of 1812 277

Welsh 50-1, 55

Westerner xvi, 151

Wild rose Alliance party 140

Winter Olympics 5, 178, 203-6

World population 9

World war II 30, 62, 102

Y

Yacob Gowon 130

Yugoslavia xxv, 112, 333

Z

Zionist ix

Zymunt Bauman 168

CPSIA information can be obtained at www.ICGtesting.com
Printed in the USA
LVOW042013121112

307004LV00002B/2/P